PRAISE FOR *SURVIVE, RESET, THRIVE*

D0149144

"Full of street-smart insight, practical steps and effective techniques—Rebecca Homkes's approach delivers for teams that want to perform through real-world disruption and constant change."
Toto Wolff, Team Principal and CEO, Mercedes-AMG PETRONAS F1 Team

"Most strategy tools do not factor in uncertainty or change. *Survive, Reset, Thrive* is therefore a timely guide for leaders as to how we embrace ambiguity and yet still develop and execute strategy in times when the goalposts keep moving. As Rebecca Homkes so eloquently puts it, 'You can't stop the market from punching you, but you can get better than anyone else at taking hits.' At its core, this is a book about how to develop the resilience that will enable companies to thrive in an uncertain world."
Steve Brass, President and CEO, The WD-40 Company

"*Survive, Reset, Thrive* is an essential compass for entrepreneurial leaders charting a course through today's unpredictable business climate. With a compelling call to embrace uncertainty and harness it for growth, Rebecca Homkes offers a pragmatic and actionable strategy for organizations of all sizes. This book is a testament to her expertise, providing a playbook that is both grounded in theory and rich in practical application. It's a must-read for any executive seeking to lead their company to sustainable performance and turn disruptive forces into opportunities. *Survive, Reset, Thrive* doesn't just offer a path to survival; it's a blueprint for flourishing in an era of relentless change. Leaders who follow this guide will not only futureproof their organizations, but position them to thrive, no matter the market conditions."
Dr. Marshall Goldsmith, Thinkers50 #1 Executive Coach and *New York Times* bestselling author of *The Earned Life*, *Triggers*, and *What Got You Here Won't Get You There*.

"*Survive, Reset, Thrive* is an immensely practical take on strategy. It empowers leaders with the 'how' to adapt intelligently, learn fast, and be ready to succeed in any market environment. It helps leaders find opportunities in an uncertain environment rather than protect against threats. At Gorilla, the

process engaged my team in the strategy process, simplified a complex world, and provided a simple approach to reset our strategy for growth."
Mark A. Mercurio, President & CEO, The Gorilla Glue Company

"Dr. Rebecca Homkes has written a highly relevant, readable and practical guide on how to formulate and update strategies to thrive in a fast-changing business environment, which should be a go-to guide for all organizational leaders."
Martin Reeves, Chairman, BCG Henderson Institute

"As Dr. Rebecca Homkes defines 'uncertainty is a series of future events that may or may not occur,' and it is amplified during times of extreme disruption. SRT asked us to embrace uncertainty head-on and find the opportunities it provides rather than protect ourselves from threats. Using SRT gave my organization the power of focus and empowered our leaders to act, not hide in fear. Result: we thrived!"
Garry Ridge, Chairman Emeritus, The WD-40 Company and The Culture Coach

"This book is an essential read for executives and leaders grappling with the enormous changes AI has brought across the economy. AI is already impacting business and operating models across companies and Dr. Homkes helps leaders to develop a strategic framework to reset and thrive in this era. I highly recommend this book for all leaders looking to succeed in constantly changing times."
Karim R. Lakhani, Professor, Harvard Business School, and Chair of Digital Data Design Institute at Harvard

"*Survive, Reset, Thrive* was energizing and empowering for leaders in our organization as they learned to adapt intelligently and we were able to succeed in any market environment."
Rich Wolowski, President and Chief Executive Officer, Gordon Food Services

"These days, uncertainty is everywhere, it seems. Unwelcome tradeoffs are rampant. The result, all too often, is analysis paralysis, leading to blissful inaction. But it doesn't have to be this way. Dr. Homkes helps us see that uncertainty can be our friend, not our enemy. By embracing, rather than fearing uncertainty, and by providing us with a pragmatic playbook, she shows us how to survive, reset, and ultimately thrive in even the most

daunting situations. If you want your business to grow through thick and thin, this book is for you."
John Mullins, Associate Professor, London Business School, bestselling author, *Break the Rules!* and *The Customer-Funded Business*

"Dr. Rebecca Homkes and the *Survive, Reset, Thrive* approach was an integral part of our recent strategy reset and helped motivate the team both internally and externally. Her systems-thinking strategy combined with clear strategic intentions, has steered our preparation for the future, improving the outcome by magnitudes."
Malek Sukkar, Executive Chairman, Averda

"*Survive, Reset, Thrive* is an inherently practical resource for leaders looking to drive strong market returns when facing radical uncertainty. It asks us to reframe what we've learned about linear strategy development when we're leading in dynamic markets and instead guides us through a process of debating, articulating and testing market beliefs, making iterative adjustments to strategy from learning, and placing and executing on growth bets. There are fundamental changes happening to industries we assumed were stable, and *Survive, Reset, Thrive* helps us face those head on and engage productively on the opportunities that this change presents."
Philip Meyers, Director of Business Development, Associated British Foods

"We applied Rebecca Homkes's *Survive, Reset, Thrive* strategic framework to triple the size of Primekss. In today's volatile and unpredictable world, SRT is uniquely the best in getting the team to translate the power of crisis into growth momentum, and it does this in an easy to grasp yet smart and comprehensive way. Highly recommend to all who want to grow fast!"
Janis Oslejs, CEO, Primekss Group, and Chair, YPO Construction Industry Network

"Dr. Rebecca Homkes's strategy approach takes away all of the buzz words and provides a set of simple steps that work. This playbook helped formulate my strategy and most importantly how to win. Using *Survive Reset Thrive* has taken the company from serval years of losses to 10% net profitability. Rebecca's work, style, and content is simple, full of gold nuggets, and importantly it is actionable."
Husam Al-Saleh, CEO of SAC-Motor, Deputy CEO, Arabian Hala

"It is rare to find a book on strategy that is well written, simple, practical and addresses an aspect of strategy that is often overlooked: uncertainty. *Survive, Reset, Thrive* is the needed resource for today's leaders to guide their team's with confidence. Rebecca Homkes asks us to embrace uncertainty because it creates opportunities. Yes, uncertainty is inconvenient, and can even be a threat. But, as with all change, it disrupts the status quo, and that creates opportunities for those ready to respond. *Survive, Reset, Thrive* will help you be ready. It provides a playbook that helps business leaders prepare for uncertainty, reset their strategies as events develop and achieve sustainable performance building on the opportunities that emerge. Facing uncertainties such as digital transformation, AI, climate, or changing customer preferences, you will find the playbook powerful. It will help you guide your team with confidence."

Andrew Campbell, Professor and author of *Strategy for the Corporate Level* **and** *Operating Model Canvas*

Survive, Reset, Thrive

*Leading Breakthrough Growth Strategy
in Volatile Times*

Rebecca Homkes

KoganPage

First published in Great Britain and the United States in 2024 by Kogan Page Limited

2nd Floor, 45 Gee Street
London
EC1V 3RS
United Kingdom

8 W 38th Street, Suite 902
New York, NY 10018
USA

4737/23 Ansari Road
Daryaganj
New Delhi 110002
India

www.koganpage.com

Kogan Page books are printed on paper from sustainable forests.

ISBNs

Hardback   978 1 3986 0788 0
Paperback   978 1 3986 0786 6
Ebook   978 1 3986 0787 3

British Library Cataloguing-in-Publication Data

A CIP record for this book is available from the British Library.

Library of Congress Control Number

2023950522

Typeset by Integra Software Services, Pondicherry
Print production managed by Jellyfish
Printed and bound by CPI Group (UK) Ltd, Croydon CR0 4YY

To the leaders who entrusted Survive Reset Thrive with their organization's growth journey and whose stories form the pages that follow; the colleagues, family, and friends who supported the writing journey; and future leaders steering their companies towards the future, may you find opportunity in uncertainty.

CONTENTS

PART THREE
THRIVE: Building a Robust Growth Organization

ABOUT THE AUTHOR

Dr. Rebecca Homkes is a high-growth strategy specialist and the founder of a boutique consultancy firm, advising CEOs and executive teams focused on growth and success through uncertainty. She is a Lecturer at the London Business School (LBS)'s Department of Strategy and Entrepreneurship, Faculty at Duke Corporate Executive Education, Advisor and Faculty at Boston Consulting Group University, and previous Fellow at the London School of Economics (LSE)'s Centre for Economic Performance.

Dr. Homkes is the director of the global Young President's Organization (YPO) Active Learning Program (ALP); a previous partner with GrowthX, a Silicon Valley investment ecosystem and innovation consultancy; and the faculty lead of fintech scaleup accelerators. A global keynote speaker, she is a member of several advisory boards, directed the joint McKinsey & Co and LSE Centre for Economic Performance Global Management Project from 2007 to 2014, and has written for publications such as the *Harvard Business Review*, *Businessweek*, *Fortune*, and *Forbes*.

A Marshall Scholar, she received her PhD and MSc from the London School of Economics in International Economy. Prior to LSE, Dr. Homkes received two degrees at Indiana University: BS (Honors) in business administration alongside a BA (Honors) in Political Science where she was a Wells Scholar and graduated as the schools' top graduate in 2005 and its sole Herman Wells Scholar. She previously served as a Fellow at the White House's President's Council of Economic Advisors and has worked in strategy consulting with Bain & Co. She lives between Miami, San Francisco, and London.

PROLOGUE

Building Uncertainty into Strategy

It was the second week of March 2020, and conversation after conversation with CEOs started with the same question.

What do I do now?

These executives were from companies ranging in revenue from a few million to several billion and scattered across industries and continents—and they all shared the same concern. They had a strategy in place, and it was working. Then the Covid-19 Pandemic happened, and everything felt like it stopped. They had no idea in which direction the world was going. Everything was uncertain. They were worried about their organization and their employees. They wanted to know how to get their organizations through this (whatever *this* was) and back to growth.

Over the next weeks, I found myself repeating the same few lines.

Uncertainty is just an unknown future; it's not necessarily bad. Periods of uncertainty (and even downturns) are a great time to grow. They aren't easy times to grow, but there's always opportunity in change. First, let's stabilize the business and ensure survival. Next, we're going to have to reset the strategy and build the capability to return to a growth pathway. Then, we can find our way back to thriving.

Eventually, I captured these main points in a long email, partly so I could stop repeating myself, and I sent it to the CEOs who had come to me for help in those first weeks. The next morning I received a flood of responses: It was the most helpful thing they had read, and they wanted to forward it to others.

The email became an article, the article became a strategy program, and that program I then combined with my over 15 years of strategy advising and experience to build a practical methodology: Survive Reset Thrive (SRT). Now that methodology is captured here so SRT can support a wider range of organizations.

What strikes me about those panicked March 2020 conversations were that they were not unlike the many I had had with CEOs during the 2009 recession, after the Brexit vote in 2016, in early 2022 after Russia's invasion of Ukraine, and even in late 2022 when AI became a part of the daily discourse.

Here's the thing: Events that cause us to pause, stop, and rethink our growth pathway are not once-in-a-leadership generation events. We'd all be better off if we built the flexibility into our strategies to absorb and even leverage these unexpected shocks when they occur.

Most strategy tools do not factor in uncertainty or change. They help to assess the environment, make a set of choices, and then force ruthless discipline in executing the plan. Change is seen as an anomaly and, when it does happen, a risk to be addressed. Complex and sophisticated tools for planning through uncertainty certainly exist: scenario planning, Bayesian simulations, or horizon mapping, to name a few. But most small and mid-size companies do not have the teams or capability to use them. Larger companies that do use sophisticated tools often feel unequipped when shocks occur to know what to do in the moment.

What I have realized is that companies simply do not have the tools *and guidance* to ensure they can survive, reset, and thrive through uncertainty.

In times of uncertainty, leaders struggle to know which tools to apply when and to know when to switch. They struggle with what feels like forced tensions: growth vs efficiency, execution vs opportunism, agility vs discipline, among others. Traditional strategy tools tell us we must make choices between these tensions, but with the right approach, capability build, and growth pathway, I have seen many of these trade-offs evaporate. Survive, Reset, Thrive is the approach I have developed to break the tension of these trade-offs and provide a disciplined path through uncertainty—through any market conditions, really—to growth.

Leaders are busy. That's why they come to high-growth specialists like me who live and breathe strategy, leadership, and execution; who know all the tools and how they work in practice; and who can create a clear path for them through all the noise. As a Teaching Fellow and Lecturer at the London Business School's Department of Strategy and Entrepreneurship and Faculty at Duke Corporate Education with a PhD and MSc from the London School of Economics in International Economy, I read everything on strategy. But more importantly I practice high-growth strategy development and execution everyday, meaning I can refine an approach that works.

Survive, Reset, Thrive brings together more than 15 years of working directly with high-growth companies (ranging in size from a few million to over 20 billion) across industries (from technology and software to construction, professional services, tourism, and retail, among many others) including not-for-profits and industry associations, across multiple countries and geographies. I've guided these companies through the Survive, Reset, Thrive loop, helping them to embrace ambiguity, proactively stabilize their businesses to survive any market condition, and then reset when they needed to clear the path to thriving. Most of these companies went on to outgrow their industries by a significant degree while enjoying their highest levels of profitability, employee engagement, and customer satisfaction. I know it works.

Survive, Reset, Thrive is different, practical, and effective. It pulls the best elements from some existing strategy tools and frameworks—all of which I have battle-tested—and it adds the critical missing element: It builds dealing with change into the playbook.

I wrote this book because I see firsthand how we can get it wrong about change. Our default is to frame uncertainty as unequivocally bad, something to be managed down. SRT shows what happens when we see uncertainty as a set of possibilities for growth. This new frame of what is possible is exciting, but it is not easy. Most books aren't honest enough about how hard it is to reset. Yes, it takes a mindset switch—and it also takes hard work, emotional resilience, and discipline as you must keep assessing and adjusting along the way.

If you are ready to embrace change as a central element of your growth strategy, this book is for you. When you are facing uncertainty and you want to find your way to leading a growth journey, SRT is your roadmap.

1

Why Survive, Reset, Thrive?

"There is no such thing as a growth industry, I believe, there are only companies organized and operated to create and capitalize on growth opportunities"

—PROFESSOR THEODORE LEVITT

A once-in-a-generation crisis. The week that will have a dramatic impact on markets for decades to come. A historic drop in confidence. Everything changes after this.

Phrases like these should define a traumatic or historic moment in time; a point when we all quickly align on the same reference point. The problem is that they could have referred to a number of cataclysmic events over the past 25 years, such as the terrorist attacks of 9/11, the 2001 dot.com crash and recession, the 2007–2008 global financial crisis, the 2016 Brexit vote, or the 2020 Covid pandemic. We are constantly facing unpredictable disruptive events that overturn the old certainties.

The problem is not that these unpredictable events happen; the problem is that when they do, organizational leaders tend to freeze or panic, and then falter through the uncertainty that follows.

Business leaders, economists, and academics obsess anxiously over uncertainty. This is an understandable but rather unhealthy preoccupation. We tend to ignore uncertainty when it is not clearly manifest and panic when it is, as if certainty were the normal, natural state of things. Unfortunately, that panic leads to inaction at best, and dysfunctional responses at worst, which can destroy a company's growth trajectory.

There is something about the word "uncertainty" that I realized several years ago, long before Covid made it a highlight of everyone's agenda. When we refer to it, we usually put a word before it that means it is bad. We speak of how we need to "manage," or "overcome," or "get through" uncertainty. We almost always precede this word with a verb that signifies this is going to be terrible.

As organizational leaders, figuring out what you are trying to achieve and then setting the organization up for success in an uncertain environment is the core of your job. How to do so is the focus of this book. But viewing uncertainty as universally negative does not prepare your businesses for growth. So our first step is to reframe how we view it.

Certainty is a delusion. Uncertainty is normal... and it is neutral. **Uncertainty is a series of future events which may or may not occur. Whether or not these events are good or bad depends on what we are trying to achieve and how we are set up.**

The fundamentals of Survive, Reset, Thrive

Let us start our journey with three fundamental propositions that lay the groundwork for the Survive Reset Thrive approach, and that I will build on throughout the book.

Three propositions

1. UNCERTAINTY DOES NOT ALWAYS HAVE BAD CONSEQUENCES
"Uncertain" is not synonymous with "bad," and uncertainty in a market is not synonymous with a downturn. The fact that our brains are programmed to view uncertainty as negative has major ramifications for the actions we take. Our starting point on the Survive Reset Thrive loop must be that uncertainty is the future, and not necessarily a negative one.

2. STRATEGY IS WHAT IT ALWAYS HAS BEEN: THE ART OF CREATING VALUE
While industries, markets, consumer preferences, and societal norms will constantly evolve, one critical thing never changes: the notion of what strategy is. You need a strategy, and the essence of strategy remains the same. Strategy was, strategy is, and strategy will always be about one thing: value creation. Strategy is an articulation of how your organization creates value.

Value creation is about driving a fundamental gap between two factors: your customers' willingness to pay for your products, services, or solutions, and your total cost (including the risk-adjusted cost of capital) of delivering that value. The best way to visualize strategy is with two needles, where the upper needle is customer willingness to pay and the bottom needle is the total cost of delivering that value (Figure 1.1). The art of strategy is focusing on the few things which will dramatically move these needles apart. Thousands of things can cause the needles to bounce, but only a few will push and keep them apart over time.

3. NO ONE CAN PREDICT THE FUTURE

Growing through uncertainty is hard because we cannot predict the future. Accept that now: you cannot predict the future. I wish I could, and I wish you could! And if you think you can predict the future, please put this book down and go use your powers of clairvoyance to make yourself lots of money in the markets! Most of us can't, and that matters. The future consists of multiple options and trying to predict attempts to simplify these into one, which blinds you to unforeseen opportunities. Predictions are also usually based on experience. In a turbulent environment the past is not always a good guide to the future, and therefore most predictions will be wrong.

Three directives

These three propositions lead to three important directives for surviving, resetting, and thriving.

FIGURE 1.1 Value creation needles

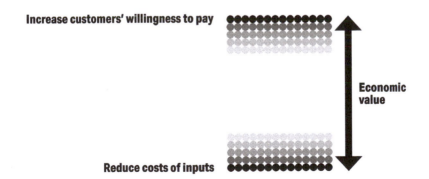

**The essence of strategy is creating economic value:
Moving the needles**

Increase customers' willingness to pay

Economic value

Reduce costs of inputs

1. MAKE GOOD DECISIONS EVEN WHEN WE CANNOT MAKE GOOD PREDICTIONS

The challenge is mastering how to **make good decisions even though we cannot predict the future.** It is the quality of decision-making that sets apart those who lead growth from those who barely survive or indeed perish. Strategy's fundamental job is providing a framework for decision-making, and the following chapters provide a playbook of tools and techniques to boost your team's decision-making capability, a differentiator in getting to Thrive.

2. STOP PLANNING, START PREPARING

In uncertainty, we cannot always plan well because the picture continues to change, and we cannot predict the end-state. We can, however, prepare ourselves so that we do not simply survive now but thrive over the longer term. Thriving through uncertainty means forgoing the notion that you can just implement a plan, and instead acknowledging you are often in preparation mode for the future.

3. PERIODS OF UNCERTAINTY ARE A GREAT TIME TO GROW

Leaders often worry about what uncertainty will bring, but they should remember that **periods of uncertainty can be a great time to grow.** Times of peril—perceived or actual—are when having true strategic insights and executing on them can make the biggest difference between winners and losers.

Anyone can grow a company when markets are booming, cash is free-flowing, and everything is going up. It looks easy—for a time. But when the boom ends and things get hazy and gray, only those with true strategic insight prevail. When there is no boom, the easy path is closed to all.

Uncertainty allows those with insights to get ahead, if you are prepared to adapt and change. If your organization can move with aligned speed, executing on these insights and adapting as you go, you can make uncertainty a growth launchpad for your organization.

The need for Survive Reset Thrive

Periods of uncertainty are a great time to grow, but they are not an easy time to grow. There is a difference between being bullish and being stupid. We need to be smart about how we think about creating value through uncertainty. Survive Reset Thrive (SRT) is the proven playbook I have used with countless organizations to develop and lead successful strategies through an unprecedented range of market conditions.

When uncertainty appears, most downshift to recession mode and hunker down. But growing through uncertainty is not just about protecting the downside; it is also, critically, about setting up to optimize for the upside and then adapting with aligned speed to grab these opportunities. Facing uncertainty does not mean you are facing a recession, but if you find yourself in a market downturn, this approach can guide your strategy approach to reset for growth. Downturns are also a great time to grow, and the Appendix covers these reasons in full.

A future shrouded in fog is what we should expect as a norm. SRT is therefore how you can develop and execute strategy for the realities of your future markets. It allows organizations to leverage any market condition: up markets, down markets, incredibly foggy ones, and even times of stability (though there are admittedly few leaders who believe that's their current environment).

The Survive Reset Thrive loop

Survive Reset Thrive is an interconnected three-mode approach to building and executing a solid growth path with purpose, regardless of your environment.

Survive is the first mode. It is about stabilizing the business when a shock hits. Shocks can be macro events such as major market corrections or reduced capital flows, or micro and specific, such as losing a major customer account. Survive must be reframed as a proactive stance and not a reactive posture; that is, successful companies are always set up to survive! This phase has several "basics" such as the cash flow runway, receivable and liability resets, and shoring up the balance sheet. Many of these will be familiar, but these moves alone will not be enough. To move into Reset and then Thrive, you must utilize what I call the power moves: repurposing and partnering, deepening customer moats, and accelerating learning velocity. Strong, robust decision-making is key to managing and moving out of a successful Survive.

Reset means exactly what it says—resetting your strategy when the situation changes. **The power of getting to Thrive is in the Reset,** and how to Reset forms the heart of this book.

While this can seem daunting, overwhelming, or just plain frustrating, Resets must happen. You change strategy when the situation changes, and the situation usually changes after the shock that triggered Survive. Reset is a revisit of each of the key questions that together make up your strategy story:

- What is the situation, and how will this change?
- What is success?
- Where will we play?
- How will we win?
- What will stop us?
- What should we do?

Within each of these steps, I interweave some established strategy tools with updated approaches for leading through uncertainty. At the end of a Reset, you will have an updated mid-term (three-year, two for smaller organizations) growth strategy.

Thrive is not a given; it must be earned. After transitioning out of Reset, companies begin executing an adaptable strategy through the evolving market conditions. Getting to Thrive takes what I call disciplined flexibility. This phrase sounds like two contradictory words thrown together, but this is true of most high growth principles. Disciplined flexibility means having a methodical approach that involves testing assumptions, verifying beliefs, and building trackers. And then when you have an insight, you must move quickly! To get to Thrive, you must combine the rigor of developing and testing insights with speed of execution. The recipe for Thrive is deceptively simple: a strong balance sheet brought from the Survive phase; strategic insights from the Reset phase; and then executing with agility and learning.

The power of SRT is that it works. It is purposely simple but not simplistic. SRT is practical, ready to implement, and adaptable to your organizational size, industry, and context.

Using this book

Survive, Reset, Thrive is for entrepreneurial leaders who want to lead breakthrough growth through any market condition. While the focus is on senior executives, leaders, and entrepreneurs, team members leading functions, units, departments, or teams will also benefit from the playbook.

SRT is not just for established companies; many start-ups and scale-ups have also used this playbook including dozens of scale-ups through the Fintech accelerators I lead. SRT also works in the non-commercial world. Several industry associations and sports organizations have executed with SRT to lead successful performance journeys.

Survive, Reset, Thrive is written directly to the leader, but going through the SRT loop is a team activity, not an individual one. You will want to work with your leadership or executive team on Survive. For the Reset discussions, it is useful to involve a few more team members to ensure the customer, market, and operational perspectives are included. Once the top priorities are set, you will involve the next level of leaders in the process of building the execution plans. And as you move into Thrive, you will be engaging the wider organization in building shared context and capability building. Along the way, it is important to communicate more widely to keep everyone abreast regarding where things are, where they are going, and why this matters.

Chapters in brief

The book walks through SRT with a focus on practical implementation, proven techniques, and examples of successful execution. In each mode, I use case studies and examples to make the concepts come alive. The chapters are explicitly written in the order of execution: Survive, then Reset, then Thrive. I recommend reading the book in its entirety first before embarking on the SRT loop so you have the big picture of the journey. While it may be tempting to start with Thrive, I promise you, you will not be ready to leverage the learnings in these chapters until you have gone through the hard work of the previous ones!

PROLOGUE: BUILDING UNCERTAINTY INTO STRATEGY
Chapter 2 provides background on uncertainty, focusing on what it is and how approaches to it have changed over the past several decades.

PART ONE: SURVIVE
Chapter 3 dives into what it means to be in Survive mode, including the difference between "steady-state" and "triggered" Survive. One of the hardest parts of Survive is knowing when to move on, so the chapter will also cover how to transition into the Reset.

PART TWO: RESET

Comprises the core of the book. In five chapters, I walk through the growth strategy questions organizations must revisit—or, for some of you, answer for the first time. Each Reset chapter introduces the strategy question and why it matters, explores how to address the question the first time, and discusses how to update it after a triggered Survive.

Chapter 4 focuses on the question "What is the situation, and how will it change?" I detail the process of building a strategic situation assessment including identifying trends, articulating beliefs, testing assumptions, and transitioning to implications.

Chapter 5 explores the critical concept of competitive advantage, or Right to Win. I simplify it to its core: you have one when you have things others do not (resources), you can do things others cannot (capabilities), and you can build moats around your advantage (barriers to entry). These resources and capabilities need to be the key, rather than just the necessary, and pass the hard tests of being valuable, rare, and inimitable. As it is uncommon to have more than a few of these advantages, I suggest ways to close capability gaps and translate these insights into action.

Chapter 6 dives into the question "Where will we play?" I explore the interrelated questions of the customers and markets you are targeting, the value proposition you are delivering, and the pathway you have taken to go to market—in other words, your Who, What, How.

Chapter 7 pulls the Reset insights together to build a picture of what winning looks like, which involves setting a "finish line" and a structure so the team can make decisions to get there. I also cover "What will stop us?" or the biggest challenges that must be addressed. At the end of the chapter, we pause to discuss what happens when you need a "hard Reset," that is, when almost everything needs to change.

Chapter 8 concludes the Reset and discusses how to decide "So what should we do?" This question comes at the end of the section, as you need the insights from the previous chapters to address it correctly. I introduce the term "must-win battles," which will be your list of clear, mid-term, executable priorities that make a major difference to value creation.

PART THREE: THRIVE

This completes our journey through the SRT loop.

Chapter 9 discusses the transition from Reset to Thrive mode, which is the movement from setting your top priorities to scoping and executing them. Strategy dies without execution, so I get granular about how to build out execution pathways in a team workshop as well as boost organizational execution capacity.

Chapter 10 explores what it means to Thrive, and I introduce the BLAST framework: Beliefs about the world, Learning velocity, Agility in decision-making, Shared Context, and Trust or reliability across the network of performance commitments. Thrive comes from executing on full BLAST with these elements.

Chapter 11 lays out the biggest reasons for failure to Thrive based on real examples. More importantly, I offer guidance on how to overcome these traps.

Chapter 12 concludes with a summary of key considerations and recommendations for making it through the SRT loop.

Getting the most from SRT: Some learnings

Many learnings have emerged from working together with leaders on their SRT journeys, and these will be interwoven into the chapters that follow. A few central ones are worth starting with, as this will help focus the discussion and your considerations for the upcoming journey:

1 **SRT is a loop, not a line.** While it is easier to consider this as a linear process, where you check off Survive, then Reset, then Thrive, that's not how it plays out. Instead, view SRT as a loop as shown in Figure 1.2. While you transition through the modes, sometimes you must go back to Survive before Thrive. You may be in Thrive for months, or years, but then find yourself needing to move into Survive to re-stabilize. Embrace the loop. Avoid the hubris of ignoring when it is time to Survive, but also avoid getting stuck in Survive or Reset.

2 **Different units move at different paces.** Your organization will not move through SRT at the same pace; different business units and regions will proceed faster or slower than others in different modes. It is more common for two or three business units to be moving on from Reset while another needs longer in the Reset and another is still in Survive. As a leader, you need to appreciate that this is not just OK, but probably better for the business. While it is easier, and therefore tempting, to manage all parts of the organization in the same way, doing so is unlikely to lead to success.

FIGURE 1.2 The SRT loop

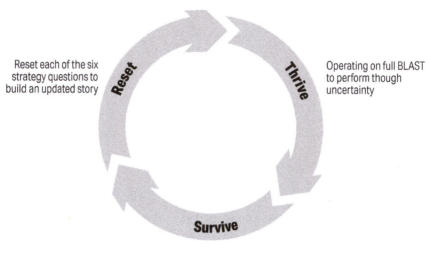

**Survive Reset Thrive:
a loop—not a line**

Reset each of the six
strategy questions to
build an updated story

Operating on full BLAST
to perform though
uncertainty

Proactive stabilization
of the organization

3 **The power is the Reset.** Don't just Survive—Thrive! While a popular phrase, and one that we hear increasingly after market turbulence, it misses the critical point. Just surviving will not get you to Thrive. If you are not prepared to go through a Reset—and if you are not prepared to manage the changes that come along with it—you will likely not get to Thrive. The power is in the Reset. Resets are hard because Resets involve change. Creating a robust new strategy is fundamentally about change. Change is hard for individuals and harder still for organizations. But if you can prepare to lead through the SRT loop and embrace the change it demands—and then lead this through the organization—you can journey to Thrive.

As you work through the book, remember that leading this journey means confronting tough choices and what feels like unprecedented uncertainty. **Strategy, however, is and has always been about making tough choices when facing uncertainty.** Making good decisions when you cannot make good predictions is fundamentally about being comfortable with being uncomfortable.

It is time to get the basics right, revisit your growth strategy, and prepare to accelerate through uncertainty, a possible downturn, or whatever conditions the market throws at you next. It is time to embark on the three-part loop of Survive, Reset, and Thrive (Figure 1.3).

FIGURE 1.3 Overview of the Survive Reset Thrive steps

Recap of key steps in SRT

Survive

Basics: The 4Cs

Power moves

Reset

What is the situation?
And how will it change trends, beliefs, assumptions, implications?

What is success?
Destination vs direction; intent and boundaries

Where will we play?
Our who, what, how

How will we win?
Right to win, our VRIN advantages

What could stop us?
Friction to address

What should we do?
Our MWBs

Thrive

Beliefs about the world:
Setting, testing, and acting on beliefs

Learning velocity:
Learn faster, grow faster

Agility in decision-making:
Making good decisions quickly, aligned with strategy

Shared context:
Intent and boundaries, MWBs

Trusted network:
Reliability across the network of commitments

2

The Challenges and Opportunities
of Strategy Under Uncertainty

"I returned, and saw under the sun, that the race is not to the swift, nor the battle to the strong... but time and chance happeneth to them all."

—ECCLESIASTES 9:11

In the 1990s, Pfizer began work on the compound torcetrapib to treat heart disease. In 2001, despite evidence that torcetrapib raised blood pressure, CEO Hank McKinnell declared it to be "an enormous opportunity." In 2005, despite worrying levels of patient mortality, Pfizer began building manufacturing facilities. In December 2006, the new CEO Geoff Kindler announced that torcetrapib would be "one of the most important compounds of our generation." Three days later, Pfizer terminated clinical trials on the drug after spending an unprecedented $800 million. The company's market value fell by $21 billion overnight.[1]

Although the scale of Pfizer's eventual losses was unusual, the company's pattern of decision-making was not. Experienced executives swept aside uncertainty, confidently predicted a positive outcome, ignored mounting evidence that their predictions were wrong, and failed to cut losses until they had no choice. This sequence of bold predictions and timid decisions is all too common. But why?

Studies consistently show that executives are overconfident in their ability to predict the future—more so than the population as a whole.[2] Often, they

This chapter is based on joint research with my colleagues Stephen Bungay and Anthony Freeling between 2014 and 2020.

do little more than guess, and then feel the need to stick to their decision in order to justify past investments and avoid being wrong. This is reinforced by organizational governance systems that reward sticking to the plan.

The only certainty in life and in business is uncertainty. Unfortunately, our natural human response to uncertainty often works against us, which impedes our brain's ability to make good decisions.

This chapter discusses how to reframe our view of uncertainty, assess it, and adjust our strategy approaches to succeed through it. We then explore the role of chance and serendipity before linking these discussions to the Survive Reset Thrive playbook.

Our natural response to uncertainty

Human beings do not like uncertainty. The most common response is to ignore it and pretend certainty exists. Others recognize uncertainty, but often have unjustified faith in their ability to predict its consequences. Worryingly, this faith is particularly delusional amongst subject matter experts. In making predictions, we pay undue attention to the information most readily available to us rather than the most relevant.

Human beings are natural storytellers. As we make sense of the world, we create stories to help orient ourselves in potentially confusing situations and ease our discomfort with uncertainty. And as soon as we have a narrative that makes sense, we tend to stop looking for alternative ones. Often, the narratives we adopt are based on the most recent rather than the most relevant experience, known as recency bias.[3] Once adopted, we get attached to the narrative, and it becomes increasingly hard to budge, a phenomenon called anchoring.[4]

These tendencies have severe impacts on organizational decision-making. We work in environments that are fundamentally ambiguous and can therefore be open to multiple interpretations. Nevertheless, we tend to anchor on the first explanation we develop and use new information to confirm this view rather than challenging it. For example, a leader who has led two successful turnarounds through cost-cutting is likely to have confidence in the story that cost-cutting is the best way to achieve turnarounds. They may then apply the same tools to different businesses, without doing due diligence to justify their confidence. Similarly, if the last time unemployment increased sharply and consumer demand paused a recession occurred, we assume the next time there is a jobless spike a recession will follow. In 2020, however, a shock to the system and unemployment spike did not lead to a global recession (or lasting unemployment), which left many businesses unprepared to take advantage of market opportunities when demand returned quickly.

A further nefarious consequence of our natural discomfort with uncertainty is to frame it as negative, synonymous with "risk" as discussed in the introductory chapter. Nearly all companies include a risk register at the back of their annual operating plans. These registers propose actions that can be taken to mitigate the risks identified, as well as assessments of the residual risk. The exercise provides a sense of comfort that potential issues are in the line of sight and can be addressed. But the entire focus is on reducing downsides, with no attention paid to capturing opportunities.

More worryingly, risk registers often fail to capture the risks that cause the most serious damage. Few banks foresaw the warning signs of the 2008 financial crisis that followed the collapse of Lehman Brothers that led to the need for a host of bank bailouts. Meanwhile, stress tests imposed by regulators in Europe had given the all-clear to those bailed-out banks within months. Likewise, while Japan's Tokyo Electric Power Company identified possible tsunamis following the great earthquake of 2010, they assumed none would be big enough to overwhelm defences. And while there had been fast-spreading viruses before—remember SARS?—few businesses had a global pandemic on their risk radar coming into 2020.

Defining uncertainty

One meaning of uncertainty is a state of reality. The future is the totality of events that may or may not occur, which makes it uncertain. This is *real* uncertainty, which makes it difficult to make good predictions.

The other meaning of uncertainty is a state of mind. Not knowing what will happen causes anxiety, makes us feel uncomfortable, and makes us prone to biases during decision-making. This is *psychological* uncertainty, which makes it difficult to make good decisions.

The combination of real and psychological uncertainty creates the double jeopardy of delusion and paralysis. If we ignore real uncertainty and try to predict the future, we plunge forward with our delusions until the business hits the rocks. But if we bow to psychological uncertainty and anxiously wait for clarity to emerge—which it rarely does—we become paralyzed by inaction, and the business drifts and sinks. This strategic "holding pattern," evident in many UK businesses following Brexit in 2016, causes businesses to falter and fall behind.

There are more options than delusion or paralysis!

To open those options requires that we first overcome the temptation to make predictions. Instead, let's *acknowledge the reality of uncertainty and build our strategy around it*—not simply adjust for it. Next, we have to overcome the fear of making decisions without having all of the information. This is important because we will never have all the information, and that's OK.

Uncertainty is not inherently good or bad, and the future is simply the totality of events that have yet to be determined. Moreover, whether the future presents threats or opportunities depends to no small extent on how we react to them. Some of the greatest business successes have come from capitalizing on uncertainty. Take IKEA.

In the 1960s, IKEA was primarily a mail-order furniture company based in Sweden.[5] It had one retail store, and in 1965 opened a second store in the suburbs of Stockholm, where low real estate costs meant they could take over an unusually large space. By chance, the Swedish government announced plans to raise sales taxes the next week. As a result, on its opening day the store was overwhelmed by 18,000 customers. Short of staff, the desperate store manager told his people to work the tills and open the warehouse so customers could pick up the goods themselves.

Later, the manager apologized for his poor planning and assured IKEA's founder, Ingvar Kamprad, that it would not happen again. Kamprad became contemplative and asked the manager once more to confirm that customers had indeed been willing to pick up their goods from the warehouse and take them to the tills themselves. "Yes," came the nervous reply. Kamprad then announced that from then on this would be the norm for all IKEA stores. The unexpected crush on opening day drove a pivotal change to the company's business model, which reduced staff costs and became a key element in IKEA's future success. The problem of understaffing was an opportunity in disguise. What set Kamprad apart, and allowed IKEA to capitalize on the opportunity, was his attitude toward chance and uncertainty.

Assessing: The Uncertainty Matrix

There seems to be a consensus that leaders must first diagnose the level of uncertainty in the environment before deciding how to proceed. Not only do leaders find this hard to do, they usually get it wrong.[6] A simpler and more pragmatic approach is to categorize uncertainty in terms of variables that teams can assess: its **degree of familiarity** and its **potential impact** on the organization. These two variables create an Uncertainty Matrix (Figure 2.1).

Plotting uncertainties, their priority, and the right approach to dealing with them is not an exact science but a matter of judgement, and it helps if that judgement is based on collective discussion with the team.

To evaluate familiarity, consider:

- Can our company's current business model deal with the uncertainty?
- If not, has anything like the current situation happened before?
- If so, which aspects of the current situation are different?
- Is the rate of change linear or exponential?
- Can we identify and control the variables driving change and how they interact?

People tend to overestimate their own levels of certainty and overemphasize the familiar aspects of a situation. Because of this, my advice is: When in doubt, move to the right (of the matrix).

To evaluate the potential impact of uncertainty on the business, consider:

- Could this challenge our basic beliefs about how our business works?
- Will we get into trouble if we continue down our current path?
- How soon do we need to decide what to do?
- How much will we need to invest?
- If new technology is involved, how could it affect us in the hands of a competitor?

Distinguish what you know from what you don't know. It's easy to confuse assumptions with knowledge. Split out what is a trend (something you are seeing) from an assumption (a proposition based on beliefs, frames, or prior experience). Often societal and technological trends take longer than expected to reach a tipping point, and then have a greater impact more quickly than expected. As Bill Gates noted, "We always overestimate the change that will occur in the next two years and underestimate the change that will occur in the next ten."[7]

FIGURE 2.1 The Uncertainty Matrix

Answering these questions about the familiarity and potential impact of the uncertainty will result in a prioritized portfolio of potential decisions and a clearer understanding of how to approach each one. Let me explain.

The uncertainties that populate the lower left quadrant of Figure 2.1 are familiar and manageable. They are high on the familiarity axis and low on potential impact. For instance, organizations routinely make budgets and sales forecasts without knowing what next year will bring. When wrong, it is annoying and adjustments are needed, but the consequences are rarely serious.

The upper left quadrant contains uncertainties that require specific experience that is learnable. Many companies have built skills and experience that enable them to make good decisions about high-impact uncertainties regarding known variables. For example, oil and gas companies make huge investments in drilling exploration wells based on only partial knowledge. These experiences have become more familiar to them—even though they would paralyze others. Established processes guide their decision-making, and these usually work reasonably well.

Despite the weaknesses of human psychology noted above, the human brain has a decisive strength: the ability to learn. If we have sufficient exposure to initially intractable problems, we can learn to handle them. Learning velocity is also one of the biggest differentiators of high-growth companies, which I'll discuss in Chapter 10.

More serious issues arise from the right-hand side of the matrix when the phenomena are unfamiliar. Here, our experience may be as much of a trap as a guide. Similarly, the key is not prediction, or making a single right call, but learning about the unfamiliar as fast as possible. For a pharmaceutical company, upper right examples would be class action lawsuits. The rising trend of telemedicine would have started in the lower right, but has gradually moved over time, and for many is now on the left of the grid.

Unfamiliar uncertainties with high potential impact must be part of the executive agenda. Others with less potential can be delegated, tracked, watch-listed, or even ignored, given resource limitations. Think about what items are already budgeted for, and then move emerging issues onto the executive agenda before major resource allocation decisions need to be made.

The degree of impact is often a function of time, as some uncertainties will move from low to high on the matrix over months and years. Additionally, as a company's knowledge, skills, and familiarity grow, uncertainties that were on the right of the matrix tend to move left. Others may fade away over time.

When artificial intelligence (AI) was first explored in the 1950s, optimistic forecasts predicted its huge imminent impact—another bold forecast that was wrong.[8] Tracking it as a critical trend made less sense then. In the decade preceding 2020, while its impact was still uncertain, AI moved quite quickly to the forefront of people's minds with many businesses investing heavily in the area. The launch of Open AI's ChatGPT in 2022, however, made AI part of everyday discourse with more organizations quickly bringing it—and its varied use cases, especially around efficiency, customer insights and enhanced centricity, and learning potential,—into strategic planning.

Different types of uncertainty require different approaches, including adjusting between planning and preparing.

Approaching strategy: Planning versus preparing

Traditional strategic plans involve committing to an estimate of future results based on several "best estimates" of things we cannot predict such as economic growth, customer demand, and input prices. We put these into a plan, which projects results for three to five years. We caveat these are assumptions, but we are committed to delivering the plan. Organizations and stakeholders reinforce this dynamic by favoring the status quo and preferring management teams that "deliver on their promises."[9]

Plans articulate a base option, but it is based on a series of events that are not only unpredictable but also often uncontrollable. This view is not new to strategy. Prussian Field Marshal Helmuth von Moltke memorably challenged the traditional approach towards strategic planning in military conflict, when he stated nearly 150 years ago:

> "The material and moral consequences of every major battle are so far-reaching that they almost invariably create a completely different situation, a new basis for new measures. No plan of operations extends with any certainty beyond the first encounter with the enemy's main body."[10]

In uncertainty, we cannot make perfect plans because we cannot predict what *will* happen. But we can prepare for what *could* happen.

There will be parts of the business where planning still applies. Leading through uncertainty is about knowing when to apply planning versus preparing. Below is a breakdown of how to determine when to apply these with your strategy discussions (see also Figure 2.2):

- **Are you working with beliefs or data?** When there are no reliable facts, we need to make decisions based on beliefs. This sounds scary, especially to companies that have invested in data-based systems and technologies. But we are not ignoring data. We are instead acknowledging that by the time something becomes a market fact, the opportunity for developing strategic insight has passed as everyone knows the same thing. If you want to outgrow your industry, you will at times need to make decisions based on beliefs about the emerging reality. Good beliefs are not guesses or fantasies, but views about the future informed by reliable information and judgement that can be tested and changed.

- **Is the situation familiar or emerging?** Familiar situations tend to have data that can be analyzed, known variables, and a relatively clear path forward. These types of uncertainty, on the left side of the grid in Figure 2.1, lend themselves to a *probabilistic* approach, one that combines planning—drawing on probability theory—and a variety of analytical methodologies. But when we move to the right, we are playing in

FIGURE 2.2 Planning vs preparing

Probabilistic strategy: Planning	Exploratory strategy: Preparing
Based on **data**	Based on **beliefs**
Variables are **familiar**	Variables are **emerging**
Set **destination**	Set **compass heading**
Goalposts are **fixed**	Goalposts are **moving**
Optimize decisions for **efficiency**	Optimize decisions for **robustness**

environments where variables are still emerging, such as we saw with Brexit, Covid-19, or more recently AI. In these situations, we should avoid the temptation to plan. Some phenomena are sudden and unexpected. In other cases, the phenomenon is anticipated but the timing and extent of the implications are unclear. These unfamiliar situations require preparing, which is a more *exploratory* approach, much like navigation in uncharted waters.

- **Should you pinpoint a destination or a direction?** In 1850, Chicago journalist Horace Greeley urged America's young men to "Go West." He didn't specify a destination, like San Francisco or Colorado. He didn't have to. The West was the land of opportunity and he strongly believed there were fortunes to be made—even though it wasn't exactly clear how the westward migration would play out. His injunction was not precise, but it was accurate. It was directionally correct. Like a ship's captain he set a good compass heading. When the future is unclear and you're in exploratory mode, setting the right general direction is more important than setting a precise destination.

- **Are goalposts fixed or moving?** Leaders should distinguish between the times when clear endpoints and related deliverables are needed versus rolling milestones to achieve further learnings. Goalposts are important in strategy, but sometimes we can only get clearer on where they should be as we move and learn. While exploring, acknowledge variables are emerging and you will keep learning as you go. As conditions evolve and greater clarity emerges, tighten the goalposts you are aiming for and adjust your pace. Aims are important in strategy, but sometimes we can only get clearer on where to set them from acting and learning.

- **Should you be optimizing for efficiency or robustness?** In a downturn, optimizing for extreme efficiency may be the right move. We have developed a wide array of tools to help us do this, such as just-in-time production and cost-cutting methods. In uncertainty, being overly indexed on efficiency can sometimes hurt you. Instead, you want to optimize for robustness—still running lean, but set up to capture the opportunities uncertainty can provide. Robustness is preparing your organization to adapt to change and perform well, continuing to produce results regardless of the situation.

In times of uncertainty, shifting from planning to preparing helps support clearer decision-making instead of rash predictions. It involves overcoming both hubris and fear to achieve decisiveness and adaptability. It generates knowledge of what is initially unknown, and so creates learning. And, as I emphasize throughout the book, Thrive companies are those that maximize their relative rate of learning.

Adjusting strategy: Adapt as you go

Strategy is not just a masterplan; rather, it is a series of goal-based moves conducted in a process of iterative reappraisal. Each move builds on the last and the new situation that move creates. In the process, planning tools may need to be augmented, and sometimes replaced, by the preparation tools discussed above. To ensure constant assessments and learning, strategy cannot be created simply by the top team, but rather people in leadership positions across the organization; what I term distributed leaders.

A more exploratory approach combines the readiness to adapt with incisive decision-making at each inflection point. The chapters that follow will break down this approach into an actionable playbook. Below is a high-level view of what's to come:

- **Defining your beliefs**: Horace Greely urged young men to "Go West" because of a strong belief that the west was the land of opportunity. Similarly, an important element of directional strategy is to clearly define the beliefs and assumptions that will guide your organization forward. This set of beliefs can become a company's true north, ensuring that everyone can make good decisions no matter how circumstances change.

- **Agreeing on a compass heading and pace**: Setting a compass heading allows a company to take coherent action and opens up future options by limiting decisions to only what is necessary at a particular point in time, without prematurely worrying about the precise endpoint. The question for the executive team is: Given our beliefs about trends and our current position, what no-regret moves can we make now to advance our interests, and how much time do we have? The focus should be on actions—such as building capabilities or gaining experience—that will get the company to a better place under any set of plausible future scenarios.

- **Choosing a strategic stance**: As you move in the direction you initially set, the situation and your position within it will change and you'll need to make a continual series of decisions about your next move. A wide range of options lie within the extremes of dithering and gambling, such as your organization's ability to be actively preparing for future opportunities or learning about the environment.

- **Reassessing the situation**: Any stance your company takes will either yield new information or alter the competitive situation, so monitoring outcomes and the changing business landscape must be ongoing. At each progress review, the first question should be: Has the situation changed? If the answer is yes, question whether your beliefs and assumptions are still valid, and whether your stance needs to be altered.

- **Adjusting the course and communicating the change**: The timing of these reviews will vary depending on the rate of change of your industry. As clarity increases, you may need to reassess and revise your beliefs, assumptions, actions, and stances, and then make updated moves. These updated moves are communicated, within the context of the evolved situation and learnings, and the organization adapts the course.

- **Building change in, and culturally rewarding it**: Thriving through uncertainty is fundamentally about building change in as part of strategy—not an exception. It involves acknowledging from the onset that not everything in the plan may happen and the situation will change. But changing without alignment is chaotic, changing without communicating is harmful, and changing without having built the capability of how to change is simply not possible. Your approach must adapt for this implied change, including what you culturally recognize and reward.

Approaching strategy in this way creates a flexibility and dynamism that traditional strategic planning often lacks. Along the way, companies often find that unexpected opportunities arise from the actions they take and from other chance events in the changing business environment.

Kickers, killers, and serendipity

Threats and opportunities often depend on our perception, our expectations, and our plan. If we have a plan, it is tempting to identify threats by trying to predict problems. The issue with predicting problems is that they form an infinite set of things that may or may not occur and may or may not be relevant. We need to stop asking "What could happen?" There are just two critical questions: **What could break us?** (a *killer*) and **What could make us?** (a *kicker*).

Visualize the varying strategic consequences from your decisions as a bell curve (Figure 2.3). With clear strategic choices and disciplined execution, most outcomes will fall under the fat middle with familiar consequences and medium to high likelihoods. Killers and kickers lie at the edges of the bell curve of probabilities. They are the outliers that writer and scholar Nassim Taleb famously christened "black swans."[11]

While tempting, I encourage you to resist imagining what could happen because the actual consequence is often something hard to imagine. It is far better to think through vulnerabilities (killers), and, once you identify them, ask:

- What would have to be true for this vulnerability to be exposed? And,
- What do we have to do to make ourselves more robust?

Unfortunately, it is easy to ignore vulnerabilities until they become exposed, by which time it is too late. Contrast the attitude of Citigroup's Chuck Prince, who in the summer of 2007 announced that the bank would maintain its enormous portfolio of collateralized debt obligations (CDOs) "until the music stops," with that of Goldman Sachs' Lloyd Blankfein (the latter claims to spend 98 percent of his time worrying about the 2 percent worst contingencies).[12] In late 2007 Citigroup lost $20bn and 30 percent of its market value, whereas Goldman, which had unraveled its CDO position in 2006, enjoyed its most profitable year ever, earning $17.6bn.

What prompted Goldman to do so was not a better ability to predict the future, but an awareness that the CDOs in its portfolio made it vulnerable, and that if, for whatever reason, CDOs were to go sour, that vulnerability would be exposed. Indeed, as the world soon learned, CDOs were a potential killer. Goldman acted to reduce that vulnerability before it became exposed and, by shorting CDOs, turned the potential killer into a kicker.

To identify the positive outliers which could give you a "kicker," ask **"How could we win big? What could make us?"** Most companies spend disproportionately less time identifying possible upside kickers versus downside risks.

When considering the bell curve of options, we rarely explore possibilities in the far-right tail, and, when others capture these, liken it to luck.

FIGURE 2.3 Kickers and killers

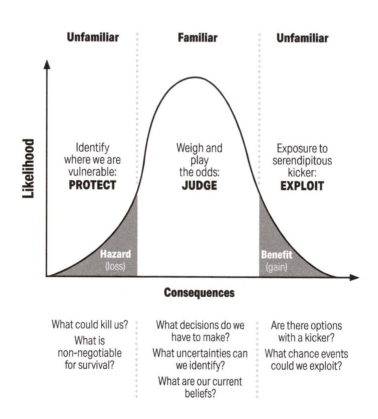

Don't ask *What could happen?*
Ask: *What will make us? What could break us?*

Unfamiliar	Familiar	Unfamiliar
Identify where we are vulnerable: **PROTECT**	Weigh and play the odds: **JUDGE**	Exposure to serendipitous kicker: **EXPLOIT**

(vertical axis: Likelihood; horizontal axis: Consequences)

Hazard (loss)   Benefit (gain)

| What could kill us? What is non-negotiable for survival? | What decisions do we have to make? What uncertainties can we identify? What are our current beliefs? | Are there options with a kicker? What chance events could we exploit? |

Business success can often be attributed to luck, but it is not luck that some companies are luckier than others. "Good luck" is the name we give to the result of a chance event that enables an organization to gain an advantage. It depends on the chance event taking place, but more so how a company reacts to it. It can be recognized or ignored; it can be thrown away or exploited. Chance is endemic in business. Good luck is less so.

There is a tendency to ignore or suppress the role of chance in business unless bad consequences flow from it, in which case "bad luck" is invoked to exonerate poor judgement. Taking a closer look at cases of successful enterprises reveals chance played a central role. Taking a closer look at how chance enabled success reveals that runs of good luck are more often systemic than random. Companies that seem to be luckier than others do two things well: They make good subjective judgements about probability, and they adapt their view of the world to fit new facts, producing stories that are more accurate, honest, and valuable than the old ones.

Consistently lucky companies exploit unforeseen opportunities through their aggression and timing. They embrace the unknown by engaging in serendipity-rich environments in which there is a lot of change that can result in opportunities. These environments are usually ones that contain threats and opportunities in equal measure. The biggest risk is not participating.

In contrast to the story of Pfizer's failed heart disease drug torcetrapib is the story of the company's biggest-selling drug, Viagra.[13] The development of the now ubiquitous male performance enhancer came down to a decision taken in the early 1990s to explore the role of nitric oxide (NO). At the time, it was known that NO played a role in raising the levels of a compound called cGMP, which reduces blood pressure, and might therefore play a role in treating high blood pressure, which kills millions of people a year. But its precise role in the chemical pathway was unknown. Interest in NO was such that in 1992 a scientific journal nominated it "molecule of the year."

Scientists at Pfizer's Sandwich lab decided to investigate further. One exploratory pathway led to a breakthrough and very profitable treatment for erectile dysfunction—a kicker. Since then, sildenafil, the active ingredient in Viagra, has been licensed under the name Revatio to treat pulmonary hypertension, and investigations are underway to use sildenafil to treat mountain sickness, Raynaud's phenomenon, and heart disease. The pathway that started with NO was a serendipity-rich environment, which is still being explored and exploited today.

Strategy creates the context in which adjustments to goals and actions can be thought through. Benefiting from chance events requires the strategic ability to adjust actions—both to overcome obstacles and to realize unforeseen opportunities. Organizations that consistently do so will be serendipitous.

No one will be successful in business without good luck. **No one will be successful in business without recognizing when they can shape reality and when they must adapt to it.**

Summary and next steps

Developing strategy requires that we assess the situation and decide upon a coherent set of actions to achieve desired outcomes. In traditional planning, this process is linear and uncertainty is catered for under the heading of "risk." With the SRT approach, this process is a loop, and unpredictable chance events represent opportunities to be exploited just as much as they do risks to be mitigated.

By building our strategy around uncertainty—not simply adjusting for it—and embracing possible kickers and not just killers, we can set ourselves up for luck. But approaching strategy in this way involves shifting from planning to preparing and being prepared to adapt as we go. It also requires the humility to forsake prediction and the courage to face reality.

Uncertainty often manifests itself after a system shock. This may trigger movement into the Survive mode, which I will cover in the next chapter.

Endnotes

1 M Herper (2006) Behind Pfizer's Failure, Forbes, www.forbes.com/2006/12/03/ pfizer-heartdisease-drug-biz-cx_mh_1204torcetrapib.html (archived at https:// perma.cc/7TAQ-4UDU); A Berenson (2006) Pfizer Ends Studies on Drug for Heart Disease, New York Times, www.nytimes.com/2006/12/03/health/ pfizer-ends-studies-on-drug-for-heart-disease.html (archived at https://perma. cc/LY68-USLA)

2 See D Kahneman (2011) *Thinking, Fast and Slow*, Farrar, Straus and Giroux, pp. 261–63. Kahneman interprets this systematic over-confidence as a manifestation of the "availability bias," a tendency to believe that "what you see is all there is." There is some evidence that élites are less prone to loss-aversion bias than the population as a whole, but more prone to over-confidence. See E M Hafner-Burton, D A Hughes and D G Victor (2013) The Cognitive Revolution and the Political Psychology of Elite Decision Making, *Perspectives on Politics*, **11** (2), pp. 368–86.

3   Known as the "availability heuristic." See Kahneman, chapters 12 and 13 (pp. 131–45).

4   Kahneman, chapter 11 (pp. 119–28).

5   B Torekull (1999) *Leading by Design: The IKEA story*, Harper Business

6   M Reeves, K Haanaes and J Sinha (2015) *Your Strategy Needs a Strategy*, HBR Press, pp. 93 and 111

7   B Gates and C Hemingway (1999) *Business @ The Speed of Thought: Using a digital nervous system*, Warner Books, chapter 4 'Ride the Inflection Rocket', p. 69. Gates was likely paraphrasing professor Robert Amara.

8   D Crevier (1993) *AI: The tumultuous search for artificial intelligence*, Basic Books, p. 109

9   D Kahneman and D Lovallo (1993) Timid choices and bold forecasts: A cognitive perspective on risk taking, *Management Science*, 39 (1), pp. 17–24

10 Helmuth von Moltke the Elder, *On Strategy*, 1871, translated by S Bungay in *The Art of Action* (2011), pp. 245–46.

11 N N Taleb (2007) *The Black Swan: The impact of the highly improbable*, Random House

12 J La Roche (2014) LLOYD BLANKFEIN: I'm A 'Highly Functional Paranoid', Business Insider, www.businessinsider.com/blankfeins-calls-himself-paranoid-2014-6?r=US&IR=T (archived at https://perma.cc/8V7J-GS2M)

13 'The Viagra Story', unpublished case study by Stephen Bungay.

PART ONE

SURVIVE: Setting Up for Continuity

3

Survive: Proactive Stabilization of the Organization

"It is not the strongest or the most intelligent who will survive but those who can best manage change."

—LEON C. MEGGINSON

Warren Buffett's fundamental rules of business are often reiterated in times of market shocks. To paraphrase:

Rule number one: Stay in business.

Rule number two: Don't forget rule number one.

As with so many of his business quips, Buffett was right.

An organization's priority is business continuity. The problem is that it only feels like a priority when it has to be—when something bad happens—and by then you are left scrambling. But stability is the foundation of growth, not the antithesis of it. If your company is not set up to survive the unexpected, you will not achieve a sustainable growth journey, or Thrive. If you want to be a Thrive company, you must always be set up to Survive.

The word "survive" carries many associations with it, most of which are unhelpful, whilst some are simply wrong. To do well in this mode, we need to start by reframing how we approach it.

First, Survive is not a reactive stance, it is a proactive posture. Survive done well is not just about getting through something that hit or disrupted you. In Survive, you are proactively stabilizing and setting your organization up for continuity.

Second, Survive is more than just recession-proofing or managing through a downturn. Recession thinking causes us to view markets only in terms of swings—there are good times when you grow and bad times when you hunker down. It asks your team to wait for the market to tell them it is OK to start growing, rather than controlling your own destiny. Markets are cyclical, but your business does not have to swing between good and bad as well. **Your strategies and approaches will adapt across different markets, but your ability to grow is always there.**

All organizations will need to work on Survive at some point, which begs the question: When do you go into Survive mode? To answer this question, consider that there are three main reasons to be in Survive mode:

- Steady-state Survive
- Triggered Survive
- Persistent uncertainty that leads the brain to think a downturn is coming

Steady-state Survive is continual, proactive stabilization. You are not necessarily managing it daily, but you are consciously and regularly ensuring you have a stable foundation for growth. Then, if circumstances produce a system shock, you are prepared to act. Proactive stabilization is a strength as long as it's not overdone and you run too lean. This discipline will support you in moving to Thrive.

Triggered Survive is onset by a sudden, significant shock or correction, either external or internal. These can be major macro events such as the 2020 Covid-19 pandemic and its subsequent shutdowns, a major foreign exchange (FX) shock such as that triggered by the 2016 Brexit vote, or central bank decisions. Shocks can also be internal, such as a major investor pulling back, an industry shift making your solutions less relevant, or major customers cancelling. Shocks trigger Survive. Assuming you were employing steady-state, when a shock hits, you pause, go through your Survive basics, accelerate the power moves, and when the timing is right move back to Reset and Thrive.

Persistent, high uncertainty Survive occurs when the effects of several events exacerbate each other leading to ongoing market concerns that make it hard for us to know what comes next. The prevalence of high uncertainty is the least compelling situation to be in when it comes to Survive mode. Our brains are programmed to view uncertainty as bad—so we either avoid addressing it or we overreact to the circumstances and go into an overly protection mode.

The power to stabilize the business during such times is in preparation—done by employing steady-state Survive. Steady-state Survive allows us to see a path forward during high and persistent uncertainty. Then, when there is a specific course-altering shock, we are set up to move into triggered Survive and restabilize. Given this, and the need to focus on the two healthy variations of Survive, this chapter only covers steady-state and triggered, but it will address how triggered Survive varies depending on the level of your steady-state.

This chapter will get you prepared, starting with the hard truths about Survive mode. Then it covers knowing how to ensure you have the necessary Survive basics in place and are proactively stable in steady-state. Next, we explore the Survive power moves that will help you get you through triggered Survive. After Survive (defense) comes the Reset (offense), so the last Survive move is learning how to ease the transition into Reset by playing offense and defense at the same time. It is easy to get stuck in Survive, so I detail pragmatic approaches to track and move out of Survive as well as how to manage the emotional energy it takes on the team.

Survive: Challenging assumptions and hard truths

Survive done well comes from accepting five truths.

Hard truth 1: Triggered Survive mode sucks

Famed boxer Mike Tyson once said, "Everyone has a plan until they get punched in the mouth."[1] Going into triggered Survive is like getting punched. You have a great strategy, you may even be thriving, and then a shock occurs, and you must go into Survive mode. Do not waste time feeling sorry for yourself or pretending you haven't been punched. You can't stop the market from punching you, but you can get better than anyone else at taking hits.

While this mode is not fun, you must be good at it, or find someone to step in who is. Being good at it is different from *needing* to be in Survive mode. Entrepreneurial literature often hypes the distinction between "wartime" and "peacetime" CEOs, building an almost heroic mythology around "wartime" CEOs who are great in a crisis. This can lead to the assumption that great leaders are the revered "wartime" architype, and you need a crisis to prove your leadership chops. But leaders who enjoy Survive too much often do not lead Reset or Thrive well. If that's the case, these leaders should consider moving to another company once their company goes into Reset so they can lead another company's Survive.

Hard truth 2: You do not choose the timing

You survive when you have to, not when you want to. This is difficult to accept: when you are in Thrive, you want to stay there. Leaders often put on blinders, refusing to acknowledge a trigger has occurred. Recently, a CEO proudly told me their company was not going to participate in the next recession. While I loved their confidence, the market determines when there is a recession, not ego. You can grow through and out of market downturns, but first you must pause to make sure you are set up to Survive.

Hard truth 3: Your company's business units will not move at the same time

It is unlikely the entire company will go through triggered Survive at the same pace. Managing disparate business and geographical entities in different modes presents a leadership challenge, but it is a challenge that must be embraced. Slowing down the whole company or forcing all units to proceed at the same pace will either hold back some units from growth or ruin others' chance at Thrive.

Hard truth 4: Survive is part of growth, not the opposite of it

One of the biggest traps preventing companies from thriving is seeing Survive and Thrive as opposites. They oscillate wildly between the two: overspending and lacking discipline in up times and over-cutting and slowing too dramatically in down times. When everyone is growing, it is easy to forget that the Survive mode is part of the loop. You build, hire, and spend assuming the future will reward you with a stronger market position. But markets can change, often unexpectedly. It is easy to get caught up in the hype of fast growth and over-spending, as we saw with internet companies in the early 2000s, real estate in 2005–2007, and cryptocurrencies in 2020. This is not a new phenomenon: industry shifts have led to growth explosions for centuries, such as the boom and bust of American ship building in the early 20th century. Going into extreme growth mode and extreme cost reduction mode means as an organization you do not build capability in either. Leading successful strategy is about building capability through the entire growth journey.

Hard truth 5: Survive, done well, happens in the good times, too

These four truths lead back to the underlying premise: Survive is proactive. Steady-state Survive is the tough balance of disciplined stabilization while allowing for investment in future growth. Balance means being prepared for when things get tough and having the solid foundation for growth. Companies in Thrive continually check in on their Survive basics, even in up-markets. Then, in down-markets they know they can rely on being stable, so they move quickly through Survive mode, faster than others, and return to innovation and growth.

Survive basics: Get them consistently right

Are you default alive or default dead? In a 2015 essay, co-founder of startup accelerator Y Combinator Paul Graham raised this question.[2] While it may be premature to ask in the very early days of a company, it can become critical quickly, and, he warned, dangerous to ask it too late.

You are "default alive" when based on current expenses, growth rate, and cash on hand, your company can reach profitability with its current level of capital (i.e. not raising another round of funding), and you are "default dead" when you cannot.

While startup lessons should be applied judiciously to established companies, this becomes THE question during Survive. Assuming your company is past the start-up stage, you can rephrase it to: *Based on current expenses, current linear growth rate, and cash on hand, will the company continue to be profitable if the current growth rate does not increase?*

For example, if your growth is five percent/year, and next year it remains five percent/year, with the same linear increase in expenses, what happens? The answer may be that you are default dead.

More companies are "default dead" than they realize. They are assuming a third- or fourth-year bump in growth numbers as the basis for their decisions. But what happens if that assumption is challenged? What happens when a shock triggers a movement into Survive mode? Understanding the Survive basics is critical, because when capital becomes more difficult to access, a small shift in one metric or another can make a major difference.

The Survive basics outlined below are moves that should be made continually as part of steady-state Survive. In triggered Survive, the basics must be tightened and metrics updated and refocused on the updated situation.

For ease of tracking and memory, a Survive basics checklist can be organized around the Four Cs: Cash, Cost, Customers, and Communication (an example of how to assess your organization across these is in Figure 3.1).

FIGURE 3.1 Survive basics checklist

The 4 Cs

	Survive elements	Rank 1 = weak 5 = best in class	What can we do to improve?
Cash	Cash reserves held	①②③④⑤	
	Cash conversion cycle	①②③④⑤	
	Accounts receivable	①②③④⑤	
	Accounts payable	①②③④⑤	
	Balance Sheet Strength	①②③④⑤	
	Bank(s) and Financing Relationships	①②③④⑤	
Cost	Fixed costs percentage	①②③④⑤	
	Fixed costs: Ability to cut	①②③④⑤	
	Customer Acquisition Cost (CAC) and Cost to Serve (w) versus Lifetime Value (LTV) relationship	①②③④⑤	
Customer	Customer loyalty / Risk of leaving	①②③④⑤	
	Customer indexing (% within one customer or segment of customers)	①②③④⑤	
	Customer satisfaction or Net Promoter Score (NPS)	①②③④⑤	
Communication	Communication: Employees	①②③④⑤	
	Communication: Customers	①②③④⑤	

Cash

CASH FLOW

Cash is always king, and market shocks show why. Those with cash on hand have more security and flexibility, and the liquidity to quickly deploy it. While numbers will vary, set minimum cash flow boundaries for steady-state Survive and stay within them as non-negotiables. In technology investing, general guidance is a 12- to 18-month runway; that is, the number of months the company can fund its current operations without raising additional capital. Some investors ask for this to be closer to 24 months, whereas for many established companies three months is a more realistic figure. An average is six to 12 months.

Your steady-state boundaries will be different from your triggered Survive ones: set both as guidelines to stay within. In triggered Survive, perform an immediate analysis of your cash flow forecast and work proactively to anticipate issues. While income variability makes these forecasts more difficult, perform a best-, medium-, and worst-case scenario for revenue this year and its impact on cash flow, and make the decisions necessary to ensure a sufficient runway. Microsoft founder Bill Gates has a similar principle: Always have enough cash on hand to pay all your employees for a year.

BALANCE SHEET STRENGTH

Strong balance sheets are important for steady-state Survive, as they are a snapshot of your overall financial health. Your balance sheet is composed of assets (items owned by or owed to you), liabilities (what others owe to you), and equity (capital paid to you). Assets equal liabilities plus equity. Healthy balance sheets are generally those with higher levels of cash and working capital and an appropriate amount of liabilities. In triggered Survive, shore up your balance sheet by increasing assets through topline revenue or eliminating non-performing assets, improving cash flow, and cost cutting. Triggered Survive can require you to bring in more cash through loans or debts. This can negatively affect the balance sheet as it increases liabilities, so trade-offs must be made. Set clear metrics for your cash conversion cycle and other critical metrics and monitor them on your Survive checklist. Understand your current credit rating and how to improve it, as being able to secure more favorable borrowing terms will help your position.

ACCOUNTS RECEIVABLE AND PAYABLE

In steady-state, have clear policies in place for accounts receivable to ensure a stable flow of cash coming in. In triggered Survive, review receivables and accelerate payments owed to you. Consider offering discounts to get cash in sooner. Do a best, mid, and worst-case scenario for how many of these you will eventually get in, but budget to the mid and worst case. Understand your accounts payable, the terms you are liable for payments to others, and how you can re-negotiate and simplify these to your advantage.

Cost

FIXED COSTS

A fundamental principle of growing through uncertainty is keeping the fixed cost base as low as possible. In steady-state Survive, fixed costs should be kept under a certain percentage of total cost. True variable costs are acceptable in Survive mode, as these ideally only rise with your revenue, but fixed costs become a drag which can trap you in Survive.

After a shock, examine your fixed costs and lower them to the greatest extent possible to allow only additive costs that pay for themselves. Many of your costs will be long-term and not easy to offload. Rank these from highest to lowest and evaluate what you can do with each one. Do not be afraid to re-negotiate payments or leases under contract. Shocks are also a great time to consider what fixed costs are most susceptible to disruption or capable of being digitized: digitizing can increase efficiency and reduce run-rate costs going forward.

Focus on necessary cuts and sizable costs that will make an impact and ignore insignificant adjustments. Don't cut by asking for something across the board, like demanding each department reduce costs by 20 percent. Not only is this usually ineffective, it also shows a lack of strategic understanding. Instead, do a value chain mapping (covered in Chapter 4) and make cuts in areas not critical to your Right to Win (covered in Chapter 5). Also, do not tinker. Small, micro cost cuts do not move the needle; rather, they annoy employees and send terrible signals about leadership intentions and the company's future state.

UNIT ECONOMICS

Deeply understand your unit economics, which are fundamental to assessing the financial viability of your business, but more importantly segments or aspects of the business, such as certain customers or solution offerings. Your unit economics show the profitability of different solutions or customer segments and the efficiency of your operations. Without a clear grasp on these numbers, decision-making in Survive becomes more difficult. The critical input measures are revenue, cost, and contribution margin per unit. Here are the most important related metrics:

- *CAC (customer acquisition cost)*: the fully weighted cost to acquire new customers.

- *LTV (lifetime value)*: the average total revenue generated by each customer segment over their lifetime with you.

- *Gross margin*: the difference between the revenue generated by each unit or customer segment and the cost of goods sold associated with each unit or segment.

Understanding the profitability of different customer segments, products, and solution offerings means you can make faster decisions in triggered Survive. At times, it may be rational to explicitly grow an unprofitable customer segment to generate volume, provide "reference customers" (those key brand names that will draw other customers to you based on working with that name), or have a total number of customers that enhances brand name. Unless you are running a land grab strategy,[3] however, over time these customers will become a burdensome cost and will need to be compensated for by either cheap capital (which dries up in market downturns) or more profitable customer segments. These are critical metrics to understand and watch, as during triggered Survive decision-making speed is a competitive advantage.

TALENT AND TEAM

For many companies, especially those in professional services or software, one of the largest expense items is staffing. While there is no one-size fits all guidance for hiring, you can avoid issues in triggered Survive by employing these principles during steady-state:

- **Avoid stacking management upon management.** Thrive companies celebrate individual contributors. Too many organizations over-celebrate managers, which means high-potential employees feel they are only rising in the organization if they have people to manage. When high-potentials want the next step in their career, they assume they must build a team, which means hiring people under them. Of these, at least 20 percent of the new team will also be high-potentials, who will want to soon replicate teams under them. Very quickly you have built an organization of people managing people and not managing growth. Break the cultural norm that potential is rewarded with people to manage, and instead reward potential with new and stimulating opportunities for value creation.

- **Approach growth problems with new solutions rather than just adding people.** Too often when we have new problems to solve in companies, we assume we need new people to help solve them. Challenge the linear assumption of more work needs more people and work back from the problem to be solved with new approaches. Reexamine and break down solutions, shorten learning loops, and experiment before adding people—topics we will explore more in Chapter 10.

- **Understand what it takes to be a great employee at your company.** From a cultural and strategic approach, what are your non-negotiables on hiring? Be very clear about them, while understanding your answers may vary across different functions and regions. Gain alignment with all leaders and managers, and do not make hiring compromises, even if competitors are hiring faster than you. "A" players who do not match your requirements should be passed over, and this filter will help with more judicious hiring.

- **Hire two types of talent: specific tour of duty vs re-purposability.** At an extreme, break all hires into two types. Sometimes, you have a specific task (such as ERP implementation), and you will need to hire specific skillsets for that initiative. With this type of hire, the employee's time with your company will be limited to that "tour of duty."[4] The second type of hire is a repurposable one. A key skillset of Thrive employees is they can be repurposed to different areas of the organization as the company shifts how it creates value. Not all employees have this capability. If you are not hiring for a specific, and likely time-limited task and the employee does not seem fit to repurpose, you probably shouldn't be hiring them.

- **Articulate your beliefs in hiring:** During steady-state, increasing your employee count more than 30 percent in any year should be done with caution and only after articulating and testing your articulated beliefs. Let's take a simple example. If demand spikes quickly for your solution and is doubling month over month, employees will demand more resources especially for support and service. But you should not hire linear demand curves on untested assumptions. Say out loud: "Our growth increased 50 percent every month for the last three months, and we believe it will increase at this rate for the next year, so we need three times as many team members in account management and support." Even saying that should give pause. Sustaining this level of growth is rare, and when it flattens you have unsustainable fixed costs. We saw this play out starkly in 2020. Many software companies seeing spiking demand hired just as fast, if not faster. Meta and Snap both doubled employee count from 2019 to 2022 and many of their competitors increased employee count by at least two-thirds, only to begin multiple rounds of layoffs in 2022 when demand started to decrease. Force yourself to clearly articulate your beliefs and testable assumptions between demand and supply, and more so, why that number of employees is needed to support that growth, especially given automation gains enabled by AI.

In steady-state, you can push these principles too far and run too lean, which means operating with too many controls on hiring. This can slow growth and critical talent pipelines. Avoid over-centralizing hiring decisions, freezing hiring prematurely, or putting too high a barrier on hires. Effective talent pipelines are a Thrive advantage, and with clear boundaries and talent principles you should trust distributed leaders to hire well. Watch for burnout of top talented people, especially those being overwhelmed by basic administrative tasks. A few hires for specific tasks can free the growth mindset of others and lead to order of magnitude returns.

In triggered Survive, examine your talent. Hiring freezes may be necessary unless the employees pay for themselves (e.g. a sales person who fully costed brings in more revenue than their salary). You may also need to cut staff. Use this time to make the tough decisions you were likely already delaying, such as laying off consistent underperformers. During and after the Reset, there will be an opportunity to hire, but during Survive the immediate response might be a freeze until the shock abates. I say more on talent below when I cover tough decisions.

Customers

CUSTOMER LOYALTY AND RISK

In steady-state Survive, you should not be overly dependent on any one customer or industry: set a boundary, such as no more than 30 percent dependence, and stay within it. Ask what makes your customers loyal to you? In triggered Survive, review your list of top customer accounts and understand the risk of any of them leaving or significantly downscaling their work with you. Build mitigation plans to address the risks, such as targeted customer outreach or shifting focus to a new set of customers (in Chapter 6 I will discuss how to segment and understand customers). If a particular customer segment is most affected, shift your focus to the next set of prioritized ideal customer segments.

Communication

EMPLOYEE COMMUNICATION

Clear, consistent communication and building shared context is key. During steady-state this is normal communication about needed efficiency and balance. During triggered, increase communication and share more not less. Perception is reality inside organizations, and your employees will make up the story if you do not give it to them. Most times their stories are worse. Trust your team members to be able to handle the truth. If you show your employees you do not trust them in Survive, it is hard for them to trust you in Thrive. Work with your leadership team on the triggered Survive story: why we are in it, what we are going to do, and the specific asks of employees. Communicate the bad news that may come, such as shutting down units or letting staff go, and then execute swiftly and efficiently on these tasks. Set a regular cadence of updates and stick to it, even if there is less to say in any given week. Have a specific leader own communication and monitor formal and informal team channels for the employee vibe.

CUSTOMER COMMUNICATION

Clear customer communication is always important, but during Survive it is critical. During triggered Survive, determine how much, if at all, your actions need to be communicated to customers. As with employees, they will make up their own narrative if you do not set it first, so tell the story. Open the communication lines so your customers know what you are doing, how you're handling the shock, and what they can expect from you. Customers are looking for authenticity, but if your triggered Survive elements will not touch customers, you can skip this step.

Survive power moves

The basics are just that: basics. If during Survive you just do these moves—you can get stuck. Too many companies drop their growth mindset and just focus on the basics during Survive. This is the generals fighting the last war. **In triggered Survive, the basics will not be enough, you also need to employ the power moves.** Moving through the SRT loop to Thrive demands getting ahead, being proactive, and moving faster and better than others.

Repurposing and partnering

Repurposing is revisiting every single asset in your organization—plants, buildings, lines, people, data. Ask the question: Does this asset add the same amount of value to the business now as it did before the shock? If not, who or what can it add value for? Which parts of the business (plants, lines, people) have been paused or under-utilized due to the shock, and how can they be repurposed?

After the shock of Covid-19, many companies repurposed their assets as an element of national security. Formula One teams switched plants to making ventilators, and in the US, Tito's vodka repurposed to making hand sanitizer, which it gave it away for free. Ford Motor Company repurposed several of its plants to manufacture face shields, medical gowns, and later ventilators and air filtration kits through its Project Apollo. Repurposing is not a new phenomenon: Black & Decker repurposed its machine and tool-kits during World War II, spurring new business lines that grew rapidly in the boom that followed.

You can also repurpose employees. In 2020, fast fashion retailers allocated employees they would otherwise have furloughed to grocery store chains. Food service companies repurposed drivers that previously delivered to restaurants to shared kitchens and homes.

AVIS Rental Company in Saudi Arabia, who saw their business shutter overnight when Covid-19 lockdowns were imposed, repurposed its fleet of cars to the top three logistics companies for online shopping deliveries. They quickly developed a new high-demand ecommerce delivery product that took advantage of the pandemic shock and allowed them to cover payroll costs. Meanwhile, competitors with idle fleets struggling to survive went into layoff mode. In addition to repurposing, AVIS focused on creative ways to cut costs, such as moving to remote management and paperless daily billing processes and reconciliation. This crisis was an eye opener for them to explore available technologies, move faster than others, and embrace a growth mindset to market disruptions.

Repurposing also links to what I call borrowing; that is, borrowing from work others did. In hyper growth, companies often do not have time to implement disciplined procedures, so where possible they borrow. For example, in its scale-up phase Google hired only referrals of current employees who went to an Ivy League school. They missed some good people, but it was more efficient way to hire than an elaborate screening process. They could not have hired at the rate they needed to without "borrowing" the vetting other recruiters did. In triggered Survive, utilize borrowing whenever possible.

Ask yourself and your executive team: Should we be on the sending or receiving end of borrowing, and if so, how? Re-examine every asset you have (including customer data and insights as well as physical assets) and perform this thought experiment on value potential.

Build stronger moats

Move beyond just protecting customer relationships and strengthen them. In strategy, building moats or lock-in around customers is a competitive advantage. You are increasing customer loyalty or deepening your relationships or service, which further pulls your customers in to you. After a shock, too often customer service and support are cut, new hires stopped, and resources reallocated away. It is an expense you feel can be saved as these customers are "safe." They are usually not.

Instead, use the power move of strengthening service and support. Dig in more to your customers and show them you are there. **Look for cost-free customization to do this:** How can you customize or specialize the experience for your customers in a way that costs you little or nothing? During Survive, many companies over-standardize, assuming all customization has costs. If you can identify value-add for your customers with little incremental cost to you, implement it. You will increase loyalty and satisfaction. You can also use this time as an opportunity to understand better how to serve your customers, including what tangential jobs you can do for them (more on this in Chapter 6). Take no existing relationships as given and build loyalty that will last through multiple market cycles.

Take advantage of imbalances or be agnostic to winners

Shocks exaggerate existing imbalances in demand and supply, so after a triggered Survive, look for new industry imbalances. How can you use these imbalances to your advantage? Does a partner need a distribution channel that you can provide? Can you adjust your supply to meet the new demand? Can you change your solution positioning to address these gaps? Map out the imbalances and what they imply going forward. Identify the major needs that are currently unaddressed or will be under-addressed going forward (so you should gear up now when things are cheaper).

Shocks can also intensify head-to-head competition. A related move is to identify markets or industries that are battling out in head-to-head competition and position yourself so you can be agnostic to the winners. For example, it is unlikely that the existing consumer space exploration companies Space X, Blue Origin, and Virgin Galactic will all win, if any do, but the parts suppliers who serve them can grow regardless of who wins that race. Cisco took this approach in the early days of the internet, providing solutions to enable business internet activity that worked across the players battling it out for dominance in the B2B space. And way before that, the makers of picks and shovels were set to win regardless of which explorers found the gold in the West! The same thought process should be applied to AI—where are the pieces of the industry value chain that will benefit regardless of the winner of the consumer interfacing search?

Employee engagement

Employee engagement is always important, but during triggered Survive it is critical. Part of getting through Survive is bringing your employees along with you. There are the basics mentioned above of consistent communication, frequent check-ins, and trusting your employees with the story. Now, here's how you go beyond communication to true engagement. Increase your light-touch measures (not just the annual survey) to get a pulse sense, make changes when friction points arise, and adjust as needed when engagement lags. Triggered Survive is emotionally draining, and while engaged employees will give their all for long periods of time, this is a different, much bigger ask than steady-state Survive.

I suggest nominating one person to "own" the employee pulse—engagement, productivity, and wellbeing—during Survive. In choosing who should do this, do not simply default to your HR Head; select the best person. Unless you are a very small company, this should also not be the CEO role. If the CEO does it, it becomes just one more thing on the list and it will get skipped. CEOs should have a regular check in with the nominated leader who owns the employee pulse to address any issues.

No-regret moves

Most companies distinguish between big and small decisions, but not types of decisions. Decision-making is a critical area where different methodologies and approaches can allow you to move faster and with more robust processes.

Accelerate decision-making by identifying and then quickly accelerating no-regret moves. There are always more than you think. **No-regret moves are defined as decisions that even if your beliefs are wrong, you will not regret making this move.** Massive layoffs are not a no-regret move, but cutting an under-performing product that has never validated assumptions may be. Ask at each decision point if this is a no-regret move and quickly execute all that are. I will go deeper into these in Chapter 4.

Jeff Bezos used another type of decision distinction at Amazon—what he referred to as Type 1 and Type 2 decisions. Type 1 decisions are "one-way doors" that once you walk through you cannot go back. Most decisions, however, are Type 2 decisions or "two-way doors." If you make a suboptimal Type 2 decision you can walk it back. Each decision type requires a different process. Type 1 decisions should be made more slowly and with greater rigor, whereas Type 2 should be made more quickly and trusted to more individuals and smaller groups.

Learning velocity

One of the essential distinguishers of a high-growth company is learning velocity: **companies that learn faster, grow faster**. Teams often go into heads-down tracking mode during Survive, moving the focus on learning aside. Leaders should instead stay heads up and encourage learning. Triggered shocks are not the time to flatten the learning curve.

To help learning, hold postmortems: What lessons can you learn from how you weathered your last triggered Survive? If you didn't experience one, or do not have postmortems, schedule a call with a Board member or another CEO to discuss what applicable lessons they pulled from the experience. Go through these lessons with your team and what implications they have for your plan.

Learning should not be restricted to the top team. Communicate to employees that data from the past is not a reliable guide to the future, so you will be building and constantly checking your beliefs. Bring employees into the process of articulating realistic beliefs about how each aspect of the value chain will be challenged now and going forward. Ask them: If this belief remains true for the mid-term, how could it affect the business? Holding "beliefs huddles" or similar light-touch meetings allows for discussions with the wider team on the evolving situation. Not discussing evolving beliefs gives the unintentional signal that everything will eventually switch back to pre-shock levels. That will not be the case.

One way to accelerate learning and improve decision-making is to avoid discussions about opinions: we all have them, and they do not matter much. During Survive more than ever we need to take out opinions as variables as much as possible.

Instead of asking "Do you think this is a good idea?" ask **"What would have to be true for that to be a great idea?"** List the assumptions, rank them by criticality, and then discuss one-by-one which are actually true, or you can make true.

I did this recently with a London-based tech company over the question of making an acquisition. One assumption they all agreed had to be true was that the founder would stay past the integration process—yet the team knew he would not. So, we concluded that it was not a good idea unless we were able to convince him to stay.

Given fast-moving situations and extreme uncertainty, there will likely be some things we cannot definitively deem true, nor can we know if they can be made true. That is OK. First, try and isolate the individual variables. Next, identify any game-changer assumptions. These are assumptions that if they are not true, put the entire business model in question. These are the assumptions that need immediate watching and testing. I discuss them in Chapter 10.

Keep trust high and boundaries clear

Companies tend to shift to micromanagement during Survive—increasing controls, centralizing decision-making authority, and removing autonomy from distributed leaders. They assume they must make a trade-off between alignment and adaptation, and they want the alignment. This is a false trade-off. Stephen Bungay explains why in *The Art of Action*.[5] Rather than ends of a single spectrum, he argues that alignment and autonomy are independent variables. You can have high alignment and high autonomy at the same time because the more alignment you have, the more autonomy you can afford to grant people. Moreover, the way to align is not to impose a lot of KPIs, but instead to develop a common shared understanding of the overall intent—what the organization needs to achieve and why. Then, you can give people autonomy to work out how.

In triggered Survive, communicate the intent or main goal and its time-frame, and the boundaries that employees must stay within in reaching this goal. Boundaries, which I discuss in Chapter 7, are non-negotiables that are usually related to the basics: cash, cost, and customers. Then, once these are set, get out of the way and allow your employees to execute towards that intent while staying within the boundaries.

Micromanagement is neither effective nor scalable, and the Survive winners are those that keep trust high. Micromanagement slows learning velocity, reduces the growth opportunities you explore, and signals to employees you do not trust them. This is a terrible message to send. Your boundaries will likely be tighter in Survive mode, which is OK, but communicate them and give employees all the space possible to move.

Make the tough choices

Survive involves making tough choices. Having a strong sense of unit economics is important so you can avoid blanket edicts and instead evaluate by solution, market, or customer segment in deciding what to stop, pause, and slow.

Know that your leadership will be remembered just as much, if not more, for the how rather than the what of making, communicating, and acting on these choices. You cannot always protect jobs, but you can protect people. Be incredibly human and empathic in the process. If forced to make tough people decisions, first re-review repurposing or borrowing options. If you need to do layoffs, do them once and early. Layoffs are like surgery: they cause short-term pain but are necessary. The body as a whole will be healthier over the mid to long term.

Go deeper than you think you may need to get things through in one round. While you can never fully promise there will only be one round of layoffs, you want to be confident enough to communicate to those who are staying that they do not need to be fearful and anxious. Multiple rounds of layoffs spread over many months are demoralizing, demotivating, and cause your top talent to dust off their resumes and look elsewhere.

Consider how Airbnb handled its March 2020 crisis moment. Just a few weeks away from its planned IPO, lockdowns forced the company to close most business units, lay off a third of its employees, and shrink back to its core. Yet the letter CEO Brian Chesky wrote to his employees[6], and the way in which the layoffs were handled—including repurposing their HR team to be external recruiters finding the let-go employees new roles—was a model for others to follow. He conveyed true emotion, owned up to his leadership responsibility, clarified their existing beliefs, and—most critically—took care of employees in their next steps. The cuts were necessary for their transition into Reset, but the way they handled the layoffs boosted their credibility and market assurance in their ability to Thrive.

How deep you should cut depends on why you are in Survive and the uncertainty in your beliefs and assumptions. Actively test and validate them so you make the right tough decisions. Some proclaim that you will never regret cutting too deep. Maybe for some companies in some industries in a deep recession this is the case, but as blanket advice it is flawed. In 2020 it was just wrong. Many companies that overcut were not able to seize the opportunities that arose quickly after the initial shock. Cutting deep might be OK in a recession, but it is far from true in uncertainty where the upsides can be significantly greater for those that are prepared.

Avoid sunk cost fallacy

Decision-making often becomes flawed during Survive due to the sunk cost fallacy. Sunk costs are payments, investments, or time which have already occurred. Nothing in the future can get them back. They can hold emotional weight, as we value our organizational time and money. Our natural human programming causes us to escalate or double-down on commitments that we've already invested in, as we have spent so much time, money, or attention on it. But shocks mean the situation has changed, and that matters. So instead of "How much have we invested in this?" discuss with your team,

"Given what we know today, would we start/ invest/ launch this project now?" If the answer is no, or even maybe, pause it and possibly completely stop it. Sunk costs are already gone and should not be factored into future decision-making.

You can use the checklist in Figure 3.2 to assess your team's ability to execute each of the Survive power moves.

FIGURE 3.2 Survive power moves checklist

The power moves

Survive elements	Rank 1 = weak 5 = best in class	What can we do to improve?
Repurpose and partnering	①②③④⑤	
Learning velocity	①②③④⑤	
Employee engagement	①②③④⑤	
Customer Moats and stickiness	①②③④⑤	
Digitization	①②③④⑤	
Ability to leverage industry imbalances or be agnostic to winners	①②③④⑤	
Clarity of boundaries and employee trust	①②③④⑤	
Ability to make tough choices	①②③④⑤	
Robust decision making (avoiding sunk costs, assumption vetting)	①②③④⑤	
Other power moves:	①②③④⑤	

Tracking and timing Survive

How long does Survive take? It depends. The timing will vary given the specific trigger, whether it was internal or external, and how strong your steady-state Survive was. It may never *feel* like the right time to move out.

When going into Survive mode, communicate a purposeful pause. Tell the company you will be in Survive for three, six, or nine months. For some smaller companies, three months is enough, but for many, six to 12 is a more realistic timeframe. It is hard to sustain full Survive mode for more than a year. There is also no time allocation to each step. They are not one-offs and may need to be worked through over the course of several weeks or months. And of course, in steady-state Survive, the basis should be ongoing practices.

Steady-state should be tracked using your normal operating metrics. Ensure you are tracking for what you need at that time. In steady-state, you can run too lean, hold too much cash, and starve your strategic priorities of the resources needed to succeed. In triggered, you can cut too deep, stay in the mode too long, and not accelerate the needed learning soon enough to emerge from it. Do not act like you are in triggered when you are in steady-state.

In triggered Survive create a separate tracking mechanism that is simple, clear, and shared. Set a clear milestone or goal for each of the steps (within the 4 Cs) with metrics, owners, and timing. Have a clear goal or finish line for each three-month cycle, specifying the outcome or results you want to have achieved at each point. Then determine the activities to get there. Do not simply track activities, though. When facing a long list of activities, employees usually focus on the shortest and easiest ones first, which means everyone is busy but doing little to move the needle. Work back from outcomes to guide the activities needed to get there.

If you have existing strategic priorities (we will cover these, or must-win battles, in Chapter 8), you may need to pause them for a period. The other option is to de-scope them but keep momentum going (playing offense and defense). If an explicit pause is needed, communicate why and the estimated timing, such as six months. Multiple pauses lessen the perceived importance of these must-wins, so use them sparingly, only during triggered Survives, and communicate the beliefs and assumptions that make the pause necessary.

Survive review meetings should examine the power moves and not just the basics, ensuring you are celebrating learning and experimentation as well as meeting the metrics. Be ruthless in setting realistic timeframes and sticking to them with tight accountability. Hold leaders to account for achieving results but be agnostic to how they got there: measure outcomes, not activities, and whether they stayed within the set boundaries. Once you achieve your 4 Cs targets and have power moves in place, you should begin the transition to Reset.

Assign one member of the Executive team to "own" Survive, usually the COO or CFO. This allows the mindshare of other team members to begin the transition. I find without this assignment a successful transition doesn't happen. It's also important the CEO does not spend all their time on Survive. The CEO's main focus should be on the business's survival years from now. If their focus is only on today, other leaders will not be preparing for what could come. If nobody is thinking beyond the immediate crisis, every future shock will become a crisis.

Above all, do not get stuck. Survive can become like quicksand and suck the team down. This often starts with Boards of Directors. A Board's job is governance and continuity: they are tasked with survival. But when you are in constant protect mode thwarts growth. I often see well-intentioned Board members go so far into protect mode it hurts the chance of Thriving. Agree on the metrics to move from Survive, task one Board member to govern these efforts working with the assigned executive team member, and free mindshare of the others to begin playing offense.

Playing offense and defense at the same time

Former Indiana University basketball Coach Bobby Knight was known for saying, "As coaches we talk about two things: offense and defense. There is a third phase we neglect, which is more important. It's conversion from offense to defense and defense to offense." While Coach Knight was referring to the fast clip of his team moving up and down the court, the same can be applied to the relationship between Survive and Reset modes.

Business commentators often remark you can't play offense and defense at the same time: they are wrong. You can, and sometimes you must. Starting to think about, and even moving into Reset is necessary during Survive. When done in a managed way, it can be the ultimate power move.

Once the Survive basics are in place, begin thinking about Reset and future growth. This can be as soon as a few weeks into the process and should not be more than a few months. You are not trying to move fully into Reset mode—yet—but you are taking some steps. Start the strategy Reset by having the first beliefs discussion (Chapter 4) and Right to Win discussion

(Chapter 5). As Jeff Bezos articulated in his last shareholder letter in 2020, differentiation is survival,[7] and you need to begin the Right to Win reset sooner than others. Moving out of Survive without a hypothesis about your current or near-future Right to Win will likely send you right back.

Mindshare is important to manage during these modes, and most people struggle to think fully about survival and future growth at the same time, so do not ask them to. Just as a football team separates offense and defense, so should your organization. The defense should be focused on the Survive steps, knowing that other teams are considering future growth. Offensive members are focused on finding and exploring future growth options with low-cost and low-risk experiments and tests, knowing that company survival is in the hands of their very capable colleagues. Separate offense and defense meetings and team rhythm to allow for the focus needed.

This was a successful move employed by Swedish-based zoo and amusement park Skånes Djurpark. In spring 2020, as with other in-person venues, lockdowns were imposed and there was little clarity on opening dates or capacity restrictions. The Park's team was forced to cancel their largest revenue-generating event of the year—a concert for recent graduates—leading to a cash shortfall and extreme uncertainty. The team set three clear Survive goals: Cash (minimum 18 months' cash on hand), Safety and Care (prioritizing employee safety and reducing costs without compromising quality of care for animals and staff), and Communication.

While globally most parks laid off employees or put them on extended furloughs, Skånes Djurpark took a different approach. They articulated the belief that without international travel, people would still want an adventure. If the Park created a safe experience, they could meet this demand. If they furloughed or fired employees and demand emerged, they would not be able to rehire quickly or well enough to meet it. If the demand did not emerge, they would be bankrupt anyway, so rather than cover for both scenarios, they prepared for the local demand assumption, building up the concept of "Safe Park."

When opening was allowed, they had to move faster than ever before. The team was explicitly encouraged to learn: mistakes were OK as long as the safety boundary was not violated. They even told customers mistakes would happen! Then a surprising thing occurred. The freedom to move not only led to fewer mistakes, it encouraged them to try new ways of approaching problems, such as integrating food trucks into the dining experience and adjusting the park's offerings with staggered schedules, allowing for more intimate guest experiences.

As Skånes Djurpark continued to update and test beliefs, they realized it was time to begin the Reset. Yet the team kept dragging itself back into survival mode. So Chairman Håkon Lund split the team into two: offense and defense. While the Survive team maintained critical financial and safety boundaries (defense), Reset team members accelerated acting to learn (offense), and many of their micro tests were later rolled out across multiple parks, such as expanded overnight stays and "glamping." The freedom to move clarified the role each team needed to play, empowered them, and boosted morale.

At the end of the season, the transition to Thrive was in place. The number of guests increased by 20 percent from the previous year (despite limiting capacity to one-third of maximum), with spend per guest increasing by 30 percent and overall profitability being boosted by 180 percent. Customer loyalty and satisfaction, as measured by Net Promoter Score (NPS), also increased significantly. In reviewing the results, Lund reflected that increased employee engagement and empowerment were perhaps the most successful outcomes, as these pieces fueled the other outcomes.

Your team can only stay in triggered Survive so long: they need to taste enough of Thrive to have the energy to Survive and Reset, so manage this transition well and be ready to move select employees into offensive teams as soon as you can while managing the rest in a clear transition.

Managing emotional energy during Survive

If you believe you can be a growth company, you must act like one in Survive. One of the biggest challenges during triggered Survive is the emotional drain it takes. When team members get stuck in Survive thinking, it starts to limit growth potential as they no longer see a path forward. They begin managing their own futures rather than the company's.

Lack of attention to emotional energy happens. Many companies get what feels like an adrenaline rush or dopamine hit after the first Survive communication and round of layoffs. Great employees want to be surrounded by great people, and often the first cut, which removes under-performers, frees talent to move faster with less day-to-day tension. Having a strong mission and clear guidelines, which a Survive goal does, also tends to galvanize employees who want to reach it. Netflix co-founder Reid Hastings noticed this after the first (and only for the next 20 years) layoffs at Netflix in 2001.[8] His Chief Talent Officer Patty McCord referred to the energy that filled the company after the layoffs as "being in love." Yes, this energy is wonderful and contagious. But you get it for only so long—and then no more. Do not confuse the initial adrenaline hit with the lasting energy needed to sustain you throughout Survive.

As Paul Graham remarked in his essay on Airbnb's refusal to die, people, like matter, reveal their nature under extreme conditions.[9] For many, Survive allows them to shine, to show their grit, tenacity, and why they won't give up. Harness and use this energy, but do not expect it to last indefinitely. You can only ask for full-out effort for brief periods of time. Growth is a marathon, not a sprint, and when your employees sprint for too long they will burn out. To keep energy high, continue to build context—more than you think you need to. Perception is reality, and the message should come from the leaders. Set a rhythm and stick to it. Communicate clear progress against the tracker, and if you are not making progress, communicate why and how you are correcting it. Consider making the Survive tracker public: everyone wants to win, and you can engage the wider team in getting to the results when you do so. Celebrate learning and progress, not just completion.

The owner of the employee pulse should go on the road and listen to get a sense of what employees are seeing, hearing, and feeling. The CEO can come along when appropriate. Keep the senior leadership team united. You will disagree on some aspects of Survive, but fight it out in the closed rooms and emerge a united front. In Survive more than ever you need to keep competition on the outside, not the inside.

Summary and next steps

While Survive is critical, triggered Survive should also be temporary. Eventually you must move into Reset. Employ the basics and execute the power moves, and while it will almost always feel premature, begin the transition as soon as possible—often by starting the offense while the defense is still on the field. Having an assigned owner of Survive will help, as will the Survive basics and power checklist that you should be continually revisiting. Keep the discipline and move into Reset while maintaining steady-state Survive.

By this point, you should understand:

✓ the difference between steady-state Survive and triggered Survive

✓ the Survive basics and your 4 Cs checklist

✓ the Survive power moves and how to employ them

- ✓ how to play offense and defense at the same time
- ✓ how to track and time Survive
- ✓ how to maintain the emotional energy during this mode

Take Survive seriously, come back to it when you need to, but most importantly get out and onto Reset. Thriving comes from playing this round to win and Thrive, and not just Survive. This starts from assessing and testing your assumptions about your situation, which is the focus of the next chapter.

Endnotes

1 Tyson was asked by a reporter if he was worried about his opponent's plan; some reports have the original quote as: "Everybody has plans until they get hit for the first time."

2 www.paulgraham.com/aord.html (archived at https://perma.cc/2BBQ-A3HV). Trevor Blackwell created a calculator for companies to determine their status as default dead or alive here: https://growth.tlb.org/ (archived at https://perma.cc/P9GD-KTU5)

3 R Homkes (2022) The three approaches to hypergrowth, blog post

4 R Hoffman, B Casnocha and C Yeh (2014) *The Alliance: Managing talent in the networked age*, Harvard Business Review Press

5 S Bungay (2011) *The Art of Action: How leaders close the gaps between plans, actions and results*, Nicholas Brealey Publishing

6 Airbnb (2020) A Message from Co-Founder and CEO Brian Chesky, news. airbnb.com/a-message-from-co-founder-and-ceo-brian-chesky/ (archived at https://perma.cc/N8HW-4DMT)

7 J Bezos (2020) 2020 Letter to Shareholders, About Amazon, www.aboutamazon. com/news/company-news/2020-letter-to-shareholders (archived at https://perma. cc/L3EV-58DD)

8 R Hastings and E Meyer (2020) *No Rules Rules: Netflix and the culture of reinvention*, Virgin Digital

9 P Graham (2020) The Airbnbs, www.paulgraham.com/airbnbs.html?viewfullsite=1 (archived at https://perma.cc/75BJ-4BTU)

PART TWO

RESET: Making Strategy Choices for Growth

4

What Is the Situation?
And How Will It Change?

"When the facts change, I change my mind. What do you do, Sir?"
—JOHN MAYNARD KEYNES

Having attended numerous Board meetings and strategy reviews, I find these sessions tend to begin with the same question. It is usually asked by someone who is well-meaning and feels they are doing their part of good governance. They always pause slightly first, and then ask quite firmly: "Are we on track to plan?"

While a perfectly reasonable question, it is not the right question to ask to start a strategy review. It assumes that the plan got everything right, that there is only one track, and that no new information has become available. These assumptions are usually wrong. Reviews that start in this way become backward looking and focus on numbers when they should be forward looking and focus on actions.

The critical issue to resolve is: What are we going to do now? So, the first question to be asked should be: *Has the situation changed?*

If the situation has changed, being on track to plan is not necessarily a good thing. So the next question should be: *Given the new situation, what should we do now?*

Strategy has always been developed under uncertainty. Strategists never know everything they would like to know about a situation, and the reactions of other actors to the situation are essentially unknowable. In high uncertainty, gaps in knowledge become acute. But that does not mean we are completely in the dark. It is a matter of working out what is going on in the half-light around us better than others and learning faster.

Having a robust and productive conversation about the situation is only possible if you have a clear and simple situation assessment on hand, so this chapter will detail how to build one. Your beliefs about the current situation will frame all your strategy choices that follow, so the situation assessment must be our starting point. We will then explore how to test your beliefs and assumptions over time, and how to adapt while executing.

Building your situation assessment

Building a situation assessment consists of four steps:

1 Identifying the **key trends** most shaping your industry

2 Articulating **your beliefs** about the implications of those trends

3 Clarifying the **specific assumptions** that must be vetted or tested

4 Examining the **implications,** or the "so what?"

Below I will detail each step as if you are building an assessment for the first time. During Reset strategy reviews, your task is to ask "What's changed?" and then update your assessment accordingly.

Identifying trends

A plethora of strategic tools, frameworks, and models abound to help teams examine key trends. While these are useful, many focus too much on diagnosing the current situation and are not forward-looking enough. The value of this step is for the team to diagnose and prioritize the most critical trends and then align on the beliefs that will shape your go-forward choices. The questions you need to explore are: "What will these trends look like over the next cycles?" and "What are their implications?"

First, lay out the major trends shaping your environment. Existing tools such as the PEST (Political, Economic, Social, Technology) framework or Porter's 5 Forces to diagnose the industry's attractiveness can help. SWOT analysis[1] (Strengths, Weaknesses, Opportunities, Threats) is another tool, but it tends to generate long lists, not prioritization, and it forces you to frame everything as good or bad. In high uncertainty it is not always clear. Many can be both, depending on how and where you deploy them. Your job is to address, shape, or exploit as many of them as you can, so move aside tools that do not help you to find opportunities in all trends.

A good analysis is not one that tries to cover absolutely everything, but instead does not miss anything big. Use these buckets to identify the major trends quickly and thoroughly enough: macro/economic, political/regulatory, social, and industrial (including customer and competition). You can also add buckets of digital or growth markets. Then start adding individual trends within each of these buckets (see Figure 4.1). The increasingly critical topic of ESG (Environmental, Social, Governance) can fall across multiple categories, so I suggest pulling these trends out rather than collapsing it into the macro bucket, as discussed below.

After these macro trends, examine the key trends most shaping your value chain. Your strategy is an articulation of how you create value as an organization, and your value chain is all the major sets of activities that allow you to do this. Popularized by Michael Porter, it's a helpful tool for several pieces of your Reset. At its simplest, think of your value chain as every major chunk of value-creating activity that allows you to go from raw

FIGURE 4.1 Trends, belief, assumptions, implications

What is the situation?

What is the trend? What are we seeing?	What do we believe to be true going forward based on this trend? How do we see this going?	What assumptions do we have? What do we need to test? What do we need to discuss?	What does this imply for our strategy? What could we or should we do?

materials and ideas to satisfied, happy customers who are referring you to others. In addition to these activities, there are supporting or enabling functions that sit across the entirety of the value chain, such as leadership, IT, and Finance. These functions are just as important, but they do not represent a discrete set of activities; rather, they enable and support the organization overall.

If your team has not drawn out your value chain before, first work with your team to map yours as part of this step. See Figure 4.2 for simplified examples of value chains for construction and professional companies.

Why do we need the value chain? Because uncertainty or shocks often impact most, if not all, steps of the value chain, and if you just consider macro trends, you'll miss something. Tease out the key trends and what they mean. How do trends like R&D spend (increasing or decreasing across the industry), supply chain disruption and/or supplier consolidation, operational efficiency demands including the need for increased automation, and changes to the go-to-market (GTM) approach, affect the activities in your value chain? Be clear on the specific trends around your talent and team as well. You may identify the trend of "increasing expectations of younger employees for mentorship," as an example.

Do not attempt to diagnose the level of uncertainty in the environment. While you should call out major risks (or potential "killers" as in Chapter 2), avoid framing trends as good or bad. Remember that trends such as inflation and cost pressures, rising oil prices, or trade flows slowing are being faced by your competitors as well. These are what I call fair disadvantages. Your industry is facing them together. If you cannot shape the environment (see strategic stances in Chapter 10), become great at managing these, but more so flipping these to build a circumstance where you can differentiate or win—building an unfair advantage. **Turning fair disadvantages into unfair advantages is what makes a Thrive company.**

Articulating beliefs

Putting together a list of trends does not make you a strategist: it makes you a journalist. Where the potential advantage lies is in building an understanding of how these trends may play out, what we believe about them, and what those beliefs could mean for the business.

Working through beliefs is hard because we are pushing what we are seeing right now into a stance going forward. The easiest way to distinguish between trends and beliefs is to think of your eyes: if you can see it, it's a

FIGURE 4.2 Manufacturing and professional services value chain

Value chain: The source of competitive positioning

Examine each aspect of your value chain
for trends to articulate beliefs going forward

Manufacturing value chain

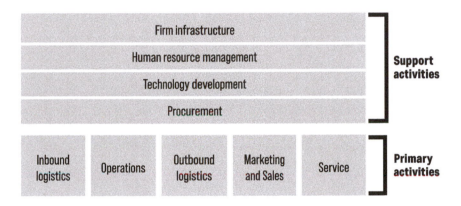

Professional services value chain

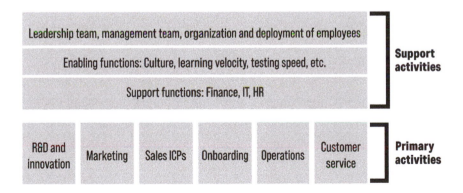

trend. I like to think of a belief as talking to yourself in the future. Imagine you are telling yourself in three years how your current self understood the world. A belief implies taking a stance, and while you need to be clear enough to be able to monitor and test your beliefs, you do not want to be so precise that you fall into the trap of trying to predict the future—because you cannot.

What makes a good belief? A good belief is one that can be watched or tested over time: if it can't move, it's likely not a belief. A good belief is something that you can get wrong. If there is no way to take an opposing view, you have just articulated a truism, not a belief. For example, I may take the belief that while inflationary pressures will abate, suppliers will continue to raise prices through this strategy cycle. This is a belief I could get wrong (and hope I do!). But, as another example, to write down "I believe employers should care about their employees" is a truism. In the most technical framing, I could perhaps get it wrong—but not really.

Some of your beliefs may turn out to be wrong. That's OK. Take a position anyway. It might make you feel uncomfortable, but taking a position is one of the disciplines leaders must learn.

It also helps to consider what you do not believe. For example, you might believe the majority of Gen Z read labels for ingredients and point of origin and will make their buying decisions based on these criteria. Additionally, you may not believe this trend will slow or reverse to where most are apathetic to labels. You may believe that label-reading will influence buying decisions, but only if price is equivalent and efficacy is not compromised. But you may not believe sustainable ingredients will influence buying if there is a major price or efficacy trade-off. By articulating what you do not believe, you start to tease out the truisms and force the team to be even clearer on the stance you are adopting.

Your timeframe for beliefs is one to two strategy cycles, and as a strategy cycle is three years, this implies a three-to-six-year timeframe. If you are attempting to cover several cycles, or the trend is happening more quickly, use the language of strategy cycles for even more clarity. That is, we believe this for one cycle, this for two cycles, or so on. Here's a way to state your beliefs I find helpful:

I am seeing ____[trend]_____, and I believe _____for the next three to six years.

For example, I am seeing [*interest rates increasing steadily*], and I believe [*while central banks will only raise a few more times, rates will remain high for the entire strategy cycle, leading to increasingly high mortgage rates and reduced labor mobility when in-person work is required*] for the next three to six years.

Forcing your team to articulate, capture, and test beliefs means you can adapt faster. Consider the automobile industry, which has gone through many shocks over the past several decades. Based in Indiana, USA, Kem Krest is a large supplier to the USA original equipment manufacturer (OEMs). In the spring of 2020, as their existing customers' businesses slowed, or shut down completely, they moved quickly to repurpose (a Survive power move!) some of their assets and capabilities into the sourcing, kitting, and fulfillment of hand sanitizer with a focus on the large business customer. They later added PPE (personal protective equipment) to their offerings. This new business unit, Kem Shield, became a testing and experimentation unit for the company. In their mid-2020 strategy session, they articulated their top beliefs, such as less commuting leading to lessened new car demand and lower sales at dealerships, the rising popularity of electric vehicles (EVs), ongoing concerns for health and safety leading to a sustained demand for PPE, and a possible recession.

A year later, while their beliefs on EVs and other shifts remained largely in place, almost all their beliefs about the current industry were challenged. While commuting lessened, supply chain shocks and a rise in local leisure travel put more cars on the road, straining local dealer inventory and capacity. The supply and demand curves for PPE went down just as steeply as they went up, with the demand curves almost flattening as supply peaked! Given they were tracking their beliefs, the updates to their strategic priorities were embedded in real time through their constant stress-testing, weekly huddles, and quarterly strategy reviews. This allowed them to update their choices and shift focus based on the emerging trends faster than others in their space.

Beliefs matter as they inform our choices. Give this step the time it deserves. Discussing and debating beliefs with your team will set you up for an effective Reset. When your belief is still unclear, or not yet aligned, ask the follow-up: What information do we need to feel firmer on this belief? When teams disagree on choices and spend time arguing, it is almost always because they have not taken the time to align on beliefs. If you find yourselves disagreeing on the best course of action, pause and discuss your beliefs. Get the necessary alignment with the team and acknowledge that when beliefs are misaligned, you need to accelerate testing.

High-growth is about moving when you have alignment, not always full agreement. It's OK to not have full agreement on precise beliefs—in the testing phase you will get closer as you learn more and stress-test the underlying assumptions.

Trends: Breaking down ESG

When you start listing trends, you will probably identify several around ESG (environmental, social, governance). These trends are rapidly evolving, so discuss them as a separate "bucket" to parse out your more nuanced beliefs.

It is highly unlikely that you are seeing equal pushes from the E (environmental), S (social), and G (governance) angles. It is also likely that you are more prepared for some pieces than others. You are probably also coming under more pressure from some stakeholders than others. So, break it down. Segment the three aspects of ESG into their different stakeholders, especially: employees, customers, end consumers (if relevant), suppliers, government/regulators, and shareholders/investors.

For each segment, articulate your belief, for example:

- "We are seeing our retailer customers ask for our ESG strategy (*TREND*), but having an audit and plan is enough for them, we do not believe they will expect a carbon mitigation strategy within this strategy cycle (*BELIEF*)," or

- "We are seeing our employees ask us to take a stance on social issues (*TREND*), and going forward we will need to be clearer on when we will take a stance, when we will not, and how we will make these decisions" (*BELIEF*).

Be clear where you believe a stance or action will translate to value creation needle up (customer willingness to pay) or needle down (total cost), as well as where you want to act to fit with your values or purpose, even if this does not translate to value creation. The relationship between ESG and value creation is evolving. A few strategy cycles ago organizations that acted on ESG were often making an explicit trade-off with value creation in that cycle to align with their purpose. We are now seeing this tension being broken. That is, notwithstanding regulation, taking explicit ESG-aligned action is becoming significant for value creation, and in some cases necessary, and can move the needles.

Even if you cannot identify immediate value creation linkage, you can still act to align with your purpose. You may decide to move faster on reducing your carbon emissions (E) or take explicit social stances with your employees (S). If that's the case, communicate what you are doing to align with your purpose and acknowledge you may be making short-term value creation trade-offs in pursuit of medium to long-term ones. That is, you believe it is the right thing to do.

After working with the team to identify your beliefs, go through the segments and identify the hot spots to create an ESG Heat Map as part of your situation assessment (see Figure 4.3 for an example of a completed ESG grid; note that this is an example only and may not represent where your organization is). Consider each of your ESG beliefs across two dimensions: amount of change required from existing strategy, and current readiness for this change. Is this belief going to have significant, some, or little impact from what you are doing now? And with respect to readiness: Are you very, somewhat, or not at all ready for if this belief is true? Hot

FIGURE 4.3 ESG prioritization grid

	E Environmental	S Social	G Governance	Notes
Employees				
Consumers				
Customers				
Shareholder/ investors				
Suppliers				
Regulators				

Change/criticality
- Significant impact on strategy
- Some impact on strategy
- Little impact on strategy

Preparedness
- We are *not* prepared for this
- We are somewhat prepared for this
- We are prepared for this

spots—the black shapes in Figure 4.3—are the grid boxes of your ESG belief set that are major and must be addressed. Prioritization here and everywhere else will be key.

Mapping and prioritizing

Once you have your full set of trends and beliefs, including those around ESG, these trends must be prioritized. You will not be able to address them all, so with the team determine which ones matter the most based on your beliefs.

Create a Trends Map with two dimensions: impact on the industry and criticality to your strategy (see Figure 4.4). Impact on the industry is defined as: **"Our industry will look fundamentally different in one to two strategy**

FIGURE 4.4 Trends mapping

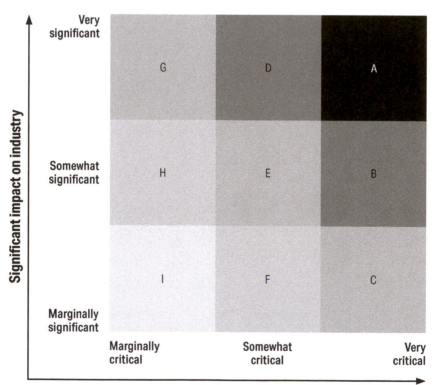

cycles because of this trend." The higher the trend is placed on the vertical axes, the more you believe your industry will be reshaped and formed due to this trend. The second dimension is criticality to your strategy, and is defined as: **"This trend is so critical it is in our strategy and/or we would change our strategy if we get our belief about this trend wrong."** The farther right on the grid the trend is placed, the more critical it is to your strategic choices.

For ease of understanding, the grid boxes are labelled A (high impact, high criticality), B (some impact, high criticality), C (less impact, high criticality), D (high impact, somewhat critical), and so on all the way to I. Be guardians of the trends in Box A and Box E. It is easy to crowd box A, as everything feels super significant, but all trends cannot be high impact and high criticality, so force the conversation on what really matters. Box E is middle/middle, and not every trend belongs here either. While the trends in box I are the least significant, they are still on the grid as you will want to monitor them for changes.

Once the trends are mapped, make a list of your top 10 to 15 beliefs based on the trends in box A, then B, and so on in order. These will go into the tracker discussed below. Seeing the list in order will be a good check whether you are prioritizing appropriately. Often one or two trends get too much priority. You may also notice an obvious trend that is missing as it was pushed too far to the left.

Recency bias can be a factor at this stage. Ensure the map is not just of trends discussed in last week's executive meeting or the last customer conversation. Discuss each one to make sure they are the one- to two-cycle trends.

Assumptions

Beliefs are our stances on how we see the trends playing out in the future. Beliefs must be broken down into distinct variables, which can then be translated into hypotheses for testing, informing choices, and deciding implications. Assumptions are the individual variables that inform our choices. They are incorporated into our strategy and can also be tested.

Every business model is based on hundreds, if not thousands, of assumptions. Part of moving faster through uncertainty is identifying and quickly testing your critical assumptions so you can make adjustments in strategy and execution to get ahead.

You will likely realize your beliefs stem from multiple interdependent assumptions. For example, if you believe cryptocurrencies will become mainstream globally *and* that more than half of Gen Z in the USA will own at least one, you are making several interrelated assumptions on the ease of use of crypto, retailer adoption, regulatory requirements, and entrants to the space. Draw these out one by one. In testing, you will keep asking whether these assumptions are true or if you can make them true.

If your environment is fast-moving, there are likely to be some assumptions where you just do not know if they are true or can be made true. That is OK. First, try to isolate the individual assumptions so that you can test each one. Also, identify any game-changer assumptions. **A game-changer is defined as a belief or assumption that, if not true, will blow up a big part of the business model.** These are rare, but they need immediate testing and ongoing observation.

For Kem Krest, noted above, their belief that the level of PPE demand would remain high going forward was their game-changer. If this belief was wrong, most of the business model of their new entity no longer made sense. The team actively tested this game-changer belief, and as the situation changed, they were able to pivot Kem Shield into new uses. The team was amazed at how quickly the situation changed and how dramatically their game-changer belief became no longer true. By 2021 not only had demand sharply declined for PPE, even their existing customers—dealerships—wanted less active sanitization displayed.

While Kem Shield was not a success on its own (it was shut down in 2023), the learnings from its operation—including how to launch a new business unit, onboard new customers (Kem Krest had only 60 customers prior to 2020), ship material directly to consumers, and integrate an online portal (versus its traditional way of connecting only via EDI) were critical lessons they applied to their next venture, EFBU, which I cover in Chapter 5.

Fast identification and testing of assumptions followed by quick action leads to competitive advantage. The founders of One-and-Only, a small Dallas-based startup that would become leading dating site Match.com, drew on a mixture of observation, experience, and analysis to derive five fundamental assumptions in 2001:

- A dating website would attract users, given that dating-focused chat rooms account for 50 percent of income at the largest internet service provider (ISP).
- Online dating ads would generate revenue, since dating ads are very lucrative for newspapers.
- Website users would be willing to pay a subscription fee, further boosting income.

- Advertising on chat rooms would attract a critical mass of users.
- A certain percentage of people would be willing to share personal details online and upload a profile.

The team determined that the percentage of people willing to share details was their game-changer assumption: if they could not prove a critical mass of single people would upload a profile and picture, this business would not work, so they prioritized testing that assumption.

They launched a simplified website with an input form for user information. Acting lean, no development dollars were spent, and instead the form emailed the information and the team copied and pasted it back to the website. They spent $2,000 for banner ads on chat sites to drive traffic to their site to test what percentage of people who visited the site would upload a profile. The answer was one in 20, or 5 percent, at a cost of five cents each. Their biggest competitors, the original Match.com, had 20,000 profiles at the time, so their goal was to match them.

The team raised $100,000 against Match.com's $10 million in funding and were able to rapidly scale to 20,000 profiles. Constant assumption testing and learning led to a compelling value proposition that adapted with the evolving market, and the small team quickly overtook Match.com in all aspects to become number one in the space. While Match.com was acquired for only a few million more than their original investment (and at a steep loss to those involved), four years later One-and-Only was acquired by Match.com's parent Ticket Master City Search for $47.5 million, and the One-and-Only team took over Match's brand.

Figure 4.5 gives an example of sets of beliefs and assumptions around trends related to supply chain disruption, ESG and the construction industry, and employee engagement.

Implications

From the assumptions, start to articulate possible implications for your strategy. Ask: If we believe X, then what could we consider doing? Play out the possibilities even if it pushes your current business model or would involve actions you do not currently take. You are still in the brainstorming portion of the Reset, so give new ideas explicit airtime and allow the team to explore the full implication set.

You may also find it helpful to break down the possible actions into **Discuss, Test,** or **Do.** Discuss is for those aspects that need a deeper discussion.

FIGURE 4.5 Trends, Beliefs, Assumptions, Implications: Three examples

How trends, beliefs and assumptions interact: If we believe X, then Y

1 Trend What we are seeing	2 Belief Our current best guess or stance on how this will look going forward	3 Assumption The variables we need to watch and/or test	4 Implications The "so what"
What are the big things moving the industry?	**What do we believe as "true" based on this trend?**	**What do we need to know? How can we improve our position?**	**What are possible initiatives to address our beliefs?**
Supply chain disruptions	*[Possible beliefs]* · Supply chain will not return to "normal" within the next strategy cycle; commitments on time cannot be trusted; and vendors will have the upperhand in negotiations. · Supply chain disruptions from post-Covid effects will abate in the next year, and we can reset assumptions to pre-2019 levels. · Post 2020 effects will pass through the system, but supply chain disruptions will cause our industry to reset what supply chain robustness means including number and types of suppliers on hand.	*[Possible assumptions]* · Can we/ how to train customers on new terms · Amount of inventory stock thus impacting working capital · Customer prioritization between speed versus reliability versus price versus quality tradeoff	*[Possible implications]* · Revisit inventory levels by technology (speed vs margin) · Use our leverage as a vendor · Review working capital assumptions for certain brands
ESG pushes for the construction industry	*[Possible beliefs]* · Carbon footprint and ESG policies will be secondary to profitability for manufacturing companies from stakeholders for the foreseeable future · Carbon footprint and ESG policies will replace profitability for manufacturing companies within two strategy cycles · Our customers will demand carbon footprint and ESG policies from us, but this will be table stakes	*[Possible assumptions]* · Customer willingness to pay for Green · Stakeholder willingness to invest for Green · Employee willingness to work for us based on our Climate and Sustainability policies	*[Possible implications]* · Move ahead of industry in specialized line of solutions to carve out client niche · Redefine employee value proposition around our leadership on climate and sustainability in the industry · Partner with a small ecosystem group of partners in testing economics of sustainability offerings
Employee experience demands changing	*[Possible beliefs]* · Next generation of employees prioritize experiences, not promotions, and are not looking for long-term employment · People and culture will maintain competitive advantage going forward, so we must actively work to protect ours · We can continue to attract and retain top talent with the strength of our culture	*[Possible assumptions]* · Our culture's ability to maintain and grow in strength in a hybrid/virtual world · We can manage the tension between running lean and burn-out of top employees · Our culture's transferability across cultures as we expand into newer markets directly	*[Possible implications]* · Redefine and relaunch updated employee value proposition · Launch reverse mentoring scheme · Move talent into key roles in growth markets while ensuring culture adapts and forms from the distributed leaders in place

Test is for the assumptions you need to test. Do is possible actions that will be incorporated in the strategy Reset based on this belief. For the Dos, add a rough timeframe: quick (within a month), short-term (within a year), mid-term (a strategy cycle), or long-term (more than three years).

If there are short-term urgent needs, quick wins, or no-regret moves (see the next section) that you can quickly execute, just do it! These are obvious actions that will be quick and low-resource to implement. They don't require more discussion or analysis. Label them JDI (just do it), assign owners and deadlines and get it done. But don't confuse these with possible mid-term priorities. The mid- to longer-term implications of your Box A (high impact, high criticality), B (some impact, high criticality), and C (less impact, high criticality) beliefs will be explored when setting your must-win battles (Chapter 8).

No-regret moves

One of my favorite parts of SRT is identifying no-regret moves. A **no-regret move is one that, even if you got your belief wrong, you would not regret making it.** Have a side flipchart (virtual or physical) to track these and start moving on them—even if you're just entering the Reset phase.

Molport is a Latvian-based company that focuses on matching rare chemical compounds for researchers. After resetting its strategy in 2020, the team began exploring new growth areas and getting some initial traction with customer segments. The team was progressing, and then the Russian invasion of Ukraine led to war in February 2022. The majority of Molport's suppliers were based in Ukraine or Russia, with a distant third group of suppliers based in China.

The company had to go back into Survive mode given stalled orders and shipments and then Reset once more. During an Survive emergency workshop, the team went through its updated beliefs and assumptions focused on their supply base. An option set emerged: Wait and hope the war ended soon and supply returned. But the team did not believe this was the right choice. They could begin manufacturing themselves in Latvia, but that would come at a significant upfront capital cost. Or they could immediately begin to find new suppliers. Waiting and watching was dismissed given the needed run rate of the company. Manufacturing—while possible—needed assumption vetting and the buy-in of the original investors. Finding new suppliers, though, was a clear no-regret move. Even if their beliefs were wrong and the war ended quickly, they would not regret having vetted and possibly onboarded more suppliers.

Testing your situation assessment

Your strategy situation may be constantly evolving and even volatile. Thrive companies do not lull themselves into a false sense of security by assuming that completing a situation assessment means it's time to execute with a fixed plan. Instead, they actively test their assumptions in parallel to execution.

Parallel pathing is a term that originated from the early days of computing when computer scientists attempted to run multiple tasks simultaneously on multiple processors. Now it is used to mean pursuing multiple paths or tracks at the same time, often within product development. During the Covid-19 pandemic pharmaceutical companies took the parallel path of manufacturing vaccines while clinical trials were being conducted to dramatically accelerate time to market.

What sets high-growth companies apart is how well they employ parallel pathing. They execute their top priorities while simultaneously stress-testing their beliefs around those priorities. That way they are getting market feedback on the strength and validity of their beliefs long before they get market feedback on the results of executing their priorities. As learning occurs, they make slight revisions and updates to their priorities. If during the testing process they find out that their beliefs were off, or just plain wrong, they pause to revise them and the related actions.

Building a "Beliefs Tracker"

As part of your situation assessment, it is helpful to build a simple tracker that provides an overview of the beliefs and how they're faring. Your situation assessment should include four spreadsheets or pages that show:

- A list of identified major trends.
- A Trends Map (as in Figure 4.4).
- All the important beliefs, assumptions, and possible implications against these major trends (as in Figure 4.1, example of a completed one in Figure 4.5).
- A Beliefs Tracker: this will be your main page. It will include a short list of the 10-15 beliefs that need active testing (sample in Figure 4.6). I will explore the Beliefs Tracker in detail in Chapter 10.

In your Beliefs Tracker page, include a summary of the trend, the current belief, where it lives in the strategy (which you will complete after Chapter 8), the status of the belief, and any updates or notes. Give access to this document to the strategy team (the set of individuals going through the SRT

FIGURE 4.6 Beliefs Tracker

Beliefs tracker example

Trend	Key beliefs	Status	Comments
INDUSTRY: Telecom operators become more like banks	More and more telecom operators will get their banking license and offer banking services. More telecoms will launch more value added services for their consumer base	Tracking ✓	Singtel acquires banking license, but moving slowly
MACRO: Demographic shifts	As US population shifts to coasts and south, these movements will create new opportunities in food service	Tracking ✓	Population from northern states is moving to Sunbelt states, but likely bringing northern values with them. ID, AZ, TN, SC, FL, TX, CO, and NC are the top 8 states with inbound moves. Inbound migration to TX coming mostly from CA.
INDUSTRY: Midterm oil price	Oil price will take up to three years to return from weak supply	Caution ‼	Brent above $100/bbl and forecast for continued increases. Good for business performance, but likely to result in asset acquisitions and M&A being more fully valued
MACRO: Market perception of EP	For public investors, returns are first and second; but short-term cash vs long-term NAV is the focus of those returns today	Off track ❗	Oil and gas companies continue to show discounts to oil price recovery suggesting a continued focus on short-term cash generation and use
OPERATIONS: New models: pivoting to try new formats	Restaurant operators will be continuing to explore and push the boundaries of what a restaurant is—delivery only, micro-store/bodega, carry-out, meal kits, prepared meals	Tracking ✓	New formats include: experimentation towards what will be the future of brick and mortar (hybrids of delivery, mealkits, bars all in one). In addition to pivoting, new players are entering the scene who only know this model and will push the industry forward. Sense from our surveys is most operators plan to keep the changes to their business model that they implemented in 2020
INDUSTRY: Increase in smaller competitive brands	Digital shelves will create a polarization of the category between the brand leader (including us) and smaller brands/new category entrants, making it easier than ever for them to take share. Our products will have to rely on point of differentiation (claims, sizes, efficacy, etc.) and cultivating a better overall brand experience to compete	Off track ❗	No new entry of any sizable scale or traction in the last 18 months; little movement in acquisition space of smallest brands that were on our radar
POLITICAL: CO_2 regulations/ carbon reduction	Countries and parliaments will push CO_2 emission regulation and taxes – especially in certain European countries and then only later the USA/UK. This provides us an opportunity to partner to help save CO_2	Tracking but watch ❓	There is no movement on regulations, but we believe this is due to slowness of regulators and not that this will not happen. We still believe we need to be ahead of this to gain advantage when it happens while others struggle to catch up

process), but ensure it has an owner who will consolidate notes on active and passive testing.

Testing and discussing beliefs

An explicit set of guiding beliefs can be tested and changed as experience and learning accrue, serving as a critical checkpoint when reviewing the strategy to decide on the next move. Once you have the Beliefs Tracker in place, discuss with the team *how* you will track your beliefs. You can do this passively, by collecting news reports, articles, and feedback or by monitoring beliefs in real-time such as by watching contrasting executive commentary and guidance during earnings calls and reports. Thrive companies also employ active testing, such as conducting interviews, running market tests, and exploring situations during customer visits. The dating company One-and-Only, discussed earlier, is a great example of a company that actively tested its beliefs and then acted quickly on the results.

The owner of the Beliefs Tracker should update it ahead of each strategy review. After the Reset, and outside of a triggered shock, these beliefs should be discussed at least once a quarter with a deep-dive once a year. These reviews build positive momentum with the team and the strategy process. Often an annual reframe shows many of the Box A, B, and C trends from a year ago have lessened in severity or were addressed more quickly than expected, which allows the team to shift to a more proactive growth mode.

When a major disruption occurs, though, you should pull the strategy team together quickly. If you have this clear summary of the beliefs you are tracking, you can quickly see which pieces of the strategy are impacted.

Testing is especially critical when a team has identified a high-impact trend but is not aligned on beliefs. This was the case for several bike companies in 2020–2022. The industry saw demand spike considerably in 2020. Supply could simply not meet the demand, leading to supplier pressures, increasing prices, and shortages. Bike companies scrambled to fulfill supply as fast as possible, but few spent the time to articulate their beliefs about what current demand meant for the mid-term, instead building supply as if those demand curves would remain high. One leading bike brand set the belief that demand would gradually start to fall by late 2022, but they did not actively test that belief. When demand fell dramatically in mid-2022, the team was left scrambling and had to undergo a hard Reset (see Chapter 7 for more on hard Resets).

Given the nature of the environment, some aspects will be static for a while whereas other beliefs will quite quickly go off track. Watch your tracker, test your beliefs, and build discussions about how these changes affect your business into all leadership or strategy reviews. More guidance on testing beliefs comes in Chapter 10.

Actively testing beliefs at Gordon Food Service

Many industries faced massive upheaval during the Covid-19 pandemic, but few were as severely uprooted as the food distribution business. The industry was already undergoing a major set of changes with the growth of food delivery services such as UberEATS, increasing demand for local and organic, and demographic changes and populations shifts altering demand. Major technological advances were also digitizing the front of house (menus, ordering) and back of house (invoicing, ordering, supplier management). While the major companies in the business spoke about these trends and were pursuing digital priorities, the industry was still relatively manual, with less than 40 percent of restaurants in the process of any major digital change in 2019.

Founded in 1897 by Dutch immigrants to deliver butter and eggs on horse-drawn carriages, Gordon Food Service (GFS) is the largest family-owned and managed food distributor in North America. Like other large broadline distributors, they serve a customer base of primarily restaurants (chains, quick service restaurants, and independent food service), schools, hospitals, and government bodies. When lockdowns ensued, demand from their wholesale customer base plummeted. The immediate effect was that their strategy needed to be completely reset. As individual states and provinces slowly eased restrictions, allowing for takeout and outside dining, restaurants began adapting in different ways. The GFS team knew agility would be critical to gaining advantage, so they held a set of virtual sessions challenging each other on their beliefs going forward.

After formulating their top trends and beliefs, it was clear that there were some no-regret moves such as offering customers a low-to-no touch digital service and delivery, which they executed. They also realized the validity of their beliefs would have a big effect on other future actions. Distribution is an industry with high capital intensity and low operating margins, so stress-testing beliefs is critical.

An advantage they had was a large set of customers, and potential customers, as there were one million restaurants in the USA in 2020[2] with another 97,000 in Canada.[3] To test their beliefs, the team pulled every trend from Box A, B, and C of their Trends Map and turned it into a multiple-choice question to get real-time insights and avoid subjective guessing. The team bought a domain, set up a user-friendly interface and surveyed 30,000 restaurants, while also sending the same survey to 1,000 GFS customer-facing employees.

The results were telling. While many beliefs were validated, a few were indeed called into question. There were also differences between the team's views and the restaurants, such as how severe both parties felt the supply chain challenges were and how long they would last. Other aspects of delivery were also surprising; team members thought that customers wanted more frequent deliveries, but many customers did not have the capacity to accept deliveries more than two days a week given reduced staff.

To test over time, they re-sent the pulse survey quarterly. Some trends were moving targets, such as the need for establishments to show their efforts to be safe and clean against the background of the pandemic. While most believed this would become a "new normal," they were wrong, leading GFS to pause some initiatives around certifying restaurants on cleanliness. Going into 2023, the team continued to send quarterly pulse surveys and make pivots within their must-win battles, including establishing new partnerships to provide updated solutions to customers, such as Gordon Restaurant Pro.

The fast testing of beliefs also led the team to trial and then scale new customer services, including small delivery vans and digital-only service models. The latter had been discussed for a while, but the fast movement and assumption vetting during led to its successful scale across the entire enterprise.

Summary and next steps

Strategy is about making choices when facing uncertainty. We cannot wait for facts, so we must make decisions based on beliefs. Articulating, prioritizing, and then stress-testing these beliefs will allow you to get ahead. During execution, you will employ parallel pathing to test beliefs while executing the top priorities, which allows for more and quicker micro adjustments.

After completing your situation assessment, you should have:

✓ a summarized list of trends most shaping the industry

✓ your priorities listed on a nine-box Trends Map by impact and criticality (Figure 4.4)

✓ a Beliefs Tracker that summarizes the top 10 to 15 beliefs (from boxes A, B, C of the Belief Map), along with their status (Figure 4.6)

✓ a next steps plan for testing assumptions and parallel pathing

✓ owners and deadlines for any just do it (JDI) and no-regret moves

These top beliefs in your Beliefs Tracker will guide the rest of your Reset conversations, including "How will we win?" coming up next.

Endnotes

1 SWOT stands for Strengths, Weakness, Opportunities, Threats; its development is credited to Albert Humphrey, who developed it at the Stanford Research Institute in the 1960s.

2 2020 report by the National Restaurant Association.

3 Statistics Canada (ND) www.statcan.gc.ca/en/start (archived at https://perma.cc/8VV6-P8GK)

5

How Will We Win? Our Competitive Advantage and Right to Win

"If you don't have a competitive advantage, don't compete."
—JACK WELCH, FORMER CEO OF GENERAL ELECTRIC

Strategy is a competitive game: you are setting and executing strategy to win.

Strategy is an articulation of how you will create value: move the needle up (customer willingness to pay) or down (total cost) or keep the needles apart. Your competitive advantage expresses how you will force these two needles apart, but, more critically, your competitive advantage—your Right to Win—articulates how you will continue to keep the needles apart over time.

A major difference exists between having a Right to Play and a Right to Win. Many companies have a Right to Play, which happens after finding a fit between their products and solutions and customers. Organizations with a Right to Win are formidable opponents as they have a hidden secret power: All employees know their organization's Right to Win and their role in executing it. And they come prepared every day ready to do it.

Playing to win is what strategy is all about, and during a Reset you need to re-assess your Right to Win and how you will execute it. That's the focus of this chapter, where I start by summarizing and simplifying the topic of competitive advantage. Next, I detail how to evaluate your competitive advantage and build an assessment. For some, your analysis may reveal you lack sufficient Right to Win, so I detail your go-forward options. To translate your analysis into winning actions you can segment them into four buckets: protect, strengthen, leverage, and buy/build.

Resources, capabilities, and barriers to entry

In the early days of strategy, the difference in performance between firms was explained in terms of the industry they were competing in and its dynamics. This notion was first challenged by Boston Consulting Group (BCG) founder Bruce Henderson, who argued we need to look at the position a firm occupies within an industry, not just the industry. Michael Porter later built on Henderson's insights in *Competitive Strategy* (1980) and *Competitive Advantage* (1985).

It was not until the late 1980s that other scholars, notably Wernerfelt, Prahalad and Hamel, and Collis and Montgomery[1], developed the resource-based view of the firm, and internal factors became important to explaining advantage. What followed was decades of scholarship on how to exploit external opportunities using an organization's existing resources rather than by continually acquiring new skills.

But let me dramatically simplify these debates. At the heart of the topic, only three avenues allow you to win:

- Resources: *You have things others do not.*
- Capabilities: *You do things others cannot.*
- Barriers to entry: *You have moats around your advantages.*

Resources are the assets an organization controls and that can be used to develop and execute its strategies. They can be tangible and physical such as plant and equipment, access to commodities or natural resources, or unique property locations. Resources can also be intangible, such as brands, culture, intellectual property, or know-how. Human capital is also a resource, which could take the form of an experienced leadership team, uniquely qualified innovators, or exceptional customer service reps. Some resources can be developed over time, such as customer networks, your base of end users, or alumni networks. Resources are powerful, but they can be easily imitated.

Capabilities are how you control, leverage, and use your resources to your advantage over time. They can also be tangible (speed of new product development) or intangible (leveraging cultural values and behaviors for speed in the market) and are most often enablers or accelerators of your existing resources. Capabilities are how you capture the value your resources provide you. They evolve to keep pace with changes in the external environment, and they become more dynamic and powerful as they lead to more continual advantage. Capabilities can arise from formal processes that are explicitly defined and communicated, such as customer experience management or budgeting processes, as well as from informal processes and practices, such as engaging employees or developing lasting strategic partnerships.

The Toyota Production System (TPS) or Lean production system is an example of powerful capabilities. In the late 1960s TPS began to launch automobiles in the USA market that were not only cheaper but also higher quality than the American incumbents. While there were distinct resources, such as playbooks and trained employees, their competitive advantage was the interwoven capabilities of their 5S system, their Kaizen approach to continuous improvement, which included empowering workers, value stream mapping, and working with just-in-time (JIT) inventory, among others. American car manufacturers tried to copy these individual pieces, but they could not replicate the end-to-end capability because it involved the complex interaction of formal and informal processes as well as lived values.

It's important not to confuse resources with capabilities. You may have a large user base as a *resource*, but that does not mean you have the *capability* of building a community amongst users. Likewise, you may have a large data set as a *resource* but that does not mean you have the *capability* to analyze and utilize data for better insights.

Barriers to entry (BTEs) are the obstacles that make it difficult for competitors to enter a market or competitive space. BTEs are commonly expressed as the advantage incumbent companies have relative to possible new entrants.[2] They can arise structurally via high capital requirements that deter new entrants, government regulations that favor incumbents, or economies of scale that make new competition financially less feasible. They can also stem from strategy, such as strong brand loyalty, patents, or intellectual property (IP).

Strategists use a range of words that essentially mean the same thing as BTEs: moats, fences, switching costs, network effects, and loyalty lock-in, among others. All of these terms mean that once you have gained an advantage, you must protect it by making it harder for competitors to come in, or customers to leave. Only then can it be sustainable. It becomes yours and difficult for others to copy or pull away.

I like to use the metaphor of an actual moat. Envision an English castle on a hill with the water-filled moat around it, dug to keep its advantages and treasures in and prevent other competitors from stealing them away. You need to do the same in building strong moats around your customers and advantages. The deeper and wider your strategic moats are, the less likely it is competitors can pull your customers away.

Assessing your Right to Win

Right to Win and value creation are intrinsically linked. Essentially, your Right to Win depends on how much more value you can create compared to your competitors. You can add more value because of things you have that others don't, or things you can do that others cannot or at a lower cost. Whatever you have or do, to sustain the advantage it must be hard to copy, which means building moats around it.

Even though it is a cornerstone of strategy, competitive advantage is often vaguely articulated inside organizations. This is partly due to when the conversation is addressed. There is a tradition of answering this question after "Where will we play?" But I have found if you first discuss your playing field and anchor there, you tend to default to tactical strategies or incremental features against existing competition to defend these choices instead of articulating your actual Right to Win.

Breakthrough growth does not come from tactical adjustments or ignoring the changing situation; it comes from having and exploiting a clear advantage in your strategic environment.

To move from Reset to Thrive, you must build your strategic playing field on a unique competitive advantage. You want to consider your advantage in the world you believe will happen, not the past one. That means addressing your Right to Win AFTER your Beliefs and BEFORE asking where you will play.

To build an assessment, start with your value chain - the series of inter-linked activities that you need to translate raw ideas and parts into happy customers who refer you to others (introduced in Chapter 4). Figure 5.1 shows the value chain of a manufacturing firm, where you would assess within each set of activities from R&D and Innovation through to sales and customer service/retention. Next, assess the the supporting functions, such as leadership, people and talent, culture and learning velocity, data/IT/tech infrastructure, among others. A competitive advantage is often held within these supporting and enabling activities that tie other pieces together.

Once you have mapped out your value chain, go through each piece, including your supporting functions, and ask: *Do we have something here that others do not? Can we do something here that others cannot? Is this where we build a moat around our advantage?*

Be clear and specific. For example, instead of "R&D" as a capability, write, "We have the capability to produce two to three new innovations consistently year on year." Remember to tease out your capabilities in

FIGURE 5.1 A manufacturing value chain

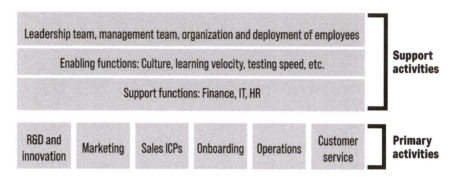

An example of a manufacturing value chain

Each aspect of your value chain must be examined; strategy going forward will be based on gaining advantage across this set of activities

Leadership team, management team, organization and deployment of employees

Enabling functions: Culture, learning velocity, testing speed, etc.

Support functions: Finance, IT, HR

Support activities

R&D and innovation | Marketing | Sales ICPs | Onboarding | Operations | Customer service

Primary activities

addition to your resources, knowing that some capabilities might cut across several value creation steps.

Why do we use the value chain instead of a blank sheet of paper to encourage more brainstorming? First, and quite simply, if you do not use the value chain, you will miss something.

Second, and more importantly, we are looking for something I call **"trapped advantage."** Trapped advantage exists when there is a Right to Win, or potential Right to Win, but it is early in the value chain. Later in the value chain you may only be at table stakes (what you need to show up and play the game, or your Right to Play), or even potentially at a competitive disadvantage. There is less opportunity to create value.

Trapped advantages need to be identified and teased out. When assessing their advantage, one company discussed the thousands of positive user reviews left on ecommerce sites such as Amazon.com. These could be a potential resource, but they were not doing anything with them! They needed to strengthen their digital and data systems, including by leveraging their growing AI capabilities, to better understand, respond, and leverage these reviews, not just for building continual end-user loyalty but also to improve their offerings going forward. If they could, they could utilize this now trapped advantage.

For a global insurer, mapping the value chain identified decades of data on insurance offerings, risks, outcomes, and rates. While this was a powerful data set—a resource unrivalled by competitors—most of the potential gains they could leverage from these insights remained trapped as they lacked data systems that pulled these insights together to inform future analysis.

Once you have your first list of possible assets, or resources and capabilities (I use the term "assets" to mean either) across your value chain, put each to two tests.

Necessary versus key: Every company has many resources and capabilities. Most are necessary—you need them to be in the game. They are table stakes, as you cannot compete in your industry without them. In fast fashion, for example, a supply chain management system is a necessary resource.

But what if you were Zara and you have a centralized design function for new fashions and an innovative supply chain management system with an average turnaround of insight to retail availability in less than two weeks? Meanwhile, most competitors average over 10 weeks from insight to retail availability. These are your key capabilities—they are competitive advantage.

If you are a hospital chain, you must have a team of surgeons. This is a resource, but you cannot be a hospital chain without one. But if you are The Cleveland Clinic[3] and most of your specialists are ranked in the top ten in the USA, this is a key resource, which means it provides you with a distinct competitive advantage.

Go through your entire list to tease out just the key assets. More than 75 percent of your listed assets are likely just table stakes, so most should fall off here. You may notice many assets used to be key but now others have caught up, the competition has changed, and these assets are now just necessary. **Thrive companies continually re-set the bar for what it takes to be table stakes in an industry**. Over time, others catch up, so Thrive companies reset their advantage and raise the bar with new "key" assets. Meanwhile, non-Thrive companies often rest on past advantages for more strategy cycles than warranted.

There is another trap to avoid. Over time, assets that were table stakes can also be downgraded to become not even necessary, and you need to acknowledge when this occurs. This was the case for big-box retail partnerships and shelf space with the advent of digital-first brands. More recently, the rampant proliferation of AI is challenging what are table stakes in many industries and forcing a re-look at what differentiation can mean. It's a needed challenge for leadership teams to constantly re-assess the value of their assets.

Next, with your shortlist, apply a VRIN analysis. A concept introduced by Birger Wernerfelt[4] and later developed by Jay Barney[5], the VRIN is the most succinct and impactful way to thoroughly diagnose competitive advantage. For each of your key assets, assess whether it passes these tests:

- **Valuable**: Does the resource or capability make you more money than it costs you?

- **Rare:** Is the resource or capability hard to get access to, or not widely possessed by others?

- **Inimitable:** Is the resource or capability hard to copy? Can others watch you, study you, make a long list of all the steps they see you doing, and still not do what you can within one to two strategy cycles?

- **Non-substitutable:** Is the resource or capability protected from being competed against by a different resource or capability? Conversely, are there substitutes that meet a similar demand or function by a different means (e.g. Zoom or Teams calls instead of corporate travel)?

You can also see Figure 5.2 for a simple visual of the VRIN assessment, and the order matters. We first test for valuable, and then we test for valuable and rare, and then valuable, rare, and inimitable. If you have something that is rare, but no longer valuable, that's a different conversation—and one you need to have—because that asset is not providing competitive advantage.

To pass the test of being **valuable**, the resource or capability should make you more money than it costs you. Does it enable you to exploit an external opportunity or better meet an environmental threat? This one feels the easiest to pass, but remember, we are only applying the test to key assets. If it is just table stakes, that's all it is. It's important to separate **competitive differentiation** from **competitive advantage**: you may possess a resource or capability that is *different* from others, but if it is not uniquely valuable, or allows you to more firmly move the needles apart, it does not pass the "V" test. Be careful with brand. While most companies quickly put their brand on the list as valuable, empirically speaking, few pass this test.

Rare means it is hard to get access to and not widely possessed by others. I purposely use the word "others" and not "competitors" when performing this test so you look beyond a narrowly defined competitive set. New or tangential entrants into your market are just as likely to chip away at your advantages as the few existing competitors you can name. Rare resources and capabilities are often linked to proprietary access, such as natural resources (minerals, diamonds, oil) or property rights, but they can also be access to key distribution channels or proprietary partnerships. How you define your competitive set also matters. For global consultancies Bain & Company, BCG, or the McKinsey Company, their brand names and alumni networks are rare when compared to the industry of management consultancies, but less rare when compared to their two main rivals.

FIGURE 5.2 The VRIN assessment model

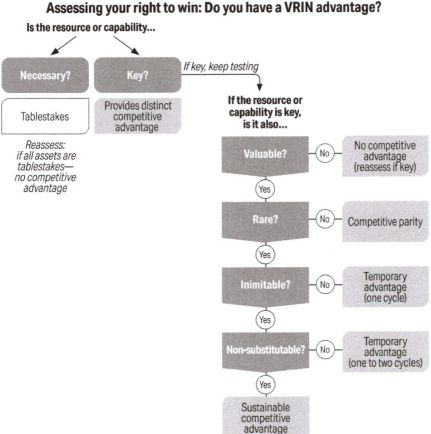

Assessing your right to win: Do you have a VRIN advantage?

Is the resource or capability...

Necessary?   Key?   *If key, keep testing*

Tablestakes   Provides distinct competitive advantage

Reassess: if all assets are tablestakes— no competitive advantage

If the resource or capability is key, is it also...

Valuable? —No— No competitive advantage (reassess if key)

Yes

Rare? —No— Competitive parity

Yes

Inimitable? —No— Temporary advantage (one cycle)

Yes

Non-substitutable? —No— Temporary advantage (one to two cycles)

Yes

Sustainable competitive advantage (at least two cycles)

Inimitable refers to the difficulty, or near impossibility, of copying your asset. These assets are so uniquely defining they allow your organization to stand out as unequalled. Becoming unique is in many ways the Holy Grail of strategy as it limits competition and allows an organization to sustain its growth and profit over time.

Passing this test means others can watch you, they can study you, they can spend more money than you have, but still cannot match you no matter how hard they try. Of course, with enough time and money anything can be copied, but building inimitability can lead to a multi-cycle strategic advantage. As our timeframe for the VRIN is one to two strategy cycles, inimitable is a hard test to pass. If you grade an "I," you are saying a potential competitor can build a clear view of your assets and invest more money than you have, and, in six years, still not copy you.

You can you build inimitability in a few ways:

- **Economic deterrence:** Economic deterrence means you have more money than anyone else. Microsoft successfully deployed this strategy for decades: its war chest of cash allowed it to essentially buy its competitors or burn them out of business by deploying extra cash towards the competition. While well-funded companies are tough competitors, in most market cycles cash is the easiest to imitate.

- **Network effects:** Network effects occur when the value of the product or service increases as the number of users increases. This happens when the value of the solution is derived from interactions among users. Most dual-sided marketplaces have an element of network effects at play, and companies that prioritize scaling both sides of the marketplace to achieve compounding network effects build inimitability. Network effects can be direct from the platform (such as social media), indirect (such as operating systems), or more local (such as data apps). LinkedIn founder Reid Hoffman understood the power of network effects, partly from his experience at PayPal, and prioritized building the dual-sided marketplace of the professional networking site more than anything else, leading to an inimitable advantage others could not copy.

- **"Land grab" advantage:** In some markets, especially where there are network effects, being the first to scale matters. When a company is the first to achieve scale, it becomes almost impossible for others to copy. As first mover, you are rewarded by the compounding effects of each step of the path taken along the way. Others will not only need to replicate the scale, they will also have to imitate the path dependency of achieving that scale. In the USA, while ride-hailing companies Lyft and Uber launched around the same time, Uber prioritized its land grab strategies by seizing all major markets quickly, de-prioritizing or completely ignoring other aspects of the experience, which allowed it to quickly overtake its rival in market share.

- **Causal ambiguity:** Causal ambiguity means that a competitive advantage has been gained, but the precise cause cannot be disentangled. Consider your advantage like a "recipe" that even if competitors list out most of the ingredients, they cannot copy how to put them together and how they interact with each other. Companies that sustain performance over multiple strategy cycles often have this at play, but newer companies can build it as well. When existing carriers like United Airlines tried to copy Southwest Airlines in the 1990s, they were consistently unsuccessful. While they could copy its policies on gate turnarounds or checked baggage, these were just pieces of its advantage that also include a unique culture of fun and frugality, as well as an intense loyalty from some passengers.

- **Historical dependence:** Historical or path dependence relates to past events that have a significant influence on future outcomes. For company strategy, we see this play out in technology adoption such as the VHS videocassette adoption over Betamax in the 1980s (even though the latter was technically superior) or the Microsoft Windows operating system. We also see this with consumer behavior: if you are used to replacing commodity goods in your life, such as laptop chargers, with two clicks on Amazon, you are highly unlikely to search for options the next time you leave your charger in a hotel and need a quick replacement. Often there is an interplay between network effects, economic deterrence, and historical dependence.

- **Time compression diseconomies:** Time compression diseconomies (TCD) is one of those expressions that contains a host of insights in a short, albeit abstract phrase, but it is worth discussing because it is one of the most powerful ways to build inimitability.

  First coined by professors Dierickx and Cool from INSEAD,[6] it means that the faster resources are developed, the higher the level of costs a firm incurs. In terms of growth strategy, it means that when a company has gained an advantage, but there was intense learning involved in gaining that advantage, this cannot be copied in less time, even by spending more money, because the resulting time compression does not allow for the learnings to occur and embed in another organization.

An example helps. Imagine your younger self trying to play a musical instrument, a story also told by my LBS colleague Freek Vermeulen.[7] Every Saturday morning you have a piano lesson. Your teacher wants you to practice for 30 minutes daily. A diligent student, most weeks you did just this. But one week you don't practice at all—between ballgames, your favorite TV programs, and just forgetting, it simply didn't happen. Suddenly it's Friday afternoon, and you realize that you haven't practiced the week's piece once! You glance at the clock and see it's only 4pm. No problem you think, I'll just practice until 7pm, and I will be fine tomorrow. Three hours is the same as thirty minutes daily for six days. So how does the lesson the next morning go?

We all know it's going to be a shambles. Your poor teacher's ears aching from the miserable attempt. But why? Quite simply because the human brain needs rest time to learn. When we take in new knowledge and information, we also need time to integrate it—to place it, frame it, and then open our minds back up for more learning. Organizations have the same problem! As organizations act and learn, these learnings compound on each other, making copying advantages that have a learning element much harder for others.

Non-substitutable is the hardest to assess as a team, as it is often difficult to imagine what could displace your current offerings with different means. For example, a substitute for Pepsi is not Coca-Cola; it's juice or bottled water. A substitute for joining LA Fitness is not joining the local YMCA, but rather buying running shoes and training in your local parks. For many new companies, not understanding how you will compete against substitutes leads to a failure to grow, and for existing companies, losing to a surprise substitute can quickly erode value creation potential.

Protection against substitutes comes from delivering a compelling product or service in a consistent manner, offering a price—performance trade-off that is difficult to compete against, and/or making it difficult for customers to switch.

Doing the assessment

Some CEOs and founders may need to step back and trust the team do the VRIN assessment without them. From years of doing these assessments, I have observed CEOs can be the unintentional blockers as they are often the most emotionally tied to the origins of the company's assets.

The first time teams do the assessment, a long list of VRIs emerge and it feels pretty good. I encourage you to do it a second time, ideally with facilitation. Re-assessing with more guidance and toughness usually cuts the list dramatically. Warning: people can get reflective and sometimes a bit upset. Many companies I work with have helpfully labelled this step as "the therapy session" as it's a lot to process. Now, do it one more time. This is when you'll get it just about right. Some assets are added back in, some others taken out, and the most honest conversations are had. If your team has the patience to go through the assessment three times, you'll have a solid list to discuss.

After you finish this assessment, you should have a short list of your assets that pass the VRIN, VRI, VR, or just the V test. Be careful, as few will pass VRIN or VRI. The history of strategy contains some celebrated examples such as 3M's ability to innovate, the Toyota production system, or more recently Google's search advertising business or WhatsApp's network of telecom operators and device manufacturers. But they are celebrated because they are few and far between.

Culture as Right to Win: WD-40 Company's and The Gorilla Glue Company's cultural strength

Can culture or another intangible resource or capability be a VRI or VRIN advantage? I find culture passes the Rare and Inimitable test much more often than it passes the Valuable test. If you feel culture is part of your Right to Win, be disciplined in the assessment and quite tough on the Valuable tests. You may decide that your culture remains important to you, as it enables and supports your other advantages, but it may not be a VRI. In practice, I can name only a few companies where culture is a clear VRI advantage; two of them are below.

CASE STUDY

When Garry Ridge became CEO of WD-40 Company in 1997, the USA-based company was looking to expand globally. Global brand building, improving distribution, and growth were the initial ambitions, but Ridge soon realized achieving these goals would necessitate a cultural shift as well. He didn't know how to do it at first, but he knew micromanagement would not allow for the fast scaling they wanted. Instead, the organization would need a global workforce with great, skilled people who were also passionate about their work, happy, and empowered to try, explore, and learn. Building this culture for growth became his top priority.

Ridge was guided by a simple equation:

Strategy x Will of the People = Outcome

His basic proposition: if strategy was 70 percent right, but the will of the people was 20 percent, that would deliver 1,400. But even if the strategy was roughly right but mostly wrong (50 percent) and there was 80 percent will of the people, the outcome would be 4,000. As Aristotle's guiding quote explains: Pleasure in the job puts perfection in the work.

Culture needs the right ingredients, which were identified as clear purpose, a hierarchical set of values that protected people and set them free, and the absence of fear to promote learning, what for WD-40 Company became codified as a "learning moment." Even junior members of the team could make aligned decisions with others within the framework the values provided.

For WD-40 company, Culture = Values + Behaviour x Consistency. The top team knew it would take more than the right ingredients: they had to live its promises daily. Without consistency, it wouldn't work. Daily effort and relentless focus led to a growing confidence and eventual global acceptance by the employees, and the building of a culture where people wanted to work, wanted to deliver their best, and left work happy. Over time, this culture began to strengthen and solidify into competitive advantage.

Ridge noticed it when employees started to talk about culture with each other, and then it started to show up in the data—they have been tracking employee engagement since 1999; engagement was trending up and attrition was going down.

The team eventually codified their Right to Win culture into six components: articulated and lived values; servant leadership mindset; high member engagement and low turnover; global nature of the business; long-term focus of purpose; and learning velocity.

But did this culture link to the company's results? Ask any leader, and they provide a one-word response: Materially.

After more than 20 years of focus on culture as their Right to Win, the company grew from 15 to 176 countries, with more than six times the revenue and a market capitalization that increased from $300 million to $2.5 billion. Ridge had consistently promised the market results, but said his focus would be on the long-term, tangible, and consistent results materialized throughout earning cycles. Current CEO and President Steve Brass, who took over in 2021, is continuing to lead with the strength of culture and learning velocity.

CASE STUDY

When the five Ragland brothers founded The Gorilla Glue Company (originally Lutz Tool), they did not intentionally try to build culture as competitive advantage from day one. But after fast early growth exposed them to what happened when the culture wasn't great, the brothers prioritized building a fun, friendly and high-performing environment. The Raglands created a space where people wanted to be because they had fun and genuinely cared about each other and the community— and where they were motivated to perform.

The brothers found that if you hired people who were a joy to be around, did their job well and with care, and wanted to grow together, it eliminated drama and inspired a place where people wanted to be. Not only did more great people come to work there (Gorilla Glue consistently wins Best Places to Work awards), the culture started to drive further performance as well.

But again, does culture lead to results? Gorilla is consistently a great place to work that also grew consistently since its founding. But there's something more there, and it's tangible. When I walked the manufacturing floor with some team members, I could physically feel the positive culture, the fast yet friendly pace of work, and the enthusiasm of the high-performing workforce—things I rarely see and feel to that extent.

If you mean it and are prepared to relentlessly focus on it, culture can be a VRI, but I have never seen it happen without this being the absolute top priority of senior leadership. Despite moving out of daily management, the Raglands still have new hire lunches with employees and spend time reinforcing the mission and values among staff in the shop and in the office.

Does this give us a Right to Win in the world of our beliefs?

Make sure to segment your assets accordingly. What do you have that is Valuable, Rare, and Inimitable? What is Valuable and Rare, but can be imitated? What is just Valuable? Is this enough? Does this give us a Right to Win in the world of our beliefs?

That latter part of the sentence is the critical one: in the world of our beliefs. You need to have a Right to Win in the world you just discussed in your situation assessment, not the past one you were operating in before the shock triggered the Reset.

Every time you cycle through a Reset, you must re-examine the Right to Win for how it holds up in the changed situation and with your updated beliefs. Especially after shocks, look for assets that were valuable but may no longer be so. Resources that were not rare may also now be rarer, which could increase their value or make them a stronger part of the VRI. Go through each piece and re-assess what it means now. Ask if your past VRI advantages still provide a Right to Win? Why or why not? Then go through each piece on your shortlist and determine what may have changed. You do yourselves no favors by clinging to old assumptions of competitive advantage.

When you have your Reset Right to Win, how do you feel? How comfortable are you that you have a compelling Right to Win for the next one to two strategy cycles with just those pieces?

There is unfortunately no easy test on what is enough, so the simplest way I express it to leaders is with the gut test. Quite bluntly, how does your stomach feel when you look at the list?

How comfortable are you that you have a compelling Right to Win for the next one to two strategy cycles with just those pieces? If you are comfortable, great! We will next test your assumptions about why you feel that way.

If you are not comfortable, that is also OK. We'll work on strengthening your position.

When your Right to Win is not enough

Many leave the assessment feeling slightly less than comfortable. First, know there is rarely a silver bullet in the Right to Win. Some companies have them: De Beers' access to their diamond mines is a clear VRI, as is Saudi Aramco's ability to explore, extract, and produce a barrel of oil for only a few US dollars. But what about the rest of us?

Your job during the Reset is to take a VR to a VRI, or to go from one VRI to two. If you do not see a clear pathway to get there, here are three options.

1. Can you turn a resource into a capability?

While you should not confuse a resource with a capability, if you have a resource the question is whether you can transition a VRI or VR resource into a capability.

One global insurer identified a valuable and rare resource in its talented leaders across its global network. This was certainly valuable; at most leadership levels they had arguably one of the best sets of talents in that space. It was rare when you consider their expansive network. Having individual leaders of that quality was not rare, but the breadth and depth of the talent was. Only a few competitors could match that.

But taken by itself, this valuable and rare resource could be imitated. A competitor with a sizable war chest and five years could certainly hire the talent away. The question they had to ask themselves is whether they had the capability to leverage their network. Were they able to pull from the right experts at the right time faster and more effectively than anyone else? If they could achieve that, it would mean this VR resource could be a VRI capability. Even if talent was hired away, they could not replicate their ability to turn this talent, and their knowledge, into global effectiveness at scale.

2. Can you re-deploy a resource or capability into a new industry?

You may have a capability that is valuable in your current industry. But can you identify another industry in which it would constitute a clearer Right to Win?

This was the case for Kem Krest, introduced in Chapter 4. The company was known for reducing their end-to-end unit logistics costs and consistently won the GM Supplier of the Year award. But this cost-reducing capability had become table stakes over time. Being a supplier to the big OEMs is a very tight margin business. Continuous end-to-end cost reduction is the customer's expectation. Kem Krest did not have many other assets on the list. They had a supplier network that was valuable and somewhat rare, but much of that depended on personal relationships between a few leaders and existing suppliers. They were one of the largest certified Minority Business Enterprises (MBE), but they knew that they were not doing much to leverage this, and there were many other minority-owned businesses.

It was a disheartening assessment that led to a grim conversation: their existing advantage was valuable and only somewhat rare in their industry. More so, the majority of their top beliefs showed possible decline in the traditional OEM business over the next decade. They had a declining advantage in a declining industry! But then they realized they were doing this analysis with their existing industry in mind. Yes, efficient and effective logistics were table stakes for OEMs, but in the fast-growing ecommerce business, which was booming post Covid-19, these were much sought-after capabilities.

A clear opportunity emerged to transition this back-end fulfillment capability to a new industry. With the learnings of Kem Shield, they launched EFBU (Ecommerce Fulfilment Business Unit) in 2021 and began building a customer base of Direct to Consumer (D2C) consumer businesses. Over a period of three months, the team portioned off part of their existing team and capabilities, focused on a brand new, small set of ideal customers, and launched their fulfilment business. This led to the company's launch of a new ecommerce technology suite allowing the ability to integrate with multiple ecommerce platforms. For the first time in the company's history, they had created an agile capability of D2C fulfillment, but more importantly developed a playbook to help non-traditional automotive or OEM customers grow.

As the electric vehicle (EV) market grew in late 2022, the company won a major contract to handle EV chargers in the D2C market—a contract that never would have been possible had they not grown this capability with direct-to-consumer fulfillment and speed to market with EFBU.

3. Can you bundle a set of resources and capabilities?

You probably have a small set of VR resources and capabilities that can be imitated. Maybe they can be individually imitated, but not ALL of them can be copied in one or two strategy cycles. Right? If so, you can build a VRI bundle of resources and capabilities. This is how you create inimitability through causal ambiguity! Each individual asset on its own does not pass the test, but as a bundle they do.

The challenge with bundles is discipline. Not every asset should fit within the bundle. Usually no more than four elements form a VRI bundle. You need to resist the temptation to put everything into the bundle—most of these are just tablestakes. And the pieces need to reinforce each other. On the other hand, if you try to reinforce too much, bundles can make you slow and overly complex. You may end up with something that your customer is not actually willing to pay for.

To build a VRI bundle, you need three pieces:

- Absolute clarity on what is in the bundle, and what is just table stakes.
- Absolute consistency of execution of each element: one piece with lagging execution or experience destroys the bundle.
- A perfect tension of individual accountability for each piece of the bundle (each team knows what they are accountable for delivering) and joint responsibility for delivering the bundle (handovers are executed flawlessly as every team member knows the value is only achieved if the pieces work together).

Building VRI bundles is difficult in practice. One Canadian home interior manufacturer found this to be the case in their strategy Reset. Initial attempts to grow their business in the USA from its Canadian base had been slow at best. When assessing the company's Right to Win, the team realized that they had no VRI advantage in the USA, and even their Canadian Right to Win had only somewhat-rare pieces. After re-assessing their Right to Win, the team concluded they had four pieces of a possible bundle: their innovative design process; their service culture; their trusted relationships with customers and partners; and their value perception of product quality. These assets were valuable and rare on their own, but when delivered seamlessly as a bundle, they would be impossible to imitate over the midterm and could provide a lasting advantage in both markets.

From insight to action

Discussions about your Right to Win are often a paper exercise. Many strategic insights may emerge, but how do you ensure they make it off the page and become actions that support your growth strategy? You can take the conversation to the next step by teasing out actions and putting them into four buckets: protect, leverage, strengthen, buy/build, each of which have separate implications and timeframes:

- **Protect:** Your VRI advantages need to fall into this bucket, but you probably have VR advantages you want to protect as well. What do you need to pull inside the castle moat and hold onto over time? What do you need to clearly label for the current and future team as assets to be protected and preserved? Remember you cannot protect what you do not have, so only existing resources and capabilities go here.

- **Leverage:** Leverage actions are your power moves. These are the resources and capabilities that you possess but are not creating enough value with currently. These can be the trapped or underutilized advantages that are often only uncovered in the Right to Win assessment. If you realize that you are sitting on an asset that you could be getting more value out of, get going! You should aim to see value creation gains within a year, as these are quicker wins.

- **Strengthen:** Strengthening actions are focused on assets that do not yet represent Rights to Win, but they could if you worked on it. The foundation has been laid but more work needs to be done to turn them into compelling Rights to Win. These could be elements of your digital platform, your customer relationships, or new product capabilities. Assets falling under "strengthen" should show value creation gains within one strategy cycle, or three years. Assets to strengthen are critical in the waging of must-win battles (covered in Chapter 8).

- **Buy/build:** Buy and build areas are gaps. These are the assets you uncovered during the competitive advantage discussion that you need and do not have. Be as clear as you can in articulating what these are and the specific gaps that must be closed. Do not assume all Right to Win must be built yourself: if you cannot build the capability in enough time, one of your options should be to buy them. Scan for "buy" opportunities like talent, platforms, or new company acquisitions. Buy/build gaps often need longer to close, so your timeframe to value creation is one to two strategy cycles. The midterm implication of these may also become must-win battles (covered in Chapter 8).

Topics can fall into multiple areas across these four buckets. For WD-40 Company, its culture and values fall into the "protect" bucket, but they also identified some Strengthen components, especially as they wanted to continue to work on their culture as a Right to Win with a younger, hybrid workforce post-Covid.

Summary and next steps

Strategy is a competitive game, and you need to hit the field not just ready to play but ready to win.

A Right to Win comes from having an advantage in **resources, capabilities,** or **barriers to entry.** Isolate your resources and capabilities that are valuable, rare, and inimitable. A true Right to Win occurs when these are also non-substitutable. Companies that have a VRIN Right to Win are powerful opponents, as the Right to Win is clear and all employees know their role in executing against it.

During the Reset, leaders must re-examine every aspect of the Right to Win and re-assess its viability going forward. Being a Thrive company means letting go of former Right to Win assets that the market is no longer willing to pay for while continually leveraging, strengthening, and building those that will provide a Right to Win going forward. During the Reset, leaders must re-examine every aspect of the Right to Win and continue to re-assess its viability as the situation changes.

After re-assessing your Right to Win you should have:

✓ a summarized list of your valuable, rare, inimitable, and non-substitutable resources and capabilities.

✓ a summarized list of the beliefs and assumptions your Right to Win is based upon, and how you will test them

✓ a prioritized assessment of which Right To Win assets belong in the following buckets so you can take action to protect, leverage, strengthen, and buy/build

Now, given your specific Right to Win, where should you play? This is what the next chapter will explore.

Endnotes

1 B Wernerfelt (1984) A resource-based view of the firm, *Strategic Management Journal* 5 (2), pp. 171–80, http://web.mit.edu/bwerner/www/papers/AResource-BasedViewoftheFirm.pdf (archived at https://perma.cc/QN2U-E925); C K Prahalad and G Hamel (1990) The core competence of the corporation, *Harvard Business Review*, 68 (3), pp. 79–91; J B Barney (1991) Firm resources and sustained competitive advantage, *Journal of Management*, 17, pp. 99–120; D J Collis and C A Montgomery (1995) Competing on Resources: Strategy in the 1990s, *Harvard Business Review*, 73, pp. 118–28

2 See M Porter (2008) The five competitive forces that shape strategy, *Harvard Business Review*, https://hbr.org/2008/01/the-five-competitive-forces-that-shape-strategy (archived at https://perma.cc/58TV-YDDK)

3 B Wanamaker (2013) Why Cleveland Clinic always wins: the solution shop business model, *Christensen Institute*, www.christenseninstitute.org/blog/why-cleveland-clinic-always-wins-the-solution-shop-business-model/ (archived at https://perma.cc/WR7V-BM8H)

4 Wernerfeld, op.cit.

5 J Barney (1991) Firm Resources and Sustained Competitive Advantage, *Journal of Management*, 17 (March), pp. 99–120, https://doi.org/10.1177/014920639101700108 (archived at https://perma.cc/FE6V-FZ42)

6 I Dierickx and K Cool (1989) Asset stock accumulation and sustainability of competitive advantage, *Management Science* 35 (12), pp. 1504–11

7 F Vermeulen (nd) "Time compression diseconomies" – too much, too fast, www.freekvermeulen.com/%E2%80%9Ctime-compression-diseconomies%E2%80%9D-%E2%80%93-too-much-too-fast/ (archived at https://perma.cc/53DL-P5FR)

6

Where Will We Play?
Our Who, What, How

"The essence of strategy is choosing what not to do."

—MICHAEL PORTER

Deciding where to compete in your market involves tough trade-offs. Many options may look attractive, and it can feel easier to have more on the table than less, a tendency which is getting more pronounced. In an era when CEO tenure continues to decline, few are willing to risk saying no, only to discover that the area they pulled back from was a key growth opportunity. But a company that tries to be everything to everyone is a company for no one. The potential playing field for any company is intimidatingly large, but to be able to win, you must draw some lines and declare definitively, "We are going to play *here*." Choices must be made.

Making informed choices comes from addressing the overlapping questions of, based on our Right to Win:

- **WHO** are our ideal customers (and customer markets)?
- **WHAT** are we offering them? What is our value proposition, or Jobs to be done?
- **HOW** will you reach them or go-to-market?

This is a lot of ground to cover, as each of the Who, What, and How could be (and is!) a book on its own.[1] If this is the first time you are discussing "Where will we play?" expect it to take longer than some of the other questions. Revisiting these questions during a Reset, however, should go much quicker.

This chapter provides an overview of the **Who** (your ideal customers), the **What** (your winning value proposition), and the **How** (launch and distribution of your winning product or service). We also discuss how to Reset these choices after a shock to ensure you continue to have a compelling Right to Win. We wrap by introducing the question: What is your strategic center of gravity? That is, of the Who, What, and How, which one should be the anchor point?

Who is your ideal customer?

A group of Young Presidents Organization (YPO) companies visits London every other year for the Active Learning Program (ALP), of which I am the Faculty Director, to reset their growth strategies. When we started this program, I thought identifying ideal customers would be one of the easiest topics to discuss, but time after time these leaders get stuck.

"What do you mean?" they ask. "An ideal customer is someone who pays us!"

If pushed, they would describe their existing customers, usually anchored on their largest or most recent transaction. But strategy is not a description of what you are doing today, it is the choices you are making going forward.

I found I had to ask a more precise question: "If you closed your company down today, and fired all your customers, and tomorrow you could open it again and hire back just the customers you wanted to serve, who would they be?"

Then, the light of realization would come on. The leaders would start describing the characteristics that make a great customer—the kind that can grow with them. Year after year, the insights gained from these discussions have been the most critical for their growth Resets.

Developing an ICP

Your Ideal Customer Profile (ICP) definition will be one of the most powerful tools in your growth strategy. It is your guide for where to seek future growth (new customers) and how to structure and service existing customers (wallet share growth and customer retention).

Developing your ICP: Scoping

Start by describing a great customer: the easiest to serve, the most profitable, and the ones who will grow with you. For a consumer-focused business this would include demographics related to gender, location, age, educational background, income, and digital affinity. For a business customer consider company size, industry, number of locations, and geographic base.

But do not stop there. Describe your ideal customer in terms of their values and concerns: What worries them? What excites them? What do they enjoy and love? What makes them anxious? These emotive questions are just as important and powerful for the B2B markets as the B2C. Figure 6.1 gives some guidance about these scoping questions.

FIGURE 6.1 Developing an ICP: Scoping questions

Identifying your ideal customer profile

	USER (who uses or consumes our solution)	BUYER (the decision maker who buys, or says yes to working with us)	INFLUENCER (does not necessarily 'use' or 'buy' but critical to getting to a yes)
Who are they? Where are they located? (Geography) What do they look like? What industries are they in?			
What do they value? What worries them? What excites them? What stresses them? What do they value most?			
Answer these questions mostly for the buyer, the decision maker What do they do? What functions do they work in? What roles or titles will they hold? What jobs are they performing?			
Who are they *not*?			

Developing your ICP: Characteristics

After scoping out your ideal customer, identify the main characteristics or set of criteria that define them.

For business customers, follow-up questions to consider are:

- How much volume or business will they bring every year? How big do they need to be for us to know they will bring in this much?
- What industry or sub-industry are they in?
- What is their main concern as a company (growth, branding, sustainability, etc.)?
- What are they looking for in companies such as yours? Long-term partnerships? Branding support?
- Where are they located? How many locations do they have?

For consumers, consider:

- What do they most value?
- Where are they located?
- How much will they spend?

Developing a good ICP is similar to building a funnel: imagine all possible customers being filtered through your ICP criteria. The ones that pass match who you are looking to serve and guide where you should allocate time and effort.

At this point leaders often push back: "We cannot afford to just think about our ideal customers. We want to grow—we need all the customers we can get!" I understand the sentiment, but it's incorrect.

The opposite of ideal is not "fire," a term commonly used to mean get rid of, or stop serving customers. Free yourself from this false dichotomy. Instead, divide your universe of possible customers into three categories. The first column is your ICP, the ideal customers you want to grow your business with going forward and who are described by a short set of criteria. The second is the "Nos," the customers you will not serve. They are bad actors, have a history of not paying, cost too much to serve, and so on— these are your true nos. And then in the third column is everyone else. You can be agnostic towards everyone else, but in a growth strategy you need absolute clarity on the ideals and Nos.

When Angela Ahrendts and Christopher Bailey engineered Burberry's turnaround in the mid 2000s, they had a strong view of their ideal customer:

the emerging market millennial. At the time, the investor market was dubious at best; many thought the brand was crazy to focus on millennials who had yet to prove a willingness to pay or maintain loyalty to brands. But the bet was successful, leading to significant growth of the brand from just under 1.8 billion in 2008 to 3.7 billion in 2014 when Ahrendt stepped down to become Apple's Head of Retail. An important part of their success was the clear focus the brand had on the few things that needed to be done to achieve their goal. For Burberry, targeting the Who—their ideal customer—created a center of gravity for their strategy. Every fashion line that emerged under Bailey's direction had them in mind: "What would our millennial guy or girl wear?" "How do millennials shop?" "How do they experience our brand?"

Burberry is also a helpful example of what an ICP is not: the opposite of a customer you refuse to serve. If my decidedly not-millennial colleague Stephen Bungay walked into Burberry to buy a scarf, they would not turn him away for not fitting their ICP mold. Stephen is certainly not on Bailey's vision board, but they would still happily sell him a checked scarf.

There is a cost to serving customers, and for many the cost to acquire and serve them will be greater than the value that customer provides to your organization. Building a better understanding of your customer acquisition costs (CAC) and cost to serve (CTS) versus customer lifetime value (LTV) can be helpful to make better decisions around which customer segments you target, service, and retain.

A & A Customs Brokers based in Vancouver, Canada, offers customs services across the USA and Canadian border. When CEO Graham Robbins and his team started their strategy Reset in 2018, they did not think that their customer focus was an issue. But as they explored their ideal customer a clear profile emerged: a "boring" customer, technically capable, easy to work with, with simple products and steady shipments. None of these criteria seemed overly surprising, but they had never put it on paper before.

Robins realized their team had been focusing on exactly the opposite type of customer: large companies with multiple product lines in new and emerging industries. They had thought these "exciting" customers were great, but in practice they were a huge burden. A home and garden center that had steady volume but also hundreds of SKUs—all of which needed to be individually entered—was the opposite of easy to work with. Other customers, while loyal, still had manual forms, and even wanted to fax them in—they were the opposite of technically capable. Many customers had been with them for ages, but they shipped low volumes. These customers got the same level of attention and care as the massive ones.

The ICP characterization involved a few variables, which they reduced to six criteria all starting with a C or an S so that their customer service and sales teams would remember them easily: Complexity in check (limited SKUs), Consistency (consistent shipments without seasonality), Capable (could integrate with tech), Size of the Prize (big enough to matter), Sophisticated (understands customs and basic valuation), and Simple partnering (easy to do business with).

When A & A analyzed their existing customers, they realized fewer than 20 percent were ICPs! Over the next months, they segmented their customers into tiers, restructured what customer service meant to each tier, and retrained their sales team to just focus on ICPs. Robins likened the eye-opening moment of discovering their ICPs to buying a new car. Once you decide you like a certain car, suddenly you see them everywhere—everyone has the one you want! It was the same with A & A's ICPs. As soon as they knew what they were looking for, their ICP opportunities became clearer than they could imagine. Meanwhile, the non-ICPs went to the wayside, clearly a distraction. The focus led to significantly revamped growth and an empowered team.

Developing your ICP: Segments

While an overall description of a single ideal customer profile works in some instances, most companies need to build out several Ideal Customer Profile segments. Segments take the characteristics of an ideal and then categorize your ideals into clear buckets of customers that make prioritizing and targeting them easier. Most companies should aim for four to six clear ICP segments ranked in terms of priority (e.g. ICP1, ICP2). A good segment has three to five "cuts" or clearly defining criteria: a cut can be industry, size of company, location, growth potential, and so on. These cuts provide an easy way to identify potential "yeses" to target and sell to.

This was the case for a fast-scaling Fintech based in Singapore. When they started their Reset, they realized the customers the sales team targeted the most were causing the most issues for product teams in terms of customization, placing heavy demands on compliance. Furthermore, they were bringing in little in terms of sustainable revenue. As licensing, compliance, and competition vary widely across regions, having one set of ideal customers globally would have been difficult for the company to determine and not necessarily the best answer to fueling growth.

They started with their Right to Win, which was their differentiated network—they connected hard to reach and access countries. Digging in, they realized few customers valued this network highly and were willing to pay more for it. Often customers found the network interesting, but were not really set up for cross-border payments or did not yet have sizable customer bases across countries to make it worthwhile. They realized that customers already operated in multiple, diverse regions and were looking to grow should be the focus.

Not wanting to limit opportunities, the team created a draft of more than eight possible ICPs per region, and still wanted to cater to the exceptions. To push for more clarity and less distractions, I helped them bucket these segments into ICP tiers: Tier 1A, Tier 1B, Tier 2, and Tier 3, with each region having no more than three segments in any tier.

Tier 1 was the focus now, but with a twist: 1A signaled that if this customer was signed, revenue would be booked within nine months, whereas 1B were customers with longer sales cycles (a contract signed today could mean a full year before revenue was seen). The sales team was to focus only on Tier 1, with enough focus on 1A over 1B to ensure that year's growth. As an example, one Tier1A ICP were digital banks with at least 500 thousand users looking to move into cross-border payments that had a money transfer license, whereas traditional banks that wanted to grow their international payment business that already had tens of millions in flows were a Tier1B ICP.

Tier 2 was "next." The company was ready for them, but they were not a focus. No resources could be expended in targeting them; only those that approached the company were contracted. Tier 3 customers were also not targeted by any sales or BD team, but the product teams began allocating small amounts of time to build future solutions for them, as they could come into focus the following years. All other segments were deprioritized. This structure maintained discipline, ensured alignment while allowing for local adaptation, and prepared the company for success in the next funding round and strategy cycle.

During a Reset, go through each segment and ask: what holds? What's changed? Based on your beliefs and Right to Win, should you shift focus on ICPs? What critical assumptions are you making about this segment for the next strategy cycle? Be prepared to re-prioritize or pause on an entire ICP segment. Firing a customer segment should be done with caution, as this is not a no-regret move.

Targeting every customer is not a strategy

Setting and using ICPs with integrity can be a significant growth accelerator for your company, but there will be resistance. A good salesperson believes they can sell to anyone, and while that enthusiasm is helpful for team building, this same confidence can be detrimental to building a sustainable growth journey.

A company with a growth mindset CAN serve almost any customer, but targeting every customer is not a strategy. Strategy is about playing in a place where you can win right now. The best (albeit gendered and perhaps outdated) way to express your ICPs is to remind your team: **ICPs are about Mr. Right Now, not Mr. Right.** Your ICP defines the kind of customer who will be the focus of your attention at this time, right now.

Your Sales department may push back by saying that the funnel has become too small, that by using ICPs you are shrinking their universe of potential. Yes, you are likely slimming down the top of the funnel, but that is a great thing! If you're concerned, however, the next step is to match your ICP segments to your market size to determine if you have too narrowly scoped your targets. In practice, I have never seen this happen: targeted ICPs always leave more growth potential on the table than a wider funnel, and more importantly, make it easier and more effective to get them.

When Frontier Dental Labs' CEO Paolo Kalaw was looking to accelerate growth in 2013, he was concerned the team of sales field representatives were becoming increasingly inefficient. The company operated labs that made custom dental prosthetics for dentists across the USA and Canada for both routine uptake and cosmetic procedures. Reps were tasked with signing new dentists and would visit offices trying to obtain appointments, but were met with resistance from front desk assistants, whose primary job was to protect the dentists' time. Even when dentists were onboarded, many sent too little work to justify the sales effort.

When I met with Frontier to develop their new growth strategy, the first insight was that the company was built from running their own dental education programs. That meant they had data on hundreds of dentists, most of whom had worked with one of the previous labs. They already had a better list of possible targets than any purchased list could provide them! Reps shouldn't be knocking on any new doors until the current contact list was exhausted.

Then, we developed an ICP to identify what a great dentist would look like. They did steady work (sent molds multiple times/month rather than once or twice a year); did more posterior than anterior restorations (because front of the mouth restorations required more trust than back of the mouth), was in an age sweet spot (under 30 and they would not have built a robust enough patient roster, so work would not be steady enough, and over 65 the team hypothesized the dentists would be nearing retirement); and wanted to grow their business.

The best ICP characteristics can allow for quick filtering of your customer universe without extensive research or interviewing. All their characteristics fit this mold except for the last: wanting to grow their business. Conducting interviews is cost-prohibitive, and most business owners would be reluctant to admit they didn't want to grow their business. And so, the team used a proxy. Most dentists rely on local work and families who stay with them over time, but the dentist who invests in promotion is probably looking to grow beyond their existing customer base. And so, we used "has a website" as a proxy for "wants to grow their business."

With these filters in place, the team culled the existing list of names and gave each rep five names at a time to target. The returns-to-focus were significant: the company was able to cut the number of reps from 12 reps to two while growing over 40 percent a year for the next four years, despite an overall declining market.

Customer circles

Building your top few ICP segments is a start; next, you must determine how you will accelerate sales and grow with these customers. Within any set of customers, there are really three overlapping circles of customers: **users, buyers, and influencers** (Figure 6.2). These circles will play a role in the value proposition and go-to-market conversations covered later in this chapter.

Accelerating growth comes from a nuanced understanding of who your three circles of customers are and understanding the best way to approach, sell, and service them. Think of the customer circles for Kellogg's cereal brand Lucky Charms. Who is the user? Probably younger children. Who is the buyer? This gets more complicated, as there are three steps of buyers: parents (who purchase from the retailer for the child), the grocery store or retailer, and the wholesaler. And who are the influencers? These range from government bodies and regulators (who influence marketing of children-based products and nutritional content), parents' groups, other parents, social media, and a host of others.

So if you are Kellogg's, who is your customer? The answer is all the above. In product development, marketing, and support and service all customers

FIGURE 6.2 Customer circles

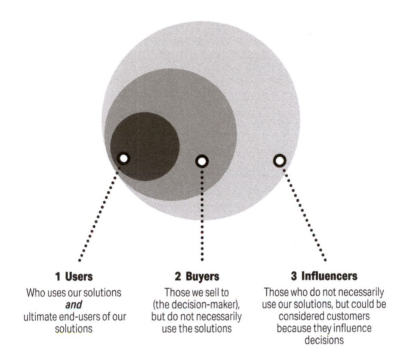

Where we will play: A way of viewing our customers

Shocks almost always disrupt one circle more than others, sometimes removing it completely

1 Users	**2 Buyers**	**3 Influencers**
Who uses our solutions *and* ultimate end-users of our solutions	Those we sell to (the decision-maker), but do not necessarily use the solutions	Those who do not necessarily use our solutions, but could be considered customers because they influence decisions

must be considered, and you should understand and deliver a value proposition for all customers. Among your circles, though, you need a center of gravity where your focus will be placed. This allows your decisions and sales pathways (the order in which you target the different customers in the circle) to be filtered through a clear focus. Many consumer-focused brands selling through retailers have their center of gravity on the "parent" buyer, with the "retailer" buyer the next focus. This can shift over time, but too many brands lose the discipline of keeping a center of gravity amongst the circles. That can lead to a communicated brand promise for one circle while energy is spent optimizing for a different one.

For each of your ICP segments, map out the three circles and identify the users, buyers, and influencers. Then discuss where your center of gravity should be. While all are your customers, you want a clear centrical force that helps filter your decisions through. This will help in finding the "fit" with your value proposition and go-to-market.

What will you offer them? Your jobs to be done

What business are you in? This feels like a simple question, but in a 1960 article, Professor Theodore Levitt suggested defining yourself too narrowly in terms of the industry rather than the customer need you serve prevents you from uncovering the insights that will accelerate growth.[2] Take railroads. If the railroad business in the USA had defined their business as transportation rather than railroads, would they have experienced the same decline?

Levitt postulated there were really no growth industries, just companies better positioned to take advantage of growth opportunities. His call for action was for companies to define themselves in terms of the customer needs they were meeting. In his 1969 book *The Marketing Mode*, he popularized the phrase marketeers would use for decades: customers do not want to buy a quarter inch drill, they want to buy a quarter-inch hole in the wall.[3]

Years later, Clayton Christensen and his colleagues asked us to consider the "jobs" our customers were hiring us to do. I have found the notion of moving beyond the features *and* beyond the benefits into "jobs" is the most effective and powerful way to consider your value proposition, including, if not especially for, business to business models.

These answers can create a powerful lock-in that outlasts periods of change. During uncertainty, if you are only providing a feature, you will be fired. If you are providing a benefit, you may have some hooks, but not many. **Only companies that articulate and deliver compelling jobs consistently build customer loyalty and moats for a sustainable Right to Win.**

Milkshakes and jobs to be done

We all "hire" companies to do jobs. Starbucks does the job of being "your local coffee shop, everywhere in the world, anywhere in the world" exceptionally well. You may not like the taste of their coffee, but that is not what they are optimizing. They are optimizing the feel of your local coffee shop: tables, more outlets in the wall, personal service (i.e. your name on the cup)—all done to do this job well. If you are looking for lipstick, you do not hire Chanel, you hire CVS or Boots or your local pharmacy. If you are looking to feel luxurious, feminine, and a little rebellious, you hire Chanel.

Imagine I was trying to sell you a milkshake. I would describe its features: sweet and refreshing, bursting with chocolate flavors, more affordable than similar milkshakes. I would also describe its benefits. You can satisfy your sweet tooth. Get great value for money. Enjoy a delicious treat. But this is still not enough to create customer loyalty, because we are defining what we are offering in ways that can be easily competed away. What about the job these milkshakes are doing?

In a version of this story told by Christensen, Cook, and Hall[4], a US-based fast-food chain was struggling to increase milkshake sales. It started with the typical tactics—it profiled customers in terms of demographics and built up customer personas. It ran focus groups to ask customers what product changes they would make. Much work was done with the feedback, but none of it impacted sales. One frustrated member of the research team suggested they just watch the customers. Doing so revealed some surprising things. One was that a large percentage of the milkshakes were sold around mid-morning. When I tell this story in Europe, I usually get an amused look and a reminder that perhaps Americans should not be eating ice cream in the morning!

These early morning customers were almost always alone, bought only the milkshake, and they were in the car on the way to work. After some questioning and probing, it became apparent the real job they were hiring the milkshakes to do was prevent boredom on the long drive to work.

They had tried other ways of carrying out this "job," but none did it as well. Toast and bagels were difficult to eat in the car, and sticky fingers did not make for a pleasant drive. Apples and bananas were eaten too quickly and with more difficulty. Customers were also not hiring health benefits—they were hiring boredom prevention. What was the competition? Perhaps other milkshakes. But what else could do this job? Podcasts, Audible, and carpooling were just as much competition as protein shakes and coffee.

How could the company do this job better? They could make the milkshakes thicker, so that they took longer to drink. They could add fruit or chocolate to make them more interesting or add more flavors. And they could move the machine to make the purchase even faster and more efficient in the morning.

This was only one group of the customers, though. The other main sales peak was in mid-afternoon. This customer was different. It was usually a parent with a child. The job they were hiring was "finally say yes to my child." Any parent of young children knows how after a long day of saying no, a chance to finally say yes is appealing. Here is something your child wants that you can agree to without feeling too guilty.

The problem for the company was that optimizing the "prevent boredom" job would hurt the "say yes" job. Making the milkshakes thicker could mean it took too long for children to finish. Adding more options to select from would mean several long (and agonizing for the parent) minutes of five-year-old deliberation at the menu. In this case, optimizing the "say yes" job meant making the milkshake smaller, with just two flavor options, and maybe packaging it with something for the parent.

What was the key insight? Attempting to improve the milkshake's features did nothing for sales. Segmenting customers by only demographic characteristics, such as gender, age, or type of car driven, would not have gotten any insights: our customer may look the same in the morning and the afternoon (it could be the same parent with the same demographic profile commuting in the morning but with their child in the afternoon), but they wanted a fundamentally different job done. It was only after identifying these two distinct jobs that the insights that made the difference were uncovered and growth was accelerated.

One of my favorite takeaways from the milkshake story is something that appears minor. To optimize the morning job, the team moved the machine closer to the register. This way customers hiring "boredom prevention" could get the job done more quickly. It really was that simple: the team just had to move the machine.

Getting to the job to be done is hard work. It may take interviews, scoping, discussions, and pushing the conversation slightly more than you want to. Often when you get to the job, though, what you need to do as an organization to optimize and deliver it even better is not dramatic. You just need to move the machine.

Discovering your job to be done

I have worked with over a hundred companies in the Reset phase. Without fail, considering their jobs to be done has uncovered powerful insights, even if these insights are not always welcome. We never get the description of the job fully right the first, or even the second time, so patience is needed.

Uncovering the jobs also usually requires customer interviews and observing your customers "in the wild." The time spent directly with customers should be preceded by several thought exercises. I like the "Five Whys" from Lean Management Training.[5] The Five Whys are about uncovering root causes of problems but they work well in this instance. Ask: Why do customers hire us? Then: Why do they care about that? Then: What makes them concerned about that? And keep going for at least five rounds. If you feel a little silly saying the fourth or fifth one out loud, you are getting close to the insight!

When I talked to the A & A Customs team about their value proposition, they were excited about their new Customs 101 training. Customers frequently told them in surveys and interviews they wanted to understand customs better, so they were building an offering to "teach" customs in an easy way. While this sounded interesting, I was not convinced.

A key insight in getting to jobs is understanding your customers want to optimize their business, not yours. Customers are selfish. If the proposed "job" you do sounds more like your business than your customers, you are not there yet. At A & A, we dug in with the 5 Whys, and then followed up with some customer observation and interviews. As we did so the real job emerged: customers did not want to learn about customs out of intellectual curiosity. Shipping across the border caused them stress as the rules changed often, and they did not want to make a mistake. Mistakes would delay shipments; delayed shipments could cost them customers. They did not trust someone else to be as concerned as they were about making mistakes, so they wanted to understand the rules for themselves. But for them, in an ideal world, there would be no customs!

That was the key: the jobs A & A had to do were "Make the border disappear" and "Treat your business like our business." Clarity on the jobs to be done was humbling, but also invigorating for the team. They acknowledged that customers didn't want to be dazzled with their customs knowledge and expertise—they just wanted everything to disappear so they could focus on their own businesses.

RPS Composites, based in Canada and the USA, manufactures and services high-performance corrosion resistant tanks, vessels, and piping systems for industrial customers. Their ICPs are in tough, highly regulated, and high-risk environments where failure is not an option. During their Reset, a key insight emerged: if the customer was thinking about the pipes, RPS was not doing their job! The job they were being hired to do was provide end-to-end risk management—not provide pipes and service them

As such, the company developed more comprehensive service offerings and focused on the heightened trust component—to great success. Building trust with the "buyer" circle (head of operations or plant managers) also reinforced their relationship with another circle, the in-plant "users" who worked with the pipes. With trust high, this gave RPS more reason for them to build deeper relationships with the users and come "inside the fence" with servicing offerings, an additional and significant revenue stream.

The power of Thrive companies is that in a company that really delivers jobs, everyone in the company not only knows the jobs they are being hired to do, but also what their role is in delivering them.

Your jobs and your ICPs

Your buyers, users, and influencers hire you for different jobs. Embrace this.

Janis Oslejs founded Latvian-based Primekss to disrupt the traditional concrete industry. Their key innovations involved using steel fibers instead of traditional steel bar reinforcements and then chemically self-stressing them. This meant their floors had improved load bearing (i.e. they could hold 50 percent more than traditional floors) and did not crack over time like traditional floors, making them ideal for robotics and automation warehouses. It also reduced CO_2 emissions. But sales had begun to slow across Europe. The sales team, almost all engineers, were constantly speaking to customers about innovation, and a deep dive into their customer circles revealed why this was a misstep.

The end users—building owners and logistic center owners—loved innovation, but they loved the floors that showed no cracks after ten years even more! Additionally, the users were not the buyers: purchasing decisions were made by the General Contractors (GCs) assigned to that job, and for the GCs the innovation value proposition was almost meaningless. No cracks was interesting, but not if it meant working in a new or different way. The GCs simply wanted to complete the job on time and under budget.

But Primekss could do this job. Because their floor was only four inches thick versus the industry standard of seven, the GCs could be in and out faster if they used a Primekss floor. This reduced the GCs' stress, and along with the longer lifetime of the floor meant that the GC had less chance of being called back to carry out repairs. This new definition of the job to be done, "reduce the stress that the job won't start on time and stay on budget", became the focus of the team, leading to a significant increase in pipeline. The company doubled in growth over that strategy cycle.

When Primekss faced the US market, though, the power within the three circles shifted. GCs had less power and were mostly focused on the lowest price, and the influencer circle had an increased role, with slab consultants becoming involved in many job designs. The team had to once again rethink its approach to work with slab consultants and designers to spec them earlier in the design process.

Further innovation in the next cycle led to the team disrupting their customer circles once more. An R&D unlock meant their new floors would now reduce up to 50 percent of carbon emissions of traditional concrete. With their slimmer floors, this was 50 percent more CO_2 savings against even the global leader. But they had to sell it. Reducing carbon was not a value proposition for GCs, but global customers building logistics centers and distribution centers were very interested! Being able to meet their carbon targets early in their expansion phases was an incredibly valuable job.

Primekss built a team of business development experts who went straight to the end users, sold the floor's ability to allow them to meet ESG targets and build longer-lasting facilities, and then recruited a GC to work with them. They flipped the power of the three circles completely—changing who the buyers versus influencers were—and this led to an incremental 30 percent growth annually.

The secret to high growth is easy to say and difficult to do in practice: it entails **delivering a distinct yet consistent value proposition, or job to be done, across all your customer circles, that you can deliver in an operationally efficient way.**

All three parts of the sentence matter. Each of your customer circles wants a **distinct** value proposition. With Kellogg's, parents want something different than children. With Primekss, the end users want something different than GCs. Yet the value proposition needs to be **consistent** – you want one powerful brand in the marketplace else you risk confusing customers with inconsistent messaging. And you need to do this in an **operationally efficient** way.

It is hard to cater to all three customer circles, so most companies optimize for one or two of them. Optimizing is about finding your center of gravity within the three circles, setting your choices around this center, prioritizing appropriately, and then winning and serving them in an operationally efficient way. And, of course, adapting this over time.

During each Reset, ask how your jobs have been challenged or changed: do your ICPs still need these done? Why or why not? What new jobs do they need done now? Does the changed situation bring about the need for additional, tangential jobs? How quickly and efficiently can you begin delivering these jobs, and can you execute any no-regret moves?

How will you reach your customers?

How can we take our product, service, or solution to the market? What is the best way for your ICPs to be educated about, purchase, and enjoy the jobs you want them to hire you to do? In early-stage investing, one of the most important questions VCs ask founders is how they will approach go-to-market (GTM). They know that growth will never accelerate without a clear strategy to get solutions into the hands of the ideal customers. If you invent something new but have not invented an effective way to distribute and sell it, you have a bad business, no matter how good the product.

Go-to-market guides how you educate the market on your solutions, how you sell them your solutions, and how you match your solutions to your customers. Established companies often become complacent around GTM and revisit this question less than other parts of the strategy. But distribution can be the biggest accelerant of a strategy—and not having one a major cause of strategy failure. Sustainable high growth through changing market conditions necessitates a thought-through, tested and agile approach to go-to-market.

Distribution varies drastically from digital to physical products, from products to services to solutions, and from complex corporates to more narrowly focused companies. Rather than trying to cover every variant, I will focus on some high-level guidance about how to set and Reset your GTM.

Start the conversation with these scoping questions:

- What is the fastest way to reach your customers?
- What is the most direct way to reach your customers?
- What is the most cost-effective way to reach your customers?
- Which routes to market translate the fastest into success?
- How do your customers prefer to be reached?

Put yourself in your customers' shoes: How would you want to be sold to? Outside of repeat work (customers staying with you or coming back), how would you want to learn about the jobs you do?

For direct go-to-market, I like to make it simple by bucketing these into what I call the **6 Rs of Market Reach**:

- **Repeat**: Retention of customers for future work; when a customer buys from you, they do so again, and this brings repeat work.
- **Referrals**: Existing customers refer you, either directly or indirectly to new customers; influencers refer new customers to you (see the three circles above).
- **Relationships**: Your relationships in the market bring you continued work through references and referrals (partly through influencers).

- **Recognition:** Brand recognition and marketing; your company name becomes associated with this job you want to be hired to do.

- **Reach outs:** Targeted customer acquisition; you directly reach out to ICPs (emails, phone calls, and so on); outside of repeat work, this is in one of the most controllable of the GTM strategies.

- **Real estate:** Your location, either in the physical world (store fronts, headquarters location) or digital world (your website, great SEO) places you in direct sight or reach of customers, making you a default purchase.

Review the past few years and ask which have been the most effective. Repeat customers are your anchors, while reach-outs and real estate are sources of new revenue streams. Referrals, relationships, and recognition are approaches that you must build up over time and work to maintain. What

FIGURE 6.3 6 Rs assessment

Go to Market approaches

	How well this works today Rank 1—5	How well this needs to work Rank 1—5	What we need to do to improve
Anchor — **Repeat:** Retention of customers for future work; when a customer buys from you, they do so again, and this brings repeat work	①②③④⑤	①②③④⑤	
Built up over time and then must be maintained — **Referrals:** Existing customers refer you, either directly or indirectly to new customers; influencers refer new customers to you (see the three circles)	①②③④⑤	①②③④⑤	
Relationships: Your relationships in the market bring you continued work through references and referrals (partly through influencers)	①②③④⑤	①②③④⑤	
Recognition: Brand recognition and marketing; your organization name becomes associated with this job you want to be hired to do	①②③④⑤	①②③④⑤	
New revenue streams — **Reach outs:** Targeted customer acquisition; with a clear view of your ICPs, you directly reach out and target this customer (emails, phone calls, visits, LinkedIn, or related)	①②③④⑤	①②③④⑤	
Real estate: Your location, either in the physical world (store fronts) or digital world (great SEO and website) places you in direct sight or reach of customers, making you a default or go-to purchase	①②③④⑤	①②③④⑤	

percentage of your ideal customers did you bring in by each of the Rs above? Which type of ICPs are best reached by different strategies? Return to your Right to Win discussions. Do any of these Rs represent a Right to Win? You may realize you do not have good enough data on how your customers became customers, so begin tracking this data going forward.

With these questions in mind, rank each R against the scoping questions. Use Figure 6.3 to help. Assess where you are today and where you need to be within this cycle, as well as what it will take to get there.

The goal is not to optimize each of the six Rs, but as a team to decide which ones are more or less critical given the emerging strategy. For a construction business, relationships with industry players are critical, as is the real estate of their work sites (such as their signage). For corporate insurers, broker relationships matter, and while corporate headquarters used to, they arguably matter much less now for GTM. But for direct-to-consumer (DTC) businesses, brand recognition or digital real estate are the ones to optimize. And don't lose sight of differentiation. How is your company uniquely set up to approach or reach the market?

CASE STUDY

Innovative approaches across the 6 Rs can spur breakthrough growth. O'Keeffe's Working Hands was founded by Tara O'Keeffe, a pharmacist who developed the formula to help her father with his cracked dry hands. It soon developed a niche following of loyal advocates in construction, farming, and similar trades. When The Gorilla Glue Company purchased the brand in 2018, some thought they would quickly bring this new brand to the mass channel (such as CVS or Walmart), efforts the previous owner had attempted but never broke through. The Ragland brothers who owned The Gorilla Glue Company knew they had a niche product that—despite its strong product/solution fit—might not take off in the mass market, which favors known brands and average consumers. And even if it did, their assumption was that they would struggle to bring it back to the hardware market (who wouldn't want to compete against mass in selling it, so would pass). They also had relationships with hardware, their proven distribution channel for their successful Gorilla Glue family of brands, and the channel trusted them immensely.

While hand cream is not something people associate with tools and supplies, the Raglands' belief was they could leverage their existing relationships with the hardware retailers. For the hardware consumer, it would be placed in the basket as an extra item, not replacing something else (i.e. not cannibalizing a sale). Providing a chance at incremental, easy revenue with an already established relationship, the hardware customer was willing to try it! They also leveraged real estate, re-labeling the jars to a brighter green so they would really pop in the stores (a similar approach they had taken with the iconic orange of the Gorilla Glue brands), and insisting the bright green jars sit only at the check out or in a floor display—never buried on a shelf.

These bets really worked—they were quickly selling the product faster in these trade channels than lotions turned at mass channels like Walmart. This success allowed them to eventually bring the successful line of brands to the mass channel as they had already proven success. The brands, including its most recent innovations such as Healthy Feet continue to sell strongly globally with consistent year on year growth.

ICP circles and sales pathway

Building and understanding GTM ties back to your customer circles and how you can leverage them for breakthrough growth. This often occurs when you view your pathway in a different way—such as RPS Composites did above when they broke through with the "user" segment. Consider the growth pathway of Slack, the enterprise communication tool. Most enterprise software companies spent decades focused on the buyer, who was typically the company CTO. They would build lists, reach out, compel, go through the influencers, and then sell the software, ideally on a recurring or subscription basis. But over time these software solutions became clunky, cumbersome, and at times removed from what a busy office worker wanted to log into, let alone use. Then along came Slack, founded in 2012 by Butterfield, Costello, Henderson, and Mourachov.

Their aim was to create a platform that was easy to use and there was no payment required to sign up. Their hypothesis was that email overload was weighing people down, and internal users were tired of the software CTO/CIOs were putting into the system. And they were correct. Users loved early versions and quickly began signing up. But user growth was not revenue growth, so how did they eventually grow monetization? When enough individuals from the same company email were using the freemium version, then and only then would they approach the CTO for a sale. The users then became influencers advocating the solution to the CTO buyer. This was successful, but the founders later remarked they wished they had turned to this business model earlier. Years later Microsoft introduced and then improved Teams, a Slack competitor, and CTOs took back some of the power.

Distribution choices in GTM

A critical question in growth is whether you should go direct to the market or indirectly via partners such as distributors. High growth comes from controlling your own destiny, which means owning the end user. But owning the end users does not mean you need to sell directly to them. There are trade-offs between the reach and depth of relationship.

CASE STUDY

When Federico Minoli came into motorcycle company Ducati in 1996, he was given a clear goal from the private equity owners: double digit growth and 20 percent profitability.[6] Under intense pressure from the existing culture, unions, and shareholders, Minoli and his team led a dramatic transformation of the company from one focused on product to an experience brand. This meant the end-to-end customer journey of discovery, sales, and experience had to be re-thought, and in doing so, it became clear that the existing distribution strategy no longer worked. It simply wasn't built to sell the experience and brand.

With less than 40,00 bikes produced a year, any single dealer they sold through had a few Ducatis at most and the knowledge of the rep was usually weak. With Honda producing over four million bikes a year, dealers had much more incentive to learn about their bikes. In a dramatic move, Minoli removed all bikes from multi-brand dealers into mono-franchise Ducati Stores where a passionate owner could sell not just the bikes, but the Ducati story. Whilst the average number of places to buy a Ducati in Italy went down from 165 to 65, average sales increased from 14 per store to 150, increasing overall sales by more than four times by the next year.

CASE STUDY

Building distribution as part of their Right to Win was something former WD-40 Company CEO and Chairman Garry Ridge helped lead during his 35-year tenure. When he took the helm as CEO, only four markets were serviced directly, but global growth was part of the strategic ambitions. He challenged long-held assumptions around distribution such as: if it worked in the USA it would work elsewhere; market research should be relied on for its insights on growth potential; and distribution was binary: direct or distributor.

Ridge insisted on learning each market and its unique channels directly, and explicitly asked the team to break the assumption what worked in North America would work elsewhere. Rather than focusing on building competency in one channel, or too quickly deciding markets were mature and moving to the next ones, the team focused on simultaneously making the end user aware of the need and making it incredibly easy to buy. Ridge pushed the team to use "get your shoes dirty research" over relying on market reports to tell them the strength of possible markets—visiting, walking stores and channels, and building relationships. In early days, every new market was indirect (serviced with a distributor), as they needed to learn. Then they started working with distributors and partners to expand capacity, and co-located team members to penetrate markets further.

When they reached a tipping point—dealers' competency and mindset was below the market opportunity—they transitioned the market to direct operations. They were also patient—they knew the market had a need and few other competitors to match them globally, and if they built this global distribution it could be a VRI advantage. It took over two decades of discipline, focus, and prioritization to build a global system that was not overly complex and could generate sustainable and profitable growth.

When Ridge retired in 2022, WD-40's iconic blue and yellow can was available in 176 countries, and the team had competency in multiple trade channels, including quickly building digital competence and leveraging partners like Amazon, and a mix of direct, distribution, and general manager models that maintained their strong gross margin as they continued to grow. The company's distribution (along with its culture) was one of their VRI advantages, or Right to Win.

Trade-offs between direct and indirect GTM approaches involve costs, and when facing extreme uncertainty the desire is to maintain the lowest fixed cost base possible. Thus, **the real secret to sustainable high growth is controlling your own destiny with a variable cost base!**

Your strategic center of gravity

Your Who, What, How must fit together coherently. In other words, your ICPs, jobs to be done, and GTM must mutually reinforce, support, and accelerate each other. But you cannot optimize all three. You must make choices. During a reset, it is important to revisit each and decide which will be your **strategic center of gravity**.

Your strategic center of gravity is the aspect of the Who, What, How which provides the anchor, or focal point, where you most have a differentiated advantage. The other two variables fit around and support it. While you need fit amongst all three, only one can be the center of gravity.

Your strategic center of gravity might be a deep understanding of **Who** your ideal customers are.

The Who was the center of gravity for Burberry during the time of Ahrendts and Bailey. Brooks Running Company had been floundering for years until CEO Jim Webb, with the support of owner Berkshire Hathaway, redefined and reoriented the company around the ICP of the performance runner. The company dropped their leisure lines of footwear (referred to as "barbeque shoes") and focused only on what a performance runner needed to wear while running. Once this clear center of gravity had been defined, Brooks streamlined all resources to support this ICP and growth accelerated. Growth even continued into the Covid-19 pandemic, as their test and learn approaches could be focused on this clear customer segment, which I cover more in Chapter 10.

With "Who" as your center of gravity, growth often comes from learning what else this ICP wants that they trust you to deliver just as well.

Or your center of gravity might be your **What**, the clear and compelling job you deliver in a consistent and differentiated way.

The Ducati story illustrates how Minoli moved the value proposition of their What from product performance and engineering to experience and lifestyle. You did not hire a Ducati to go fast; you did not hire a Ducati to go really fast; you hired a Ducati to escape the world, while knowing there was a global community of others enjoying this same adrenaline-fueled escape. The emerging sporting and racing bikes delivered a compelling "jobs" combination of "adrenaline escape and community affiliation."

The What was also key to IBM's turnaround under Lou Gerstner.[7] When he began his tenure, Gerstner realized IBM had become too siloed with internal functions and departments competing against each other for customer wallet share and had in many ways lost its place in the technology landscape. Gerstner led a dramatic internal and external refocus around the key job IBM could do better than any other: deliver integrated technology solutions that gave CTOs and CIOs peace of mind.

With "What" as the center of gravity, further growth came from identifying additional segments of ICPs who wanted this job to be done. For IBM, this prioritized their ICPs as the world's largest companies in terms of technology needs.

Finally, your center of gravity may be **How** you go to market in a competitively differentiated way.

Construction and mining equipment manufacturer Caterpillar shifted their How to prioritize their distribution and product support. Their hypothesis was that the "customer" was the dealer, and these loyal experts would be the face of the brand to the end-user customer, recommending products but also providing ongoing support, service, and advice. Caterpillar became known for its wide-ranging dealer network and strong after-sales service excellence. The company bore the high inventory and parts cost this focus necessitated, as well as the additional step between them and the end user, because it accelerated growth as dealers were the eyes and ears of the market. They would keep referring and using Caterpillar as they could trust the availability and quality of parts. The cost to build the network paid for itself in market intelligence, and the trusted relationships paid dividends in long-standing loyalty from its dealers which transferred to the customer in the fields and plants.

With "How" as your center of gravity, growth comes from identifying additional value propositions you are uniquely set up to deliver or additional ICPs you are uniquely positioned to serve.

Define your center of gravity. You need focus, fit, and clarity on each aspect of the Who, What, How, and they have to fit together, but you can only have one center of gravity. Determine the base around which you will fit the rest.

Summary and next steps

Strategy is dynamic, and maintaining advantage may mean shifting where you will play. After a shock that triggered Survive, revisit your "Where will we play?" choices based on your updated Right to Win by asking "Who is our ideal customer?" and "What job will we do for these customers?" and "How will we reach these customers?" Together, these help to answer the question of what business you are in, and the role you want to play in that space. As you revisit and reset your choices within these questions, remember that your center of gravity lies in either the Who, What, or How. Determine the base around which you will fit the others.

At this point in the Reset, you will have:

✓ developed Ideal Customer Profiles (ICPs)

✓ defined and ranked your ICP segments

✓ mapped your three customer circles by ICP and considered your sales pathways through each

✓ defined your jobs to be done and how these apply across your top ICP segments

✓ defined and tested your Go-To-Market approach across your 6 Rs: repeat customers, referrals, relationships, recognition, reach-outs, and real estate

✓ identified and prioritized your strategic center of gravity

Now that many of the critical strategy questions have been answered, let's pull together our learnings to address: What will success look like?

Endnotes

1 For simplicity, this chapter only covers the Who, What, How portion of "Where will we play?" and does not cover which markets or geographies to compete within, or a corporate strategy view of which business units to compete with. More background on these topics is available at surviveresetthrive.com (archived at https://perma.cc/W4BU-9V8J).

2 T Levitt (1960) Marketing Myopia, *Harvard Business Review*, https://hbr.org/2004/07/marketing-myopia (archived at https://perma.cc/V59G-3WVR)

3 T Levitt (1969) *The Marketing Mode: Pathways to corporate growth*, McGraw-Hill Book Company, chapter 1 'The Augmented-product Concept', p. 1. Levitt attributed the quote to Leo McGivena, but it is frequently attributed directly to him in subsequent works, notably C M Christensen, S Cook and T Hall (2005) *Marketing Malpractice: The cause and the cure*, Harvard Business Publishing.

4 Christensen, Cook and Hall, op.cit. The story is told in more depth in their later book: C M Christensen, K Dillon, T Hall and D Duncan (2016) *Competing Against Luck: The story of innovation and customer choice*, Harper Business

5 The 5 Whys method is part of the Toyota Production System (TPS). The TPS was detailed originally in Taiichi Ohno's 1973 book *Toyota Production System*, and the 5 Whys are credited to Sakichi Toyoda, founder of Toyota Industries.

6 HBS Teaching Case 9-701-132 Giovanni Gavetti Ducati, 2001

7 L Gerstner (2002) *Who Says Elephants Can't Dance? Inside IBM's historic turnaround*, HarperBusiness

7

What Is Success? And, What Will Stop Us?

"With darkness all around you, you have to develop a feeling for what is right, often based on little more than guesswork, and issue orders in the knowledge that their execution will be hindered by all manner of random accidents and unpredictable obstacles. In this fog of uncertainty, the one thing that must be certain is your own decision... the surest way of achieving your goal is through the single-minded pursuit of simple actions."

—HELMUTH VON MOLTKE

When Lewis Carroll wrote *Alice's Adventures in Wonderland*, the last thing he was thinking about was company strategy. But the famed tale contains at least one powerful observation that is important to resetting strategy.

When Alice is wandering through the woods, she gets to a point where the path diverges, and she does not know where to go. Luckily the Cheshire Cat is there. When Alice asks the Cat which path to take, the Cat asks Alice where she wants to go. "I don't much care where," Alice says, to which the Cat replies: "Then it doesn't matter which way you go."[1]

It is the same with your organization: if you do not know where you want to be by the end of the strategy cycle, then any path or set of priorities may or may not take you there. Like Alice, you will get somewhere, as long as you carry on for long enough. But to accept that just getting somewhere is good enough is to abandon strategy completely.

At this point in the Reset process, your team has gathered insights to inform your beliefs, your Right to Win, and where you should play going forward. You have completed the perspective generation, gap identification, and brainstorming to ideation phase of the Reset. Now it's time to ask, given these insights, where should we be trying to go? What does success look like?

This chapter explores this question. We start by discussing why we need a strategic finish line as well as a decision-making structure to get there. Sometimes the situation is so uncertain or fast-changing that you cannot articulate a clear endpoint for the finish line, but you still need a direction. So I discuss distinguishing between a direction and destination. Then I break down the criteria for building a good definition of success.

The next part of the chapter asks: What will stop us? It explores how to distinguish between friction and tension and how to focus on prioritizing the few challenges that must be addressed.

Last, we pause to discuss the notion of a hard Reset. That is, what if during the Reset process you realize you need to reset everything? If that's the case, I lay out your next steps.

Finish lines matter, and so does the course of the race

Why do we have strategies? Organizations operating with limited resources in competitive environments need strategies because as the situation changes, leaders must make decisions that are aligned with other leaders' decisions as they all execute towards what we have defined as success.

So strategy needs to tell us where we are going—where the finish line is.

But **strategy has another job: help us understand how to act and react as we execute towards that finish line,** as unexpected things will happen along the way. Prussian Field Marshal Helmuth von Moltke said it best: "No plan of operations is valid beyond first contact with the enemy's main body."[2] Meaning in the fog of uncertainty, surprising things will happen. So team members cannot expect strategy to give them a perfect checklist of things to do to get to that finish line because there are too many possibilities, most of them unpredictable, for strategy to script them all out. Instead, when these things happen, the team needs to understand how to make good decisions.

So strategy's job—its main job—is to provide a framework for decision-making. Then team members can make decisions as opportunities and obstacles arise along the way in a way that allows for agility without losing sight of the strategic finish line. The finish line and the decision-making structure of how to get there are strongly linked.

The story of space exploration strategy in the 1960s in the United States is a good illustration of creating a finish line that helps guide decision-making. Space exploration did not begin with President John F. Kennedy's administration, but it undoubtably accelerated during it. There was a strategy and a set of goals articulated by the National Aeronautics and Space Administration (NASA) when President Kennedy came into office, outlined in the National Aeronautics and Space Act of 1958, codified into eight goals, as follows:

1 The expansion of human knowledge of phenomena in the atmosphere and space.

2 The improvement of the usefulness, performance, speed, safety, and efficiency of aeronautical and space vehicles.

3 The development and operation of vehicles capable of carrying instruments, equipment, supplies and living organisms through space.

4 The establishment of long-range studies of the potential benefits to be gained from, the opportunities for, and the problems involved in the utilization of aeronautical and space activities for peaceful and scientific purposes.

5 The preservation of the role of the United States as a leader in aeronautical and space science and technology and in the application thereof to the conduct of peaceful activities within and outside the atmosphere.

6 The making available to agencies directly concerned with national defenses of discoveries that have military value or significance, and the furnishing by such agencies, to the civilian agency established to direct and control nonmilitary aeronautical and space activities, of information as to discoveries which have value or significance to that agency.

7 Cooperation by the United States with other nations and groups of nations in work done pursuant to this Act and in the peaceful application of the results, thereof.

8 The most effective utilization of the scientific and engineering resources of the United States, with close cooperation among all interested agencies of the United States in order to avoid unnecessary duplication of effort, facilities, and equipment.[3]

When Kennedy reviewed these, he felt they lacked clarity and, more to the point they would not help in execution. In November 1962 he called NASA Administrator James Webb to a meeting at the White House to discuss progress on the space strategy, NASA's request for more funding, and how to speed up progress.

The two began the discussion, with President Kennedy asking for clarity on strategy and success. Webb continued to reiterate that there was a higher intent: *"preeminence in space."* President Kennedy insisted that this was not clear. It could dissipate efforts to execute it, in part because it was open to many different interpretations. Space exploration was a race, he insisted, and you needed clarity around what it meant to win that race. He thought we should be landing on the moon. After several minutes of conversation, they got closer to the goal many now know well: "We will land a man on the moon and bring him back safely before the end of the decade."[4]

Consider the aligning force this clear intent provided. It focused all action on landing on the moon. When that happened in 1969, not only was President Kennedy's proclaimed race won, but the USA became the leader in space. The general goal of preeminence in space was achieved by realizing the specific, measurable one: landing a man on the moon.

Just as with NASA during the 1960s, your definition of success should provide the clarity of a moon-landing, else your team cannot make decisions and trade-offs to get there.

Finish lines: Destinations versus directions

A common question asked during the Reset is: If the future is so uncertain, should we even set a clear finish line? So much is going to change along the way, so how can we set an end point for the next three years? Do we really need to set, or reset, a definition of success when facing uncertainty?

The answer is yes, but you have a choice of which type of definition it is.

A paradox of uncertainty is that the more uncertainty your organization faces, the more a team will beg their leaders for clarity. Unfortunately, the more uncertainty there is, the harder it is to clarify the end-state. You do not want to head straight for what could be the wrong destination, especially if your focus on getting there means you speed past the unforeseen opportunities along the way.

You can resolve this tension by determining whether you need a destination or direction.

Destinations are appropriate when you have a relatively clear line of sight, when a clear outcome is needed to satisfy a stakeholder demand, or a major event is anticipated. For a publicly traded company's established business units, a major shareholder event such as an Initial Public Offering (IPO), or an organizational turnaround—destinations are needed. You are making it clear to your shareholders that you will achieve a certain set of outcomes by a certain time. The NASA example above is an example of a destination, as President Kennedy felt a clear outcome was needed to justify the program's funding and resources as well as ensure alignment of the varied projects and priorities that were undergoing at the time.

Not all situations demand a destination; sometimes determining a general direction is needed. In the earlier days of the space program, a direction was likely more appropriate—they had to explore before knowing where they wanted to go.

A direction is needed when you are facing extreme uncertainty, a business model shift, or disruptive innovation in your space. In these cases, sometimes setting a destination can even get in the way.

A direction is a compass heading. A compass heading opens future options by limiting decisions to only what is necessary at a particular point in time, without worrying about what the precise end-point will be.

We need to separate achieving accuracy from achieving precision (see Figure 7.1). Accuracy measures how close the result is to what you were trying to achieve, whereas precision measures how close results are to each other. A compass heading must be accurate, but it does not have to be precise. Precision comes with time. Remember when Horace Greeley urged America's young men to "Go West"? His injunction was not precise, but it was directionally correct. There was gold to be found somewhere out west and fortunes were made from it. With a direction, you set the compass heading and keep updating as you go. During a Reset, your team needs alignment, so tell them where they are going, but do not prematurely anchor on a destination until it makes sense.

Either a destination or direction may be appropriate; it depends on the circumstances your organization is in at that time. As above, major shareholder events usually demand a destination. Having worked with many technology company IPOs, I developed the ReCiPe formula for the destination to force clarity about the few variables that will really matter. ReCiPe stands for:

- Revenue
- Recognition
- Cash
- Customer Retention
- Product
- Presence

FIGURE 7.1 Precision vs accuracy

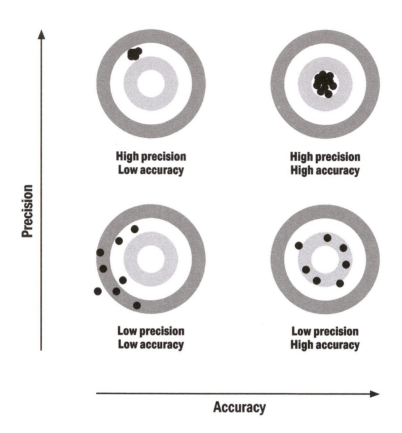

Do not confuse precision with accuracy

High precision
Low accuracy

High precision
High accuracy

Low precision
Low accuracy

Low precision
High accuracy

Precision

Accuracy

The ReCiPe provides clear guidance for what must be in place for a successful offering. Normally at this stage of growth, boundaries—covered more below—are looser, and may be focused on culture and values, basic risk indicators, and a pathway to profitability rather than explicit margin. For a Switzerland-based technology and logistics company, its pre-IPO success definition looked like Figure 7.2.

A large consumer-based cleaning company was in the middle of a transition from a product-based company, that sold almost exclusively to large, big-box stores such as Walmart, to one focused on emerging markets with larger growth potential in ecommerce and digital sales. When formulating success, they needed to leave more room to move and learn than the destination ReCiPe example above, but they still needed to clearly call out the shift the company was making. Their definition of success was directional (Figure 7.3).

Neither a destination nor direction is necessarily a better finish line than the other: it's about knowing what your organization needs at that time. In both examples, you are seeing the word "intent" for the finish line, but you are also seeing the word "boundary." These two terms, furthered below, are how we guide the decision-making along the way.

FIGURE 7.2 Destination example: ReCiPe

Destination as a finish line

Our main intent:

At the end of our three-year cycle, TechCo will have:

- Revenue of >=500mil in revenue and >=50% subscription revenue and 50% growth y/y

- Recognition: Recognized by leading analyst (e.g. Gartner)

- Cash: Cash flow neutral

- Customer retention: 90% renewal rate

- Product: Solid technology and valued product

- Presence: Proven success in five target geographic markets

Main intent
is our goal:
What we aspire to achieve

Held within our boundaries:

EBITDA
EBITDA of 15%

Culture and team
Live the values and enhance our culture

Sustainable path
Growth is sustainable (building towards midterm and beyond)

Risk tolerance
Wall Steet Journal test

Boundaries
are the non-negotiables we will not cross:
*We cannot go outside of them
to reach our goals*

FIGURE 7.3 Direction example: Cleaning company

Direction as a finish line

Our main intent: **Held within our boundaries:**

At the end of our three-year cycle, Cleaning Co. will be the trusted leader in safe and effective products having grown new users and uses to achieve net sales of 10bn by focusing on Ecommerce, Industrial, and geographic expansion.

EBITDA
Minimum EBITDA of 20%

Culture and team
Live the values and enhance our culture

Leverage ratio
Leverage ratio 2.5

National accounts
Defend and grow sales in top 5 accounts

Employees
Employee engagement at or above 90%

Health/Safety
Health and safety (regulatory /No cancer causing products)

Main intent
is our goal:
What we aspire to achieve

Boundaries
are the non-negotiables we will not cross:
*We cannot go outside of them
to reach our goals*

Decision-making as you execute towards the finish line

An issue with most strategy statements often crafted over hours of debate is that they do not provide guidance. Most say something along the lines of: "Our great people will drive profitable growth to make us the [*adjective*] leader of the [*industry*] by delighting our customers."

These statements might be motivating, but they do not articulate a strategy. In a growth strategy, it is better to be clear than to be motivating. To provide clarity, a definition of success must guide team members in making decisions that align with other decisions as they go towards the finish line.

To do this, break down all possible strategic goals in four categories:

- **Main intent:** What are we trying to achieve above all else? What is the finish line?
- **Boundaries:** What are the constraints or non-negotiables within which we must achieve the main intent?
- **Task:** What steps must we complete to achieve the main intent? These are not the main goal, but pathways to get achieving it.
- **Outcomes:** What secondary effects will we achieve by completing these tasks and achieving the intent?

Main intent

The main intent is the end goal, the answer to the question "What does success look like—what are we trying to achieve above all else?" While there can be more than one main intent, the points within it cannot conflict or give rise to a trade-off. Revenue and margin, for example, cannot both be the main intent, as there are potential trade-offs between them. The main intent is the finish line. The visual imagery for your team is that we are all crossing the line together at the end of this strategy cycle.

Boundaries

Boundaries are the non-negotiables that you cannot breach in reaching the main intent. The visual imagery is of an electric fence you are placing around yourself. The challenge is to acknowledge the importance of boundary conditions and then articulate them clearly enough to be useful. There is a paradox here: boundaries are not what you are trying to optimize. You are trying to optimize the main intent. But boundaries are actually more critical as they cannot be compromised, even in pursuit of the goals.

Tasks

You will achieve the main intent by accomplishing a set of high-priority tasks. A task is an action that is the responsibility of an individual member of the team and that can be completed by a deadline. The rule to follow in defining tasks is "no gaps, no overlaps"—don't miss anything out and don't duplicate effort. The challenge is to distinguish the main intent from the tasks needed to accomplish it. It is not as simple as it sounds, as everything feels important. Force the team to tease out what really matters above all else—the intent you collectively must achieve—from the things you must do, or the pathways, to get there. The top tasks will be your must-win battles (MWBs), explored in Chapter 8.

Outcomes

Outcomes are the positive side effects of achieving the main intent. Let's say your main intent is to have employee engagement at or above 65. A side effect or outcome may be "being a great place to work," which may seem motivating and appealing, but it lacks clarity and actionability. Outcomes like this can lead to potentially conflicting actions and a lack of consensus around whether they are achieved. Consequently, they can be distractors, so keep your team's focus on the other three elements and the outcomes will take care of themselves.

Intent versus boundaries

The challenge of crafting a strategy statement with this level of clarity— apart from the fact that it takes time—is that the leadership team must articulate what matters most as well as the non-negotiables—the boundaries.

The temptation leaders often face is either confusing boundaries with intent or not wanting to call out the true boundary.

In traditional strategy, the goals are all written as intents, they are all pushing (that is, barely achievable) and there is little to no guidance on how these are prioritized. In the SRT strategy, you are guiding decision-making, so you must specify with absolute clarity the most critical things that cannot be broken—the boundaries—and separate those from your pushing but achievable goals—the intents.

With goals, you are usually trying to optimize a value. Values can be higher or lower. A boundary, however, is absolute. In a game, the goal or intent of every player is the highest score. But the boundaries are the rules of the game. If you break the rules, you are disqualified and you get no points. It sometimes takes teams time to understand this: the things that form your playing field are the boundaries, not the main intent. Many of the Survive basics (from the 4 Cs) like safety, cash, margin, customer risk, and govern-ance will likely live as boundaries in your definition of success.

A failure to distinguish between intent and boundaries can become an obstacle to execution. For example, a CEO will say to their Head of Sales: "This quarter, we need to make $100 million in revenue with a 10 percent margin." When the Head of Sales asks which of the targets is most important, the typical reply is, "Both are important!" which of course is true. But, by giving our team two goals that are potentially in conflict, rather than spurring action, we have just slowed the company down.

Here is why. Let us say it is the last day of the quarter, and your top salesperson can sign a deal that will allow you to reach your revenue goal, but if they do so profitability will drop below 10 percent. What should they do? If they make the deal, are they a hero, or are they in trouble? What typically happens is that one third of them freeze, ask what to do, and by the time guidance comes back to them it is too late. Another third make the deal—a sale is a sale! And another third walk away. As an organization, you have simultaneously stalled and misaligned actions. Conflicting goals slowed everyone down. You cannot blame the salesforce: it was the result of poor direction. The stated goal should have been: "This quarter, we need to make $100 million in revenue within the boundary of 8 percent profit. 10 percent profit would be great, but the absolute boundary is 8 percent." With this guidance, a salesperson knows that while they are aiming for 10 percent, they can go as low as 8 percent to reach the intent.

A good goal gives explicit, not implicit, permission and does not require constant clarification. An effect of distinguishing intent from boundaries is that you empower people to make decisions without having to ask for permission. This empowerment helps them make good decisions quickly, which brings your organization the aligned speed needed to win. Thus leadership's job is setting a clear intent and boundaries for the team, and then getting out of their way as they execute towards that.

Boundaries, when clearly articulated, give leaders freedom

We tend to associate boundaries with constraints or challenges, but boundaries are liberating. Boundaries show your team the space they have to move within and how far they can go: they provide freedom.

Boundaries enable speed in execution when they follow these principles:

- **Clarity is key:** Boundaries must create clarity. "Profitable growth" is not a clear boundary because it encompasses a double goal. A better boundary would be: "Gross margin >40 percent and at least 30 percent for new product launches." Having vague or ambiguous boundaries is like having an electric fence and not knowing whether the electricity is on.

- **No stretch:** There is no such thing as a stretch boundary. Boundaries are limits the team can stay within. There is no wiggle room, and you cannot set a boundary that you have never achieved (for example, a gross margin that you have never hit cannot be a boundary as you are starting the strategy in violation).

- **They are not problems:** When defining boundaries, some people list things like "New IT system may not deliver" or "Customer reaction to price rises may be negative." These are problems or risks that need to be addressed, but not boundaries. If you identify a problem, don't make it a boundary; turn it into a task—e.g. "Liaise closely with IT to ensure minimum requirements are met on time" or "Develop pricing strategy with a view to demand elasticity."

Intent and boundaries are critical elements of growth strategies because they show the team when and where they can make trade-offs in changing situations. For example, after Facebook launched its advertising model in 2007, it had a very simple intent vs boundary trade-off: Make money on ads, but do not be intrusive to the customer experience. The ads team could place ads as needed to maximize revenue, but they could not do so at the expense of the customers' use of Facebook and their defined journey. This boundary was loosened considerably in the years that followed.

In the cleaning company example in Figure 7.3, the boundaries were critical in guiding trade-off. Their main intent was new growth channels in Latin America and online, and not physical retail store growth. But the statement helped clarify they would only be able to play in these new markets if their existing customer base remained stable and continued to generate cash. Maintaining retail sales was a necessary boundary condition of success, as this cash was what was allowing them to grow in new places.

Crafting your definition of success

To craft your definition of success it helps to follow a set process, especially the first time.

Start by scoping all possible points that may matter. Ask yourself: "What will we look like in terms of financials? If we only had three words to describe us, what would they be?" The tables in Figure 7.4 suggests some scoping questions to think through.

FIGURE 7.4 Success scoping

What does it look like to succeed?

If we are sitting in this room at the end of this three-year cycle and we are overly satisfied with our progress on executing our strategy – we would call it a success – what does it look like?

Success question	Response by end of three-year cycle
What will we have accomplished? Where will we be as a company (look like)?	
What will we look like: Financials?	
What will we look like: Offerings?	
What will we look like: Geographical coverage?	
What will we look like: Customers/partners?	
By our customers, we will be known as the company that...	
In the industry, we will be known as the company that...	
If you had only one to three words to describe us, they would be...	
In three years, I will not be happy if we have not... (*Do not write* SEE ABOVE—*only write something if it's new!*)	
In three years, we will only be considered successful if we have: (*Do not write* SEE ABOVE—*only write something if it's new!*)	

After you have laid out all your points, go through them again and ask which is the most important. Once you've narrowed them to about 10 to 15, write each one as an individual bullet point. For example:

- Our customer effort score (CES) will be at or above 6.
- Our employee engagement survey participation rate will be above 90.
- We will have over $100 million in revenue from our German business.

Next determine whether each one is an intent, boundary, task, or outcome. A common trap is to categorize everything as an outcome. You should cap the outcomes at three and use the rule of "no orphan outcomes," which means, if you write an outcome down, it needs to be a consequence of achieving the intent or have a task directly associated with it. An outcome cannot stand alone: something must be done to attain it. Not everything needs to stay on the list: eliminate success points that are not powerful enough to be part of the final definition.

As an example, let us say you had the following success points in the left column of the table below. Possible categorizations are in the right column.

Increase revenue to $80 million	Main intent (or boundary if doing land grab, which is unlikely)
Increase net margin to 15%	Boundary (or intent if doing a land grab, which is unlikely)
Reduce operating costs by 5%	Task – will need sub tasks
Build out the Latin American sales team	Task
Negotiate a new contract with site in Monterey	Task
Open two new distribution centers	Task
Increase employee satisfaction scores to 95%	Task or Main intent
Introduce the new credit control system	Task
Increase customer NPS by 4%	Task but could be main intent on customer retention or growth
Increase brand index recognition to 80%	Task but depending on criticality to success, could be main intent

Once you have gone through the categorization process, pull them together into a success statement with the following structure:

By (end of strategy cycle), our company will have (achieved its main intent of XX)
Within the boundaries of XXX
And completed these tasks XX, XX (in rank order)
And achieved these outcomes XX, XX

The tasks should be ranked in order of how much they contribute to achieving your main intent and linked to value creation.

Your intent should provide clear guidance rather than being a long list of things to do. If there are more than five intents, you likely have too many and team members will struggle in decision-making trade-offs. Also make the tough choices now. You are at the point in the Reset where you need to provide guidance on what matters: what is the main intent versus just a task to get there.

I also like to say, "the math has to work." The term BHAG—a "Big Hairy Audacious Goal"—coined by Jim Collins is often used in building strategies.[5] While BHAGs are supposed to unleash creative effort and stimulate action towards a goal—in practice they have a relatively poor track record. Here is why. When you give the team an impossible goal that they know cannot be achieved, rather than spurring aligned momentum, it can create recalibration. Faced with mission impossible, every leader will calibrate for themselves where the real goal is. For example, we all know that we cannot launch in 10 new countries in the next two years, so some people assume the real number is eight. But others will recalibrate to five, or seven. One or two newer people will take the ten seriously and start scrambling to achieve it. This recalibration leads to misaligned action and wasted resources.

Trust is critical to being a Thrive company, and one way you start building trust is to give your leaders the real number. Breakthrough growth is just that—breakthrough, so this should be a push. The math should be demanding; it can and should inspire extra effort, and it should force the team to reapproach how they solve the problem, but it must work.

Resetting your success definition after a shock

You set your success definition with the expectation it will last the strategy cycle. But if a shock triggers Survive, you likely need to adjust it.

For the main intent, or finish line, it is tempting to keep the goal as it is, but if there was a big change in the situation, be prepared to update the intent. If you do not reset it, you risk months of futile effort where team members are desperately distracted by misaligned actions to close the gap.

Sometimes the success definition stays mostly intact, it just needs updating. For example, you might decide a destination is still needed, but it now makes more sense to alter this to a range ($85 to $100 million rather than $100 million). If uncertainty is extreme, you will likely move to more of a direction.

Uncertainty will manifest itself in different ways; sometimes it calls for wider boundaries, but it often demands narrower ones until more is learned. Survive mode almost always calls for tighter, clearer boundaries to guide daily decision-making. If boundaries are too general ("live our values") or only expressed as an annual profitability figure, consider providing more clarity, such as defining the behaviors linked to the values to execute within, or defining profitability threshold by project, job, or within a shorter timeframe.

The top tasks will be your must-win battles (MWBs), which we will discuss further in Chapter 8. Do not be anxious about pausing or stopping initiatives during a Reset. This is not a reflection on the people working on them; it is an appropriate reaction to the changed situation. Your outcomes are likely to adjust as well at this point, so review the top communicated outcomes and update as needed.

What will stop us: Top challenges

After resetting your definition of success, you want to make the path to get there as clear as possible. You do not want to be thrown off course, and the best way to avoid that happening is to think through what could do that. You want to prepare by asking the next question **"What could stop or break us?"**

People often ask, quite naturally: "Why should we talk about our top challenges before setting our top priorities? Shouldn't we set the top priorities first and then ask what the challenges to execution are?" In my experience, it's better to identify the biggest challenges the organization is facing first, because sometimes addressing them becomes a top priority in itself.

Your definition of success should not be achievable without effort—if it is, what is the point? But neither should it ignore the realities of the market. Forewarned is forearmed. You cannot count on getting a forewarning, but you can think through the challenges so that you are prepared. Then if a crisis arises, you won't turn it into a drama, but a play for which you already have an outlined script.

To avoid being caught off-guard, prepare to deal with what could most hinder your ability to achieve your intent—both internally and externally. From working with many companies on execution, I find most of the time the biggest challenges that derail strategy are internal.

Tension vs friction

Growth companies are said to have ruthless focus on a few priorities at a time. What is less appreciated is that this same brutal prioritization comes into play in what challenges these companies decide to address.

While growing through uncertainty, everything can feel like a challenge because things feel hard. Growth strategy often feels uncomfortable, and high growth is very much about getting comfortable with being uncomfortable. Attempting to address everything leads to the dissipation of effort and prevents the focus needed to tackle the big things. Successful high growth companies learn to differentiate between tension and friction. Tension should be tolerated. Friction must be addressed.

Tension is day-to-day frustrations. Tension is the result of annoyance, inconvenience, and being uncomfortable with the day-to-day things that just do not work. Reporting lines that are not perfect, tracking documents that are not capturing everything, recruiting that is too slow… the list can get long. Every organization has tension, and this is not a bad thing. Some tension is also good. Just as a rope needs tension rather than slack to do its job of providing strength, an organization needs some tension to keep it taut.

Friction is different. Friction is something that gets in the way of value creation. If the current organizational structure is slowing down decision-making or your employee onboarding system is losing a high number of people in the first 90 days, then you are dealing with friction.

Whenever a challenge is raised, ask: "*Is this hindering or preventing us from creating value?*" Picture the needles of customer willingness to pay and total cost: will this challenge stop them from moving apart? If so, it is friction. Add it to the list and discuss how to resolve it. If not, it is tension. Let it go. High growth is fundamentally about letting a lot of things that don't affect value creation go so you can focus on just those few things that do.

Start with the friction inside the organization or your ecosystem. Be clear on what could stop you. A challenge is not "talent." A challenge is: "We do not have the data or digital talent to execute at the speed we need." Limit yourself to the top three to five internal challenges.

Then consider the external friction. Examples might be industry consolidation leading to price wars, changing consumer preferences, inflationary impacts, or supply chain disruption. Again, identify the specific nature of the external friction. It's not supply chain, but it could be "supply chain uncertainty is leading to shipping delays of greater than 12 months, making project estimates we give to our customers unreliable." When you have identified your top three to five, check them against your top beliefs to ensure you have not missed anything.

With a clear idea of what the challenges are, go through each one and discuss how you will address them. To be as concrete as possible, use timeframes to sort the actions: immediate quick wins (within the next three months); what you can do within the next year; and what will take the entire strategy cycle (three years). Internal challenges are more likely to have clear action plans to address than external challenges. For the external ones, you might need to wait and prepare rather than take immediate action. This is also where you might need to explore different strategy stances (covered in Chapter 10), especially "acting to learn" and "acting to shape."

Remember, a triggered shock that led to Reset may fundamentally alter your top challenges. Some former tension points may become friction, and other challenges may fade away as they are now less critical to address. Or you may realize that the friction now runs so deep that the best course of action is a hard Reset.

A hard Reset

What if I need to Reset everything?

It's a sobering question, and it happens. Sometimes an agile, shorter transition into Thrive will not be possible. After going through the strategy questions, you may realize every piece needs to change. A hard Reset is different from needing longer in Survive mode: you can need a few more months in Survive without a hard Reset, and sometimes a hard Reset occurs without a triggered Survive.

Hard Resets are the acknowledgment that the situation has so fundamentally changed (either due to a system shock or internal underperformance, or both) that you need longer to determine the scope of everything that must be reset, as well as how to go about doing it. It happens when:

- *What is the situation?* The top trends are new, and all or almost all of your beliefs are fundamentally challenged.

- *How will we win?* Your Right to Win has been significantly compromised or weakened, and your historical Right to Win will not provide differentiation (or you realize perhaps it never did).

- *Where will we play?* Previous assumptions about your ideal customers, value proposition and go to market are no longer valid (these growth areas no longer provide opportunities, or you are no longer set up to win in those spaces). Moving forward will require a Reset of your markets and customers.

- *What is success?* Your definition of success is no longer achievable, and more critically, your intent needs to look dramatically different going forward—it is a complete reshape of what success means for you and where the finish line should be.

- *What will stop us?* The list of internal and external challenges is new, daunting and must be addressed in new ways.

When this happens, embrace it. It does not mean you will never Thrive; it just means you need longer in the Reset and transition mode.

Take the appropriate amount of time

You may need a minimum of three more months in Reset, but likely more. If the hard Reset involves a transformational change, tackling your new set of must-win battles (covered in Chapter 8) may be more than six months away, and you will be working with rolling milestones in the interim.

Refocus and reset the team

Re-examine the team you have with you on the Reset process. Hard Resets are not for the faint of heart, and many will not want to go on the journey of leading this level of change. Ask each executive team member to recommit to the strategy process within this new reality, and be prepared to lose team members who don't want to sign up for it. It's better to start with a smaller team who will commit to the change. While you want a small inner circle, you will need to actively engage a wider stakeholder body to help test beliefs, vet assumptions, and utilize your acting to learn stances. Think of this as a small tiger team who will work on the Reset and a wider Reset council to engage with for testing and learning.

Cycle through the Reset questions

A hard Reset cycles through the questions in the SAME order, and it starts with revisiting your beliefs. Discuss and debate your updated beliefs with the team and build a plan to actively test the ones you disagree on or have the most uncertainty about. On Right to Win, determine if you still have a competitive advantage (you probably don't—otherwise you wouldn't be in a hard Reset). Glean what elements you can use to strengthen and build an advantage going forward. Over-index on the assets you can strengthen and buy or build.

Your "where to play" choices are based on your future Right to Win, so be open to new ideas, but also be realistic around which customers you have a Right to Win with. Continually and actively test the market to learn and get more nuanced in your future choices. You usually need to cycle through all the questions two or three times to get to the key insights.

Set milestones

During a hard Reset, develop rolling three-month milestones set towards a six-month definition of success. Limit these milestones to ten or fewer focused tasks. Each should be of the scope of a supporting battle, as covered in Chapter 8, and they should not have many sub-elements under them. Remember you are executing these milestones while continuing the Reset process and related discussions, so be realistic with what you can achieve and avoid including mere operational tactics on the milestone list.

Track these milestones in a focused tracker that I call a DDD, which stands for Define-Do-Deliver. For each milestone goal, determine the following:

- *Define*: What do we now know that we need to know to execute this?
- *Do*: What activity needs to be done?
- *Deliver*: What result, ideally quantifiable, will this produce for the organization?

Each DDD should have an owner and a deadline with the goal of having all "Defines" completed one-third of the way through that execution time-frame. Meet frequently to review progress. Celebrate and communicate progress along the way and keep learning velocity high, as you will incorporate these learnings into the updated Reset MWBs when it is time for them.

Find your center of gravity

Successful transformations from a hard Reset necessitate a clear center of gravity to move forward. Your transformation center of gravity is the key guiding principle or insight that encapsulates the value-creating transition needed. It is the critical outcome of cycling through the Reset questions, and the main frame for all future decisions. It will only emerge after vetting and testing multiple assumptions. Let it emerge and do not force it. Once you have it, communicate it incessantly and put all other choices through this lens. Do not Reset the strategy until you have a firm grasp of your center of gravity, else you will falter repeatedly.

Below are some examples of centers of gravity:

- **UK grocer Tesco's 2015–18 turnaround under CEO Dave Lewis:** *Fresh and UK-focused*

  o Tesco could not out-compete the low-cost carriers like Asda and Aldi on straight price, but they could match on key items and always out-deliver on fresh at that range. To do so they needed to embrace their local British focus and lean into local British suppliers.

- **Ducati's 1996–2000 turnaround under CEO Federico Minoli:** *Ducati is not a bike company: Ducati is an experience-based community*

  o Ducati needed to move from a product focus to an entertainment focus. They needed to embrace the heritage and legacy that were theirs in the industry to claim, which included building a museum, celebrating the bike's story, and building a worldwide community, now with hundreds of thousands of members.

- **IBM's 1994–2000 turnaround under CEO Lou Gerstner:** *IBM is not a mainframe company, IBM sells integrated solutions to the world's largest companies*

  o IBM was not the best at all, some would argue any, sub-sector of corporate technology, but they were, the most trusted overall and they were one of the only companies that could provide integrated solutions to CTOs and CIOs. These tech leaders wanted a sense of security that the technology would all work together more than they wanted to pick individual winners and make it work themselves.

- **Burberry's 2008–12 turnaround under CEO Angela Ahrendts and Designer Christopher Bailey:** *We offer a trench-coat centric, British focus to emerging market millennials through digital and social media, flagship experience stores, and our London focus*

  o The Burberry customer is digital, so they needed to speak digital to meet them. Burberry needed to re-own its trench and British focus—be proud of it and use this legacy to build the next generation of fashion consumers.

CASE STUDY
SAC's hard Reset

One company's hard Reset involved shutting down the complete business and opening a new one. Specialised Automotive Company (SAC) was founded in 2011 as part of a Saudi Arabian family conglomerate. Originally focused on new car sales with a smaller division focused on aftersales service, the company reset from selling one exclusive brand to becoming a multi-car dealer. While they had some initial success, the market significantly weakened and the company growth stalled, so CEO Husam Al-Saleh (one of the brothers who came in to lead SAC), decided to reset again for growth in 2017.

After cycling through the questions, the team hypothesized that they had competitive advantage with a premium consumer. As they built possible "Where will we play?" choices, they segmented the market into four potential ideal customer profiles (ICPs): premium consumers, budget consumers, Western brand-focused buyers, and a corporate buyer. The team acknowledged they were not set up to win with Western-brand focused consumers or the B2B space, so those were thrown out as potentials. After several weeks of acting to learn and assumption testing, they concluded the premium consumer was not there, despite how much they wanted them to be. And they did not want to play in the budget space. Given the strategic situation, the lack of ICP space to play, and a Right to Win that no longer matched any consumer demand, the team felt defeated: there was no clear strategy to set. They concluded this would be a hard Reset.

Cycling through the questions again, the team identified a few core beliefs. While the overall market and economy would remain challenged for the next strategy cycle, there was an influx of new drivers on the road. Women in Saudia Arabia were able to earn drivers' licenses for the first time in 2018 and more younger consumers getting licenses earlier. The government was also considering several reforms to the insurance industry, including making comprehensive insurance more affordable and introducing mandatory reviews of post-accident repair work to ensure it was performed as specified.

As the team turned to Right to Win, they realized this growing market of insurance would intersect with a competitive advantage that they had earlier "trapped." Their small after-sales service business had initially been de-prioritized, as it was seen as only a necessary part of the new car sales business. They had key advantages, though, in end-to-end service, total quality control, and high customer satisfaction with almost no returns due to dissatisfaction with the original repairs. SAC excelled in resolving customer issues quickly and returning owners to their cars.

This was seen as interesting but not critical before, but with a shifting market, could this be the business?

Their center of gravity became their Right to Win—unmatched quality and trusted service with industry-leading turnaround times, combined with their beliefs on the growth of the insurance market going forward. The team Reset their ICPs to insurance companies (as the strong influencer) and corporate fleets (as the users). The new "jobs they were hired to do" were to reunite the consumer with the most expensive thing they owned as quickly as possible, and to make the insurance claims managers' jobs as stress-free as possible.

With these insights, the team made the tough decision to shut the entire new car sales division. Al-Saleh closed the business he had been charged to turn around, but in the process pivoted to a new, more stable and growing market. And the strategy fit: two years into the three-year cycle they had over-achieved most of their original targets, including signing 10 new insurance companies from their original goal of three, and they continued to grow revenue and profit significantly after that.

CASE STUDY
Dell's hard Reset

Massive shifts in industry trends can also lead to hard Resets. Dell was the world's largest seller of personal computers in 2000. In the decade that followed, there was a race to the bottom in laptop margins, and the market became divided between high-end laptops and low-margin Chromebooks, with little room for a middle player. The server and storage business, another of Dell's strengths, became increasingly obsolete in the industry's movement towards cloud computing and the Internet of Things (IoT).

Founder Michael Dell returned to the company to lead the hard Reset. This included taking the company private to make big changes outside public market scrutiny. The small team, with Michael Dell at the helm, renewed focus on where the technology world was going and made deals to match it, including the enormous $67 billion takeover of EMC, which owned an 8 percent stake in VMware. Using the VMware spinout to boost cash and collateral, the company eventually went public again in 2018.

Dell Technologies, its new trading name, was able to successfully compete in a renewed PC industry on the bet that companies would keep some historical data housed in servers for diversification. Its key insight was around the future of a bundled B2B offering around data, becoming one of the largest players in data center servicing, and being able to offer a powerful bundle in data storage, services, and technology infrastructure. Adding a cloud-management subscription added recurring revenue, and from 2018 to 2022 Dell had a CAGR of 6.6 percent compared with less than 5 percent for the IT industry.

Having to undergo a hard Reset does not have to be bad. For many companies, such as SAC, Dell, Tesco, or others such as Best Buy, the hard Reset led to dramatic growth journeys. What is bad is to ignore the insight that you need one. When you need to press the Reset button in full, assume all existing assumptions have been challenged, test and vet your new beliefs, and be prepared to build a new business.

Summary and next steps

Strategy is an articulation of the choices you make to create an order of magnitude differential in your ability to create value. To build a strategy for execution, you need to give actionable guidance to your team, which comes from setting a clear finish line, or intent (either a destination or direction) as well as the boundaries (electric fence) they need to stay within to get there. The "how" of reaching this finish line is made up of your priorities or tasks, which we will cover in the next chapter.

Next, consider the internal and external challenges that could prevent you from achieving your intent. Each should have an action against them, even if this involves watching and learning. And if you need a hard Reset, give it the time it needs.

At this point in the Reset, you should have:

✓ a decision on whether you need a destination or a direction for your finish line

✓ a definition of success broken into main intent and boundaries

✓ a list of prioritized tasks (in rank order) to achieve your intent and the related outcomes

✓ a list of top challenges, both internal and external, and how you will address them

✓ clarity on whether you need to do a hard Reset, and if so a start on the deeper process

During a Reset, the course tends to change more than the finish line. This is what the next chapter will explore—given our definition of success, what is our path to get there?

Endnotes

1 The full conversation is: "Would you tell me, please, which way I ought to go from here?" – said Alice / "That depends a good deal on where you want to get to," said the Cat. / "I don't much care where–" said Alice. / "Then it doesn't matter which way you go," said the Cat. / "–so long as I get somewhere," Alice added as an explanation. / "Oh, you're sure to do that," said the Cat, "if you only walk long enough." (L Carroll, *Alice's Adventures in Wonderland*). The precise quote most often associated with it is from George Harrison's song *Any Road*. Carroll seems to have had a talent for putting his finger on things of wide significance. The now often quoted "Red Queen syndrome" comes from *Through the Looking-Glass and What Alice Found There*.

2 H von Moltke (1900) *Moltkes Militärische Werke: II. Die Thätigkeit als Chef des Generalstabes der Armee im Frieden (Moltke's Military Works: II. Activity as Chief of the Army General Staff in Peacetime)*, Ernst Siegfried Mittler und Sohn, Zweiter Theil (Second Part), Aufsatz vom Jahre 1871 Ueber Strategie (Article from 1871 on strategy), p. 291.

3 NASA (nd) National Aeronautics and Space Act of 1958 (Unamended), https://history.nasa.gov/spaceact.html (archived at https://perma.cc/ZH4Y-8L5J)

4 NASA (1962) Transcript of Presidential Meeting in the Cabinet Room of the White House: Supplemental appropriations for the National Aeronautics and Space Administration (NASA), https://history.nasa.gov/JFK-Webbconv/pages/transcript.pdf (archived at https://perma.cc/4WEU-F26L)

5 J Collins and J Porras (1994) *Built to Last: Successful habits of visionary companies*, Harper Collins Publishing

8

What Should We Do?
Our Must-Win Battles

"It's not enough to be busy, so are the ants. The question is, what are we busy about?"

—HENRY DAVID THOREAU

During Steve Jobs' tenure as CEO of Apple, he regularly took his top 100 employees on a retreat to reset strategy and renew focus. During the session, Jobs would spend time aligning the team members on the future direction and key trends, critical insights, and the top growth priorities. He then would wrap up the discussions with the question: "So, what are the ten things we should be doing next?"

Debates would ensue as each manager fought to get specific priorities on the final flipchart list. Once completed, Jobs would walk to the flipchart, cross through the bottom seven priorities, and announce to the team, "We can only do three." And so they did, repeatedly. They focused relentlessly on a few priorities at a time, with the result that they added nearly $350 billion to the firm's market value during Jobs' second 14-year tenure.[1] That is the power of focus.

Few companies are as extreme about focus as Apple was during Jobs's tenure, but every organization could benefit from more focus around the few things that matter most. Most organizations have a long list of priorities, partly due to a lack of understanding of how to set and scope top priorities, partly due to a lack of discipline in completing a results-focused process, and critically because uncertainty makes us constantly fear we will get this list wrong. Too many leaders fear the one priority they de-prioritize will be the one that matters, so they keep expanding the list.

This lack of prioritization causes people to feel increasingly stretched, with less bandwidth to accomplish the key things that will do the most for value creation. As Peter Drucker noted, "There is nothing so useless as doing efficiently that which should not be done at all."[2]

Figuring out what to do – and more critically what not to do—on your path to success is the focus of this chapter where I first detail how to identify your top priorities, or must-win battles (MWBs). Next, I break down how to structure these priorities in terms of corporate, business unit, and supporting function priorities as well as how to account for your supporting functions. I then discuss how to conduct an annual reframe or a Reset of these priorities post a shock.

Clarifying top priorities: Must-win battles

A plethora of language is used within modern organizations to label the areas of focus: goals, objectives, Key Performance Indicators (KPIs), Objectives and Key Results (OKRs), aims, targets, rocks, pillars, and priorities, among others. Many companies even use several of these terms at once! This leads to considerable confusion. Consider that the dictionary definition of all these terms roughly means "the most important things." For employees with all these competing lists, how do they know what they should be working on at any moment in time? In most cases, they do not.

Clarity on the few things that matter is critical to Thrive. To rise above this noise of wordage, I use the term "must-win battles" (MWBs). The term originated from Killing, Malnight, and Keys,[3] although I have adjusted the definition and usage.[4] Within the SRT playbook, MWBs are the key mid-term priorities most critical for value creation and growth, and the critical bridge from strategic insights to execution.

Let's break down the characteristics of an MWB:

- **Mid-term:** MWBs should roughly last the length of a strategy cycle— three years. If it can be done in a year, it is a project, and while it may be nested within an MWB as a sub-battle, it is not an MWB on its own. MWBs are also not longer-term: if they cover more than three years, they become too vague and generic. Even if asset and investment cycles for your organization stretch longer, as they do for many industries such as oil and gas and construction, keep a mid-term focus. Occasionally an MWB will run a slightly shorter duration such as two years and "graduate" early from the list, which is OK.

- **Linked to value creation:** A MWB must have a direct role in value creation, either increasing customer willingness to pay (needle up), reducing costs (needle down), or keeping the needles apart over time (enabling capability). It is important to identify which value creation role each MWB plays. No more than one or two should be about enabling capability—while this is important, it does not help the organization grow. Most MWBs should be explicitly focused on moving the needles.

- **Significant impact:** MWBs are not just priorities that make a difference; they make a dramatic difference. Many things are important, but only a few things are critical to the growth journey. Avoid putting everything important on the list: focus on what will fundamentally move the needles.

- **Limited in number:** Four to five is the ideal number, with six being the upper max for a single company. Much of what you do is important to running your business, but not a true must-win-battle. No team can focus on and win more than a few priorities, so keep the list short. For corporations with a business unit structure, this list may be slightly longer, as discussed later in this chapter.

- **Tightly scoped:** It is tempting to make MWBs pillars—such as "innovation" or "revenue growth"—that capture everything, but pillars lead to buckets of things to do. When your strategy is generic buckets, every leader's project can somehow be justified as strategic. Each MWB should be clearly and tightly defined into one execution-based priority.

- **Market-focused:** MWBs are about growth and to win them will require engagement across the organization. A list of priorities about "fixing ourselves" rarely gets the needed engagement, but a market-facing focus will. If you are in a period where the list needs to be mostly internal, then you are still in Survive mode and should wait to Reset your MWBs.

- **Set at the value creating level:** Set MWBs at the level of the organization at which value is created. For most companies, this is the business unit level. Not every team, function, and department needs its own set of MWBs; some will play the role of enabling, supporting, or accelerating the company's MWBs.

A sloppy or haphazard application of the terms "must-wins" or "must-win battles" does more harm than good. If you embrace the term, you must also embrace the rigor it demands. A good list of MWBs sits in the "Goldilocks zone" of priorities: more than just a few projects but not a re-classification of everything under an MWB label.

You do not need to set MWBs during the Survive phase, a purposeful pause, a hard Reset, or the early stages of a company (pre-$1,000,000 revenue for bootstrapped companies and/or pre-A round funding for VC-backed). Instead, set the rolling milestones most needed for shorter-term checkpoints and track them via the DDD (Define-Do-Deliver) approach, which was outlined in Chapter 7.

Defining your must-win battles

A typical strategy offsite starts with an ice breaker. Then there is a brainstorm where everybody's ideas about what the company should be working on are logged. Ideas are thrown around, markers are used to capture top insights, different colored stickers are used to "vote" on favorite priorities, and a list is created within a few hours. It's quick and everyone gets a voice, but it is not the most effective way to define MWBs. Strategy and its top priorities are not something to gamify.

During the Reset, the definition of success (from Chapter 7) is WHAT you will achieve at the end of the strategy cycle. The MWBs then are HOW you will achieve this WHAT. As such, defining your MWBs should be the last question to discuss during the Reset.

To move from the Reset questions to the final list of MWBs requires a series of steps, from a long list to a short list, then testing and scoping. The good news is you have done most of this work already!

A diagram that shows these steps can be seen in Figure 8.1.

Start by building in the appropriate amount of time and ensure the right people are in the room. Even experienced executives become prey to a few common biases when making decisions, such as wanting to keep their pet priorities on the list, pre-judging what needs to be on the final list (a red flag is the phrase: "There's no need to discuss this, we know it has to be on the list") or projecting past experiences onto new, possibly unfamiliar situations (red flag: "This is just like two years ago when we tried a partnership"). Follow a structured process to safeguard against personal biases and ensure key insights are accounted for appropriately.

Step one: Get the people and the timing right

CEOs are often tempted to deliver the team the list of MWBs to speed things up, but please don't do that. The leadership team—everyone who has been

FIGURE 8.1 MWB setting process flow diagram

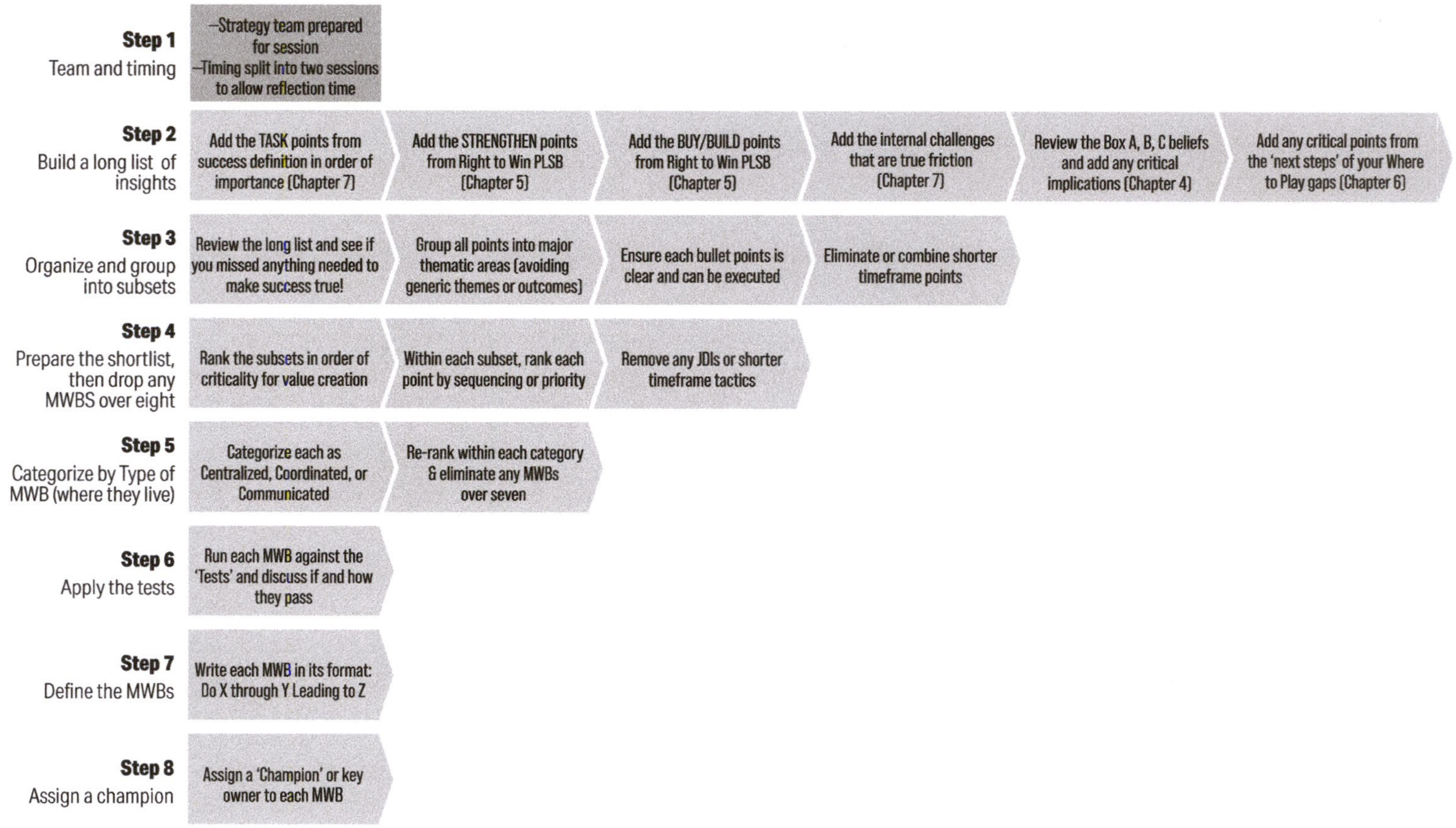

Step 1
Team and timing
- Strategy team prepared for session
- Timing split into two sessions to allow reflection time

Step 2
Build a long list of insights
- Add the TASK points from success definition in order of importance (Chapter 7)
- Add the STRENGTHEN points from Right to Win PLSB (Chapter 5)
- Add the BUY/BUILD points from Right to Win PLSB (Chapter 5)
- Add the internal challenges that are true friction (Chapter 7)
- Review the Box A, B, C beliefs and add any critical implications (Chapter 4)
- Add any critical points from the 'next steps' of your Where to Play gaps (Chapter 6)

Step 3
Organize and group into subsets
- Review the long list and see if you missed anything needed to make success true!
- Group all points into major thematic areas (avoiding generic themes or outcomes)
- Ensure each bullet points is clear and can be executed
- Eliminate or combine shorter timeframe points

Step 4
Prepare the shortlist, then drop any MWBS over eight
- Rank the subsets in order of criticality for value creation
- Within each subset, rank each point by sequencing or priority
- Remove any JDIs or shorter timeframe tactics

Step 5
Categorize by Type of MWB (where they live)
- Categorize each as Centralized, Coordinated, or Communicated
- Re-rank within each category & eliminate any MWBs over seven

Step 6
Apply the tests
- Run each MWB against the 'Tests' and discuss if and how they pass

Step 7
Define the MWBs
- Write each MWB in its format: Do X through Y Leading to Z

Step 8
Assign a champion
- Assign a 'Champion' or key owner to each MWB

involved in the Reset up to this point—should be involved. Trust the process and your team to get to the right list of priorities.

Leave enough time to get the MWBs right without letting the discussion linger too long, which makes spaces for minor points and exceptions to seep back into the discussion. Place reasonable limits to maintain the urgency and force clarity of thinking without rushing. In a virtual session, this usually means splitting the discussion into two, with at least a full day in between to give leaders time for individual reflection. Some leaders may want more time to consider potential MWBs on their own. These are big commitments, so allow for that time. If the discussion is held face-to-face, break out the MWB finalization between two days of an offsite rather than squeezing it into the final part of the day.

Step two: Build a long list of insights

You triangulate into your MWBs by pulling the insights from the earlier stages of the Reset. Do not create a new list: you already have it!

- **Prepare template:** Prepare a template that will help structure the insights you have already gathered (see Figure 8.2).
- **Start with the tasks** (*from Chapter 7*): List the tasks from your success definition points, in order of criticality. Some of these will not fit within the three-year timeframe. That's OK; they will be reviewed in the next step.
- **Add the "strengthen" points** (*from Chapter 5*): Add the actions from the "strengthen" list you developed during your Right to Win discussion. There will likely be some overlap with your tasks, but do not worry about that yet.
- **Add the buy/build list** (*from Chapter 5*): Add your buy/builds from your Right to Win discussion. There will likely be overlap here as well, and the buy/builds may stretch longer than three years, but still add them to the list.
- **Add the challenges** (*from Chapter 7*): Return to your list of internal challenges from the "What will stop us?" conversation. Are any of the internal challenges so critical that not addressing them will hinder you or prevent you from creating value?
- **Review the box A, B, and C beliefs** (*from Chapter 4*): Review the trends and beliefs you mapped in boxes A, B, or C of your Beliefs Tracker. Any of these that can and should be addressed with a strategic, mid-term priority should be added to the list.

FIGURE 8.2 MWB gathering points template

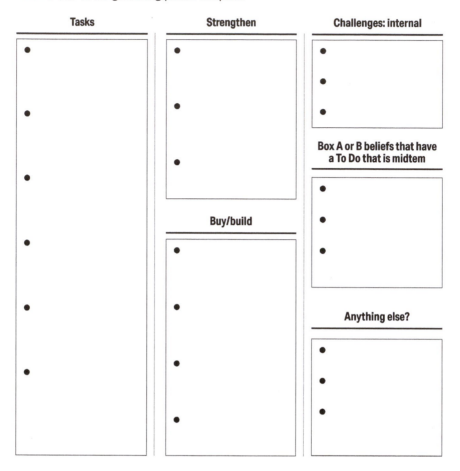

Step three: Regroup and organize into subsets

Now that you have your long list, regroup, or classify them into the major thematic areas. You may have several points around digital transformation, which you could group together. You may have different points around upskilling or building the team. Organize these into subsets so you can see the major areas in which the MWBs may fall, which could be around "digital transformation" or "accelerating growth in our new direct market." Creating subsets will help to quickly determine overlap.

Avoid having a subset around "profitable growth" or anything similarly generic, as these are outcomes. Rather, the MWB would be what to do to achieve profitable growth, like winning and retaining a new set of ideal customers or strategic revenue management. Also avoid having "innovation" as a subset, as this may be a catch-all for many different insights. Distinguish different types of innovation, such as new product development and introduction from others such as new business models or value propositions. Let execution be the guide: if you cannot map out what executing it would look like, you do not have a MWB subset.

Once you have your subsets, go through each one and ensure the bulleted subpoints are clear and specific. Now eliminate overlap. If you had "strengthen" and "task" subpoints that are roughly equivalent, combine these into one. Cut or tighten any subpoints that are too vague or generic to be executed. Update the points so all are mid-term; for those that are less than two to three years, note the approximate timing (such as six months). Shorter timeframe points might be a critical project or initiative needed to win a MWB (a supporting battle), but will not be a MWB in themselves, so nest any these under the possible mid-term must-win battle.

Step four: Prepare the shortlist

Rank the subsets in rough order of criticality for value creation. That is, the top of the list is the one that will do the most for value creation (needle up or needle down) over the next three years. You will not be able to do the full ranking yet, but a quick force-ranking to help you prioritize.

Then, within each subset, rank the sub-points from most to least critical. You will take sequencing into account (i.e. the order in which they need to be done, which may be different than criticality) in a later step. You should have no more than four to five subpoints within any subset; eliminate overlap or redundant points and rewrite these as mid-term priorities. To shorten the list, consider the impact of winning each of these points, and cut the bottom ones—that will give the least impact—from the list. Also remove any JDIs (just-do-its) to a separate list for immediate execution unless they are a critical sub-component of a MWB.

After cutting some, re-rank the updated list of subsets by criticality to value creation. There should be a big difference between one and seven, but at this stage, do not spend time arguing between three and four. Eliminate everything that ranks less than eight, as you will eventually need to reach five or six. Once you have this shortlist, move the key MWB possibilities to a new sheet (digital) or flipchart (in-person) and move onto the setting process.

Setting the must-win battles

The final list of MWBs must be short. Everything is important, but only a few things are critical: cut the important and only keep the critical ones on the list.

Step five: Categorize your MWBs as business unit or overall corporate/ company

You now must determine whether you will set MWBs at the company level only, the business unit level only, or a mix of company-wide and business-unit MWBs. When I refer to company-level, though, this is your company strategy and explicitly not corporate strategy. Company or business unit strategy is different than corporate strategy, the former is this book's focus. Corporate strategy is about making portfolio decisions (which businesses should we own and invest?) and parenting decisions (how should we manage the businesses?). While a corporate center could set MWBs for portfolio and parenting initiatives, the corporate center is relevant here to the extent the center is supporting the BU strategies.

Your final number of MWBs depends on the level of the organization that you are setting the MWBs for—whether these are company-wide or business unit specific. Strategy is set at the level of the organization where you create value. For most companies, this is at the business unit (BU) level.

There are three types of MWBs, Centralized, Coordinated, or Communicated, set at the different levels of the organization (see Figure 8.3):

- **Centralized (company-level):** For smaller or heavily centralized companies, strategy is set at the overall company level, in which case you need one list of MWBs for the entire company (even if you are split across different countries). These MWBs are centralized at one place in the organization, usually in the company or corporate center. There will be one execution plan and one owner, or champion. While these MWBs pull on different parts of the company, it does not make sense to sub-divide them into the business units. For these MWBs, more value can be created with a centralized, unified approach than by optimizing pockets of expertise. Typical Centralized MWBs are around supply chain robustness, building the organization for growth, or increasing talent density. If you are only setting Centralized MWBs, skip to step six, and the total number of MWBs should max at six, with four or five a better number.

FIGURE 8.3 Three types of must-win battles

A Centralized
- Cuts across entire organization
- No major differences in how interpreted/ executed across the company or units
- Champion should be centralized (one champion, one action plan)
- Will pull from teams/insights/actions in units but lives centrally
- Does not make sense to sub-optimize this priority

B Coordinated
- Cuts across entire organization BUT interpreted differently within each business unit/brand/trading block
- Makes sense to sub-optimize BUT also work in coordination across the units
- Champion within each unit that actively work together
- Specific/ customized to the unit
- Differences in how interpreted/ executed within the units

C Communicated (specific)
- Makes sense to sub-optimize these
- Champion within each unit

Combination of A+B+C for any business unit should not exceed 6 or 7

- **Coordinated (company and BU levels):** These MWBs are set at both the central AND the business unit level because executing them requires centralized activities as well as specific sub-battles within the BUs. They are useful when there is a common area of strategic priority that is a critical must-win across business units, such as end-to-end operational efficiency, launching a new solution area, or growth with a new vertical or set of ICPs. Given that coordination adds cost to the organization, these MWBs are the hardest to execute, but they can contribute the most to value creation when won. Typical Coordinated MWBs would be around customer growth/excellence or new solution areas, such as growing your services business. The number of Coordinated MWBs should be limited, as they demand the most resources to execute.

- **Communicated (BU level):** For companies organized into discrete business units with separate and distinct branding or GTM approaches and "Where will we play?" choices, you will need MWBs at the business unit level only and should not have company-wide MWBs. These should be tightly scoped value creation opportunities focused on explicit needle movement (up or down) for each business unit. While they may cover a similar theme or topic to MWBs at other units, for these priorities there is more value creation gains potential from local or specific focus rather than from the possible gains from coordination or centralization. If you are setting only at the BU level, skip to step six and know this process will be repeated at each BU. The total number of MWBs for each BU (with no company-wide MWBs) should max out at six, with four or five a better number.

Note for larger organizations and companies organized into discrete business units under a company-wide brand that have, or need, coordination across units, MWBs may be set at all three levels: Centralized (lives in the central, corporate level), Coordinated (lives within each BU and coordinates action), and Communicated (lives only in a BU). Even with these three types, the total list for any employee to remember should be no more than seven. There is science to this number. In 1956 George Miller studied the maximum number of things a human can remember and concluded that seven is the upper limit.[5] Pushing above seven MWBs creates the risk that people will not remember them, and what people do not remember, they do not do.

Step 6: Applying the tests and avoiding the traps

Once you have the short list of MWBs, see how they stack up against the characteristics of a good MWB, which you can do by assessing each against the tests in Figure 8.4.

After running the tests, and to ensure these MWBs deliver order of magnitude growth, there are some common traps to avoid:

- **Do not mix outcomes (e.g. growth or profit) with a battle:** Separate the WHAT from the HOW. The MWBs are how you are going to achieve a specific outcome.

- **Avoid the obvious candidates:** If the MWB seems generic, take it off the list. MWBs should be the true must-wins—growth, digital, and efficiency are not MWBs. Make sure it is a clear battle to be won.

FIGURE 8.4 MWB tests: Are these our MWBs?

Are these our must-win battles?

Question to test	MWB1	MWB2	MWB3	MWB4	MWB5	Notes
Is this linked to value creation? Move the needles? Or does it address a key challenge?						
Is this focused on the midterm (3 years)?						
Is this market facing (external)? Note, ideally no more than 1-2 are purely internal						
Is this cross-silo / functional? Engage more than one unit/department?						
If we win this, will it truly move the needle?						
Is this actually winnable? If not, why?						
Is this motivational? Could we get excited about this?						
What are the consequences of not focusing on this?						
Is this something our competitors (as defined) are potentially also working on?						
Will this help get us to our midterm success definition?						
As a group: • If we win all of these, which will move the needle the most? • What are the sequencing effects of our proposed must-win battles? Do any have to happen first? • Can we win all of these at the same time? If not, why?						
Missing: What is not on this list? • Are we comfortable with this? • Will these take care of themselves? • Are these others less of a current priority? • Can we really make the argument that these should displace something on this list?						

- **Not every department needs a MWB**: Balance and fairness are not considerations when it comes to MWBs. Most departments will not have a specific MWB but will instead be supporting other MWBs across the organization. This can be a great thing for the company, as it focuses teams on winning in the market versus just optimizing their department or area. Test for value creation and growth potential, not for whether or not each executive committee member has a MWB sitting under them.

- **Do not assume you need a people/talent/culture MWB**: For some organizations, especially after a tough Survive phase, there is a need for a People MWB, but it is not a given. There are no guaranteed spots on the list. If there's a people-related MWB, make sure there is a true battle to be won with your talent (e.g. revamping recruiting for the type of talent you need to attract and retain) or organization (e.g. changing the structure and systems to enable sustainable growth).

- **Watch both needles**: Often a first draft list has three needles moving up (customer willingness to pay), no needle moving down (total cost) and two keeping the needles apart. Watch out for this. If you don't have an MWB that moves the needle down, you are sending an implicit signal that your current levels of efficiency are solid enough to sustain margins through this cycle and prepare for the next one. If this is not an assumption you can make, then consider what needle-down MWB you may need. Often there are power move MWBs that move both needles.

- **Resist pausing innovation-related priorities during a Reset**: If a priority is still relevant (e.g. a focus on commercializing RD or accelerating innovation), it should remain in place. If the MWB is still aligned with your beliefs, then it is still needed. Remember to play offense while others are in triage mode to set up to the next stage of growth. Winners in Thrive are those who continue to innovate—selectively and with resource allocation in mind—during uncertainty.

- **Do not make a decision-point a MWB**: You may have a critical decision to make as a leadership team, for example: Decide long-term future of the Indian operation. This decision is not a MWB, though. Make the decision, and then possibly the execution of the conclusion may be a MWB.

- **Watch for linear growth traps**: Avoid reframing and slightly updating your current list of initiatives and priorities every time. Doing the same things a little better every strategy cycle is not a growth strategy. There are real limitations to linear growth, and breakthrough growth usually necessitates MWBs that multiply the additive nature of the existing initiatives.

- **Distinguish marching along the flat from climbing the hills:** One of the biggest traps companies fall into is mixing business operational priorities (what we must do to run a good business) with MWBs. Here's the visual that I've found helps the most in the final ranking. Imagine the team is standing on one side of a field. On the other side of the field is the finish line for your strategy cycle (see Chapter 7). To win the strategy the team needs to proceed from this side of the field to the other. In doing so, there are many things you need to do. You need to move forward every day, make food, and sleep occasionally. Yes, if you stop doing any of these things, you will not make it to the other side. Just as for your company, there are many things that if you stop doing, you will not be successful (like invoicing customers, improving processes, or implementing best practices in operations). This is what I liken to marching along the flat. But on this field, there are five hills, and you know that if you do not take these hills, you will not get to the other side and win the strategy. The hills are your MWBs, and this is where you need to invest your resources. Prioritize, articulate, and then win the hills without wasting time and energy on the daily marching. Keep asking this question to your team as you go through the list of possible battles: is this MWB really a hill, or is this just marching?

After the growth discussions and emerging insights for Angela Ahrendts and her team, Burberry set its top priorities as follows (see Figure 8.5).

Step 7: Define your MWBs

A final test is if you can define the actual battle to be won. I recommend using this "fill in the blank" structure: We will do __X____ through ___Y___ leading to __Z____ .

X: What are we doing, the action we want to take

Y: The main projects needed to complete that main action

Z: The impact or success we will achieve when we win

If the MWB can't be stated in a single sentence, the team likely needs more clarity on what you are trying to achieve. Figure 8.6 shows some additional examples of how to turn generic ideas into specific, winnable MWBs.

Step 8: Assign a champion

Following the definition of each MWB, you will move into the critical next steps of execution, which includes building out the high-level execution

FIGURE 8.5 Burberry MWB examples

Strategy for execution and top priorities at Burberry
Example adapted from Burberry's 2009–2012Top Priorities

How to create and capture value over time

We will offer a British-focused, Trench-centric range of products (**WHAT**)
targeted to Emerging Market Millennials (**WHO**)
through our flagship stores, social media, and a London focus (**HOW**)

Must-wins

- Leverage the franchise by building one brand (Trench and Check)
- Intensify non-apparel (esp watches, men's, festive, fragrance)
- Accelerate retail-led growth
- Invest in under-penetrated markets
- Pursue operational excellence

FIGURE 8.6 MWB examples for scoping

MWB examples

Not an MWB	Better...
Be innovative	Strengthen organic innovation and start commercialization of three to four 'blockbusters' by increasing R&D spend to 3% of sales, implementing AI in early-stage approaches, and capturing further potential from M&A leading to 100 million in innovation revenue.
Cost reduction	Pursue an end-to-end cost competitiveness model along the entire value chain, reduce fixed costs in supply chain and warehousing by 10%, and automate three back-end processes to reduce overall cost levels by 30%.
Customer-centric	Identify, target, attract, and retain our ICP customers through building an attraction framework, increasing GTM partnerships, implementing tiered service levels, and strengthening our NPS leading to 100 million in incremental growth.
Grow China	Drive profitable growth in China through joint ventures, establishing a local manufacturing footprint, and launching at least 10 local products leading to 100 million in incremental growth.

plans (covered in the next chapter). The first decision is assigning one leader to own each MWB. If you cannot identify the right leader to own a MWB, discuss whether or not it can really be won. Often a new set of MWBs necessitates new hires to bring in the appropriate talent, and that's OK! Pause the MWB until they are in place, or assign an interim champion.

CEOs often want to own several MWBs themselves, but resist this temptation. My preference is for the CEO to own the MWB execution overall, which involves assisting and guiding champions including their coordination and removing roadblocks, rather than becoming champions themselves. If as a CEO you insist, know you must then uphold the same responsibility and accountability as the other champions, including updating the Strategy tracker and attending champion huddles, discussed in Chapter 9.

Supporting function strategy

As companies start on a MWB journey and momentum builds, other functions and teams may want to set their own. While excitement spurs execution, you must avoid strategy proliferation. Again, you set strategy at the level of the organization at which you create value; for most companies that is the business unit level, for some it is the regional or country level. But there are no companies in which MWBs need to be set for every function or team. Some must play a supporting role. When functions have separate strategies and MWBs, parts of the company try to optimize themselves rather than the whole organization. This often puts competition on the inside, slows external growth, and dissipates focus on what matters the most.

To ensure supporting functions are engaged with the strategy process, hold a separate, shorter session with them to define their supporting strategy. These sessions should happen after the execution workshop on the MWBs (covered in Chapter 9) and involve all functional heads. For each of the supporting functions, set their functional priorities by breaking them into three types: Core, Support, and Future, as in Figure 8.7.

- **Core:** The two to three critical priorities for that function (i.e., the top strategic issues that function must address). Ask: Which initiatives are critical to overall company growth, and will not get done unless this function does them? These should be articulated as two to three important priorities that are not just normal functional objectives or someone's job.

- **Support:** Each function takes the list of the company MWBs, and for each one breaks down what they can do to:
  - **enable:** Ongoing background activities to enable the MWB to be won
  - **support:** Deliver specific activities and outputs to deliver that MWB plan
  - **accelerate:** Move the company closer to the finish line at a faster speed
- **Future:** Watching and addressing emerging and accelerating trends, setting and testing beliefs, and building capability for the future. Go back to your trends and beliefs and identify which beliefs impact the type of support this function must provide in future cycles. Given the current beliefs, what capabilities must they begin building now to be able to better support growth in future cycles?

FIGURE 8.7 Supporting function strategy overview

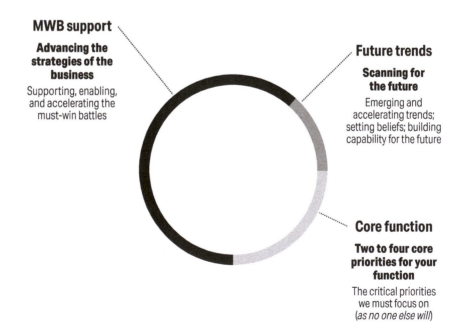

Think about your strategy as falling into three areas:

Core *functional* priorities
Supporting the business's value creation strategies
Getting ahead of future trends

MWB support

Advancing the strategies of the business

Supporting, enabling, and accelerating the must-win battles

Future trends

Scanning for the future

Emerging and accelerating trends; setting beliefs; building capability for the future

Core function

Two to four core priorities for your function

The critical priorities we must focus on (*as no one else will*)

These functional initiatives are not MWBs, but a small set of priorities that guide members of the functional team as they "march through the flat" and support the organization in winning MWBs. While there is no perfect split, Support should be more than 50 percent of resource allocation; Future approximately 10 percent and the remaining 40 percent or so focused on Core.

Resetting and reframing MWBs

Reset the list of MWBs at the end of the three-year cycle AND after every triggered shock. You should also conduct an annual reframe to dissect and update the list for the next year of the cycle. MWBs are set based on the beliefs current at the time, and if these have been challenged—which a system shock often does—priorities likely need to change as well, even if you are only a few months into execution.

During these Resets (those after strategy cycle completion or after shocks) or reframes (annually), for each MWB determine which should:

- **Stay:** Keep this MWB on the list going forward. Based on your beliefs, which MWBs remain a top priority? It is rare for all to drop from the list (even in major shocks such as Covid-19). Many stay on the list during the annual reframe, whereas in a cycle or post shock reset expect more to change.

- **Reframe:** Revise the scope. The main topic of the MWB remains, but you reset the sub-components. For example, you may have had a supply chain-focused MWB that shifts from restoring to rebuilding. Reframing a MWB is the most common case during the Reset as well as the annual reframe.

- **Take away:** Drop this MWB from the list. During a reframe, this can happen as you realize this is just "marching" and should be business as usual, or this has "graduated" from the list and won early. During a Reset, this is often because some priorities are now no longer as critical.

- **Add:** Add this MWB to the list. Based on the previous insights, what growth area or operational improvement are the new needle movers?

When you take away, especially if you are also adding, make sure you really drop that MWB. Do not just take it off the list but continue to give it your time and attention.

Be ruthless and disciplined: only a small set of priorities will be won, and they need to focus to do so.

Changing a list of MWBs can sometimes be met with pushback. Resistance often comes from not wanting to seem indecisive and therefore weak. CEOs will explain that they cannot change the list, as "the Board knows the MWBs," or "They will have to communicate again," or—my favorite—, "We already have the strategy posters on the wall."

Address pushback by linking back to your beliefs. Communicating your beliefs gives you permission to change. When you communicate the strategy, start with the beliefs and then discuss how the MWBs stemmed from them. Remind the team that you set the priorities based on beliefs, and now that they have been challenged, the MWBs must change. This is what I call having "or" discussions rather than "and" discussions: Resets are the time to be clear on the "ors" as well as the must-stops. Keep building the context that as you are executing you will also be doing ongoing testing of beliefs to allow for adaptations. And as silly as it sounds, never make the strategy too pretty or label it FINAL. Once crystalized and memento-ized, there is a reluctance to change even when the situation demands it. Posters, binders, and coffee cups are great, but do not let a ceramic cup prevent a critical change should it need to occur.

Summary and next steps

The Reset of your strategy must eventually answer the critical question: What should we do? Your must-win battles are the answer. Effective MWBs are clearly linked to value creation, tightly scoped, mid-term, and focused on what they will deliver, not the activities involved within them. To ensure you get to the right list, answer this question last in the Reset process, as it should be the result of the earlier insights, and be ready to change the list, when the situation changes.

At this last point in the Reset, you should:

✓ have a short list of must-win battles, categorized as Centralized, Coordinated, and Communicated, if relevant

✓ have a champion for each MWB

✓ have identified the role of the supporting functions and teams

✓ understand the process of the annual reframe or post-shock Reset for the list of MWBs

With this Reset, you are ready to move to Thrive. This is an exciting part of SRT but also one with many potential traps, so the next section will discuss how to successfully manage the transition from insight setting in the Reset to execution and Thrive mode.

Endnotes

1 Tim Cook became CEO in 2011, after which Apple's revenues grew from $108 billion to over $394 billion in 2022, or a CAGR of over 10.5 percent.

2 P Drucker (2006) *The Effective Executive: The definitive guide to getting the right things done*, Harperbusiness Essentials

3 P Killing, T Malnight and T Keys (2006) *Must-Win Battles: How to win them, again and again*, Pearson Education, Inc

4 While military metaphors can be overused in the strategy context, the term "battles" originates from the few things rising above the rest (see later in this chapter). Organizations wanting to avoid any military connotation should use the term "must-wins" instead.

5 "The Magical Number Seven Experiment" was published in 1956 by cognitive psychologist George A Miller of Princeton University's Department of Psychology in *Psychological Review*.

PART THREE

THRIVE: Building a Robust Growth Organization

9

From Reset to Thrive: Building While Executing

"What is strategy? A mental tapestry of changing intentions for harmonizing and focusing our efforts as a basis for realizing some aim or purpose in an unfolding and often unforeseen world of many bewildering events and many contending interests."

—COL JOHN BOYD

CASE STUDY

Brahma had been instrumental in shaping the brewing industry in Brazil for more than a hundred years—but always as a follower to its competitor, market leader Antarctica. In 1989, after a tough decade of ongoing shocks challenged the industry including price controls, increasing material costs, and rampant inflation, Brahma emerged from Survive mode with new owners Garantia Partners Investimentos.

Garantia placed industry outsider Marcel Telles to lead the brewer's dramatic Reset. Telles brought only two leaders with him and built the rest of the management team from the existing workforce. He admitted to having little knowledge of the industry so instead focused on what he knew well: recruiting, training, and keeping great people, and building and maintaining a performance culture.[1]

Telle's first steps involved building an open working environment. He dismantled bureaucracy and removed all status symbols based on tenure and role, instead focusing on rewarding performance. Lacking the information systems to set and track metrics and reward individual performance, he tasked one of the talented new leaders, Carlos Brito, with building a system from scratch with clear metrics for all. Rather than resetting the vision, Telles and his team set three strategic priorities: improve product quality, improve distribution, and reduce operating costs.

After executing the initial Reset, the team added an additional priority: growing its second brand, Skol, which soon became the fastest growing beer in Brazil. Ongoing testing and learning prompted the expansion into soft drinks as well as new geographic markets. In less than a decade, the lagging number two overtook Antarctica to become the market leader. Later it merged with Antarctica (with 93 percent ownership) to form AmBev.

Operational excellence, strong balance sheets, and a short, focused set of priorities, including recruiting and empowering great talent kept the company growing cycle after cycle. In 2004, under the same leadership team, AmBev merged with Belgian-based brewer Interbrew, becoming ImBev—the largest beer company globally. In 2005 Carlos Brito, Telles's hand-picked successor, became CEO and helped lead the acquisition of Anheuser-Busch. In 2016 they acquired SAB Miller, gaining the dominant global position and holding nearly one-third of global market share. Brito stepped down in 2021 after growing the company to nearly 58 billion US dollars in revenue.

CASE STUDY

After surviving the financial crisis of 2008–09, Ron Johnson was brought into US-based JCPenney to Reset the struggling department store. A former Apple executive, he immediately began a dramatic transformation of the company based on his prior experience. He attempted to shift the focus towards younger consumers, slashed high-low pricing (where clothes start at a premium and move dramatically lower in price over time), and revamped the look and feel inside the stores. Wanting to move fast, he pushed the changes through from the top rather than involving the wider group of leaders and managers. He also fired almost all the top executives at the company.

Johnson wanted a more dramatic change, so the new initiatives were executed all at once, and there was little trialing the changes first in a few stores. New customers did not materialize, however, and existing customers, who were used to waiting for discounts, left stores without purchasing—and then stopped coming at all. Employees became disengaged and felt powerless, leading to higher turnover. Less than two years into his tenure, revenue had dropped more than 25 percent, the largest drop among similar retailers, and Johnson was fired. JCPenney filed for bankruptcy in 2020 and in 2022 was acquired by two mall landlords.

Taking a company from the Reset into Thrive appears exciting—and it can be, but it is also challenging. Telles and his team at Brahma led a successful transition, whereas JCPenny is one of many examples of when the opposite is the case. Many more stories exist of successful and failed transitions from Reset into Thrive, the latter outnumbering the former.

The transition between the Reset and Thrive mode is when you are moving from setting the must-win battles to preparing for midterm execution. The transition includes:

- clarifying what executing the must-win battles will look like
- beginning to execute on initial insights
- building execution capacity to ensure you are set up to win
- bringing the wider team along, and
- ongoing vetting and testing of beliefs and assumptions

This transition mode requires an exquisite balance of focus between starting to move and execute *and* preparing for what's to come in the next three years (i.e. the rest of the strategy cycle). This transition presents the area of greatest leverage for learning velocity—and one of the likeliest places for progress to stall. It is too simplistic to blame strategy or execution. Both are needed, and it is their interconnectedness that determines success. In uncertainty, strategy development and strategy execution are a distinction without a difference: the real strategy is the one that is enacted.

To address the varied pieces of this transition phase, this chapter is structured differently than the others and is broken into three distinct pieces. The first part of this chapter explores the key principles of a successful transition and how to start moving on your Reset insights. The second part details the methodology and specifics of building execution plans for your MWBs and setting an execution rhythm. The third part discusses the Black Box of Execution and how to reset your execution capacity to support the new strategy.

Starting the transition: Key principles

As you start this transition, you need to start moving and executing even while you are still preparing! You do so with the principles below, which should be ongoing disciplines rather than one-off checklists.

Start moving

The hardest part of the transition is starting. As you go through the Reset, start small tests and movements. If you identify quick wins, or JDIs (just-do-its) during the earlier steps, do them! It is always tempting to wait until everything is perfect and captured in writing, but don't wait until the final strategy presentation is complete to begin moving.

Companies often confuse moving with resourcing. Yes, you should wait to commit major resources until insights are vetted, beliefs are tested, and prioritization has occurred, but low-cost movements to act for learning or shaping can and should happen along the way. For Skånes Djurpark from Chapter 3, constant experimentation—such as new dining experiences and payment methods—and ongoing belief testing allowed them to move into Thrive and profitability before their competitors. For Brahma, starting to move from the initial Reset led to its second brand—Skol—and later low-cost test-and-learns in exploring soft drinks allowed for further expansion. Acting reinforces learning and gives the team confidence their leaders are committed to making the Reset strategy happen.

Do not rebuild your old business

It is easy to unintentionally rebuild your old organization. Instead, your job is to build an updated one based on your Reset. At every single step of the SRT loop, ask: "We used to do it this way because we made these assumptions. Are these assumptions still valid? If not, what new assumptions are we making?"

As an example, if you sell solutions to manufacturing plants across Europe, you may have organized your sales team into country-based territories before 2020. You assumed plant managers were the buyers, and they would want to build relationships with their sales reps with at least monthly visits. In 2021, both of those assumptions would have been challenged. Fearing a potential downturn, many companies centralized decision-making, so purchasing choices at the plant level moved to the country or region level. Most plants also continued to limit visitors even after Covid-19 restrictions were moved. Your entire approach to structuring your sales team, and what skills you need to build and accelerate, would have to adapt to meet the new situation.

As you move into execution, avoid the knee-jerk reaction of structuring and executing as before, and instead work with your team to challenge each move and its underlying assumptions, and then update them appropriately.

Automate—what can be digitized should be

Return to your Right to Win and the testing of your necessary versus key resources and capabilities. Anything not labeled "key" in that test should be a candidate for automation or cost reduction. Automation that was in progress before the pause should be accelerated, especially in areas that will reduce fixed costs. Legacy and physical assets can potentially hinder your ability to fully move. Thrive requires agile efficiency and being able to shift to and grab strategic opportunities as they arise while maintaining a low cost base.

Avoid premature worries about scale

One of the biggest traps for established companies is being reluctant to explore or test initiatives as they fear even if they work, it won't scale. Determining how to scale something that creates value is a nice problem to have, and one you shouldn't worry about until you have solved the harder problem of value creation. Sort out value creation, and then figure out how to scale it.

This was a lesson learned in the early days by the founders of Airbnb. When the team joined Y-Combinator (YC)—Silicon Valley's fabled accelerator—in 2009, they were on their last legs. In the early days with YC, they were generating traffic to the website, especially in high density New York City, but these visitors were not converting into customers. One hypothesis was that the grainy, fuzzy images on the listings led to travelers being concerned about the quality of the apartment. They therefore lacked the confidence to book. A reasonable test would be to take high quality photographs and see if it made a difference. Some leaders thought that was a terrible idea, as even if it worked, you could not cost effectively scale taking professional photographs of every listing! Luckily the scrappy founders were willing to try it: they flew to NYC, rented camera equipment, and went to the hosts' homes to take photos. And it worked! The listings with better photographs had significantly more flow through, and the founders picked up even more growth ideas from the in-person meetings with the hosts.

They also solved the scale issue. They made basic FAQs about how to photograph living spaces on the site, and they offered a listing of local freelance photographers. This list was first managed by the founders, then by an employee until it became a digitized, easy-to-use system for the rapidly growing host community.

Keep testing beliefs

Beliefs embody strategic insights and form hypotheses that become tests and those tests inform choices. Examine your list of beliefs and play out the implications: *If X happens, what does that mean for our business? How are we set up to take advantage of this? How can we exploit that moving forward?* Draw out some likely hypotheses and the choices you would make if they were correct. Then identify the assumptions you can start testing now. For JCPenney, Johnson had firm beliefs about the validity of discounting and willingness to pay of new customers, but these were not actively tested and vetted before committing to resource-heavy execution. Active belief testing will be covered in Chapter 10.

Build internal predictability

Management literature, articles, and business school lectures stress a consistent theme: to do well in external uncertainty, you need to be outside-in and market focused. This is true but incomplete. There is a more powerful distinguisher, and it's internal. Speed is a competitive advantage in most markets, but aligned speed provides true differentiation. This happens when leaders around the organization are making good decisions quickly and acting in a way that aligns with other leaders in different parts of the company.

What differentiates high-performing companies facing uncertainty is they have internal predictability. The external market will continue to throw things at you, and new shocks and opportunities mean people across all levels of the organization will find themselves in situations where they must exercise independent thinking and action. They can only do so if the organization has provided them with the information they need to make decisions without fear of consequences, so they know how to react and how others will as well. This occurs in companies with internal predictability. Brahma, above, excelled at internal predictability, which fueled their competitive advantage.

You have internal predictability when people in your company can say yes to the following:

1   I know what we are trying to achieve and why it matters.

2   I know where critical decisions take place.

3   I can rely on others to do what they say they will do.

4   When I do adapt, within the boundaries of strategy, it is recognized and rewarded.

As each depends on the one before, the order of these four principles matters. First, team members need clear context of the strategy, why it matters, and what their role in executing it is. Second, as they are executing strategy, when they encounter decision points they must know if they are empowered to make them and, if not, where to quickly route the decisions. Third, organizations are networks of commitments or promises, and for fast execution to work these networks need to be reliable—that is, people can trust the work will be done. When reliance is high, team members are freed to execute their commitments without worry or concern about others not being met.

For all the speeches and townhalls CEOs give on the fast-changing and complex environment, they spend considerably less time speaking about how to operate within it, and less still recognizing and rewarding leaders who do. This is what makes point four so important. As most organizational means of recognizing performance focus on hitting numbers on time, this means leaders are rarely praised for stopping or changing something even if new information was learned. But Thrive leaders are the ones who can adapt and make fast decisions that stay within boundaries, especially when the plan is challenged by market uncertainties. As such, they should be celebrated.

Building internal predictability and the ability to move with aligned speed is an important part of becoming a Thriving organization. It is the critical linkage that takes the wider team from strategic insights during the Reset phase to beginning to execute at scale in Thrive.

Execution scoping, kick off, and setting cadence

Now that you have grounded in the principles of moving from insight to action, let's discuss what building out execution will look like—how you win your must-win battles. Thrive companies dedicate time to execution enablement, and it usually starts with an execution workshop. It takes a couple of days, but it is necessary to successfully move through the loop into Thrive.

The execution workshop

MWB execution involves working across functions and units, so you need to build coordination into the workshop. To determine the attendees, use the MWBs as a guide. For each MWB, ask which two to four leaders in addition to the champion will be critical for success, knowing they may cut across levels of official roles and responsibilities.

Hold a kick-off call at least two weeks before the workshop, so that leaders who were not involved in the Reset discussion can be briefed. Provide them with the key insights that came out of asking each of the Reset questions and explain how they led to the MWBs. Emphasize that while a small team formed the initial insights, it is this next step with this wider group of leaders that will be critical to translating them into action. The strategy is not "done" yet; these next sets of discussions will be when the organization builds what it will look like.

The workshop agenda is as follows:

1 **What the MWBs are and why they matter**: Using this wider team and the benefit of more time, define each MWB in one sentence based on the draft you formulated in Chapter 8. Use the sentence structure: "Do X through Y leading to Z." Then write a one sentence description of why this MWB matters. If you are going to your organization with a list of five Must-Win Battles, you better have a compelling reason for why each is on the list!

2 **What it will look like to win**: Be specific about what success looks like at the MWB level. Have the team set a clear finish line for the three years as well as for each year-end mark. As you execute, you will be able to drill down further. Remember, the summation of the five MWBs' success should get you to the overall company definition of success.

3 **What we will do to win (supporting battles)**: Supporting battles are the three to six key projects, priorities, or initiatives that work together to win a MWB. They should not be overly generic nor an exhaustive list of micro steps. Draw out what will happen in year one to have a clear shorter term action orientation, otherwise three years feels too long and progress starts too slow. A good test is to ask: If midway through year three of the strategy the supporting battles are all won, will we be more than 90 percent confident that the MWB will be won? If yes, you have your supporting battles.

4 **How we will track progress**: What gets measured gets done, so define the small set of metrics that will be most useful to track. A metric serves one of two purposes: it shows whether you are going to meet the goal, and provides information for decision-making. As you brainstorm your list of metrics, make sure each one fulfills at least one of those purposes (and ideally both).

   Separate metrics into leading and lagging, as both are needed. Lagging metrics measure the goal: did we win the battle or not? They present a challenge, though, as by the time you have the metric, it is usually too late to do anything about it! Leading metrics help guide you along the way.

They have two characteristics: they are predictive (if they are on track, the MWB is probably on track), and they are influenceable (the team can take actions to move them). Each MWB should have a core set of metrics, three to five each of leading and lagging.

5 **What we need to make it happen:** Work outcome-back rather than resource-forward to identify what the company will have to resource in order to win. Resourcing is a later agenda step as we want each champion to determine what they can achieve within the timeframe, and what will push the most for value creation first. The more typical pattern is to start with a resource set and then work out what you think is possible to achieve. This leads to linear, incremental thinking that holds back growth. To build growth mindsets, allow the teams to think freely, knowing there will be a back and forth when all the preliminary resource asks are presented. There are three critical resources in any organization: time (whose and how much), treasure (the cash), and talent (what people and skill gaps do we need to close). Champions should attempt to forecast needs across all three.

6 **Challenges to overcome:** MWBs are difficult to execute as they often involve new ways of working. Be open about this reality from day one. The teams should list the top challenges they will face internally (e.g. siloed ways of working, lacking talent or capacity) and externally (e.g. unknown regulatory changes or customer adoption speed). You can proactively address challenges by building out how you will overcome them into the supporting battles.

7 **Assumptions: What we will need to test and how it might change:** Free yourself from the notion that everything in the plan will happen. Even calling it the strategic plan builds an assumption it won't change, but it will! Build that in from the start. Although you are going to hold the team accountable for their commitment to results, let them know you expect aspects of the plan to adjust as they execute and learn. Ask the teams to list out the key beliefs and assumptions that are most shaping their MWB and, critically, what assumptions they need to test. Some teams will need help building testing mechanisms and integrating new information into the MWB plan.

Building execution plans and trackers

After the workshop, allow teams two to three weeks to refine their MWB execution plans and build a more detailed first-year outline. Leadership should provide detailed feedback and have final sign-off on the plan, including the resources and assistance needed to execute it. After the sign off, resourcing, and discussion around coordination, the champions and battle teams will move their plans into a shared Strategy Tracker that summarizes each MWB including owner, key activities, supporting battles and outcomes. For most organizations, it takes about two months to move from the execution workshop into the tracker stage. I know that sounds long, but I rarely see it move faster.

As you move into execution, you will have two main trackers. One is the Beliefs Tracker (introduced in Chapter 4 and discussed further in Chapter 10). The second is your Strategy Tracker, which allows for one home for your overall strategy, a summary of each year's supporting battles and their outcomes, and the plan for each MWB. The Strategy Tracker is also where champions will place quick updates ahead of the champion huddles, discussed next.

Execution rhythm and champion huddles

To build a cadence of execution, add a touch point for champions in the form of a huddle, either monthly or bi-monthly. Everyone wants fewer meetings, so to add this to the calendar try to remove another one. Keep these huddles short, focused, and an opportunity for discussion and joint problem-solving. Champion huddles are for quick alignment (are we still executing towards the main intent?), coordination (are we avoiding overlap and duplication and synching up when needed?), and adaptation (as the situation changes and we learn, are we updating our actions accordingly?). These huddles are not the forum for detailed discussions of everything people are doing.

Avoid merging MWB huddles into standing business reviews. Strategy discussions demand a different part of our brains, and you will hurt the MWBs' chances of success if they are framed as another operational concern. You need to give strategy its space. Emphasize results (not activities) and learning in these meetings, and ensure that they are a safe space to discuss what is not working, just as much as what is. The meeting cadence I suggest is:

- **Major updates:** What the champion said they would do, what they did do, and what results were generated since the last meeting.
- **Current testing:** If a champion is not testing, they are not learning, and if there is no learning, the organization will not be growing. Ensure belief and assumption testing is occurring within each MWB plan.

- **Projections:** Keep commitment cadence high by having champions make clear promises to the team on the progress they expect to make by the next meeting.

- **What's working:** Celebrate what's working, especially as these learnings could help other MWBs.

- **What's not working:** A lot of things will not work; talk about them.

- **Major challenges and help needed:** Separate out major roadblocks or challenges so these get due attention and the necessary resources to overcome them.

- **What needs to be socialized more widely:** Keep the organization updated and encourage champions to incorporate key updates into company communications.

Focus on the commitments made and what is being tested. Avoid cancelling champion meetings because "not much new has happened." Thrive companies are disciplined. What a company cancels is what it does not care about. These meetings should allow for continual alignment between the MWB and the overall strategy, coordination across teams and units, and adaptation as things change. Keep things short, light, and consistent, and follow up on major items after the meeting.

The Black Box of Execution

Picture this: You've reset the strategy and have a new set of MWBs. You've held the workshop and developed execution plans. It's time to start executing, but it doesn't feel like execution is happening. People are having meetings, but you are not seeing results. You get frustrated and call for meetings to understand why, which leads to more meetings. You continue to wonder why the execution is not working. What is happening? You have fallen into the execution gap between strategy and results.

The gap exists because different strategies demand different execution approaches. Time after time, executives reset the strategy and then hand it off to existing teams, processes, and structures expecting it to work and are surprised when it does not. Building out high-level execution plans is a step, but the next, critical one is determining how to reset your organization's execution capacity.

When the strategy changes, the execution approach must change too. Dedicate time to reshaping your execution capacity as it becomes clearer what the new priorities will take to win. This demands a system-wide view of your execution capacity, identifying gaps, and closing them. I call this the Black Box of Execution, which summarizes the five elements of capacity needed to translate strategy into results: shared context, distributed leadership, top leadership, hardware (supporting infrastructure) and software (company culture). See Figure 9.1.

To better understand execution as well as bring more research and quantitative rigor to the topic, my colleague Donald Sull and I developed and conducted a detailed execution survey designed to gather real analysis on companies' readiness to execute. We asked questions framed in multiple

FIGURE 9.1 The Black Box of Execution

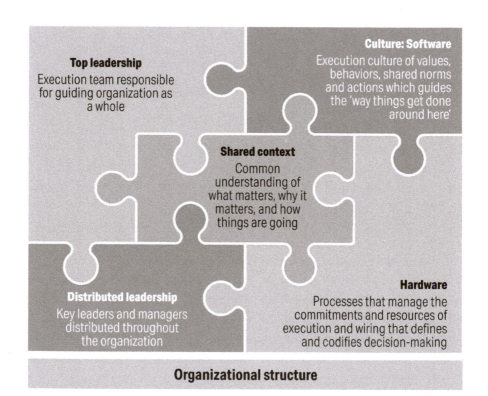

Inside the black box of execution
Elements needed to translate strategy into results

Top leadership
Execution team responsible for guiding organization as a whole

Culture: Software
Execution culture of values, behaviors, shared norms and actions which guides the 'way things get done around here'

Shared context
Common understanding of what matters, why it matters, and how things are going

Distributed leadership
Key leaders and managers distributed throughout the organization

Hardware
Processes that manage the commitments and resources of execution and wiring that defines and codifies decision-making

Organizational structure

choice or open response to remove the bias of self-assessment. Over 500 companies and 12,000 respondents participated in the survey over five years, providing a significant dataset (see box for the survey background), and some of these findings are integrated below.

One of the biggest obstacles to understanding execution is a lack of good data. With my colleague Don Sull, I developed an in-depth survey which we have administered to 11,890 respondents in 442 companies across 35 industries. This state-of-the-art survey incorporates best practices in collecting and interpreting data, and is based around the following principles:

- **Focus on complex organizations in volatile markets**. When an organization is simple and the market is stable, strategy execution is fairly straightforward. Execution is exponentially more difficult in complex organizations with more units and global scope that face regulatory, competitive, and technological volatility. The typical firm in our sample is large (median sales $430 million and median 6,000 employees) and competes in a volatile sector: Financial services, information technology, telecommunications, and oil and gas are among the most represented of the industries studied. Over one-third of the companies are based in emerging markets.

- **Target those in the know**. Rather than sending the survey to everyone in the organization, we asked companies to identify the leaders most critical to driving execution, and sent them the survey. On average 30 managers responded per company representing multiple layers in the organization. Respondents were composed of the top team (about 15 percent), their direct reports (approximately 30 percent), other middle managers, team leaders, and domain experts and other SMEs.

- **Gather objective data**. Most surveys pose broad questions, like asking if the senior management team does a good job of communicating strategy, and elicit subjective responses. Whenever possible, we structure our questions to gather objective data. To assess how well executives communicate strategy, for example, we asked respondents to list their company's strategic priorities for the next few years, code the responses, and test their convergence with one another and consistency with management's stated objectives.

- **Engage the respondents**. Respondents often slip into autopilot when filling out surveys that use the same question format throughout. To prevent respondents from checking out, we vary the question formats and pose questions that managers can answer, view as important, and have not been asked before. As a result, the typical respondent spends 40 minutes completing the online survey, allowing us to gather a rich abundance of data.

Shared context

Shared context is deliberately placed in the middle of the Black Box because it is central to building execution capacity. It is defined as **the common understanding of what matters, why it matters, how the pieces fit together, and how we are doing**. A good strategy is realistic, coherent, and makes choices. It clarifies where the company is going to play, how it will win in that space, and critically, what the company is trying to achieve—its main intent based on its current beliefs and assumptions. To execute towards that intent, all potential decision-makers must understand what they are trying to achieve, why it's the highest priority, and how the many pieces of the strategy work together. The execution workshop started this discussion, but these distributed leaders will need context building continually, which they can help maintain, as they execute the strategy. Achieving shared context requires rigorous thinking and communication discipline. Telles and his team did this by keeping the priorities limited to three, repeating them constantly, and linking all other efforts and incentives in the company to them. A detailed discussion of how to build shared context is covered in Chapter 10.

Distributed leadership

When facing uncertainty, execution requires constant trade-offs to ensure the continued alignment of activities and resources with strategy, the agility to adapt to circumstances, and the ongoing coordination among different parts of an organization. Leaders who occupy key positions throughout the organization are the ones best situated to make these trade-offs because they are closest to the situation and can respond most quickly. **Your distributed leaders are the key leaders and managers spread throughout the organization critical for execution.**

To empower your distributed leaders, you need to first know who they are. The question to ask is: "Who are our people that if they understood the strategy, were committed to it, and had the resources they needed, we would be more than 90% confident we could execute it?" They do not need to manage a team to be critical for execution; they could be domain and functional specialists.

Once identified, ensure they have what they need to succeed. Distributed leaders play a critical role in building shared context with their units, so they need to know the big picture. They shoulder much of the burden of working across silos, so if commitments are unreliable, they can falter. Distributed leaders also carry a heavy load in adjusting as circumstances change. They need the time and information gathering resources to understand how the situation has changed, what beliefs are being challenged, and what opportunities or threats it presents. Distributed leaders should also be empowered to make decisions and have access to capability building to succeed in the changing environment.

Building and equipping these distributed leaders was one of the top priorities of Telles and his team as they transformed Brahma, and they continued to give these leaders more opportunities to use their skills in the global expansion. During Ron Johnson's brief time at JCPenney, however, these leaders were not brought into the change, much less empowered in their roles to lead the transition.

Top leadership

Top leadership is the senior or executive team with responsibility for leading and steering the organization overall. The role of top leaders is *not* micromanaging distributed leaders or second-guessing their decisions. It is shaping the strategic and organizational context within which execution can emerge after the Reset.

If Right to Win is found lacking, top leaders are charged with strengthening and building it so the company can win in future strategy cycles. Once the MWBs have been set, top leaders need to be a united force: discord is quickly noticed by distributed leaders. Nearly one-quarter of survey respondents observed limited overlap or open disagreement among top executives in terms of strategy and priorities. One-third of distributed leaders believed there were top team members or factions within the C-Suite members focused on their own agendas rather than what was good for the company. If the top team cannot agree amongst themselves on a shared strategy and common strategic objectives, they cannot blame distributed leaders for failing to execute.

Shared context is the ultimate responsibility of the top leadership. At Brahma, Telles communicated the three strategic priorities for the company consistently and also ensured that all managers' objectives linked directly to them. Former CEO of IBM Lou Gerstner, who led the technology company's turnaround in the 1990s, also understood that shared context was one of his biggest responsibilities. Years after leaving IBM he was asked by a reporter what was the hardest part of the transformation. He quipped it involved saying the same thing every day, in every meeting, for years: IBM is not a mainframe company, IBM sells integrated solutions to the world's largest companies.

Attracting, developing, and empowering distributed leaders is another critical role of the top leadership team. Top leadership must invest personally in talent attraction; it is not something to be outsourced to HR. At AB InBev, recruiting new graduates was the responsibility of the executive leadership team, as was ensuring they were set up to succeed. As a result, distributed leaders were trained, empowered, and quickly promoted to hold more responsibility allowing for faster adaptation and aligned speed in execution.

Hardware

Hardware is your supporting infrastructure for execution: real-time information systems and processes, including your AI architecture; shared data and the ability to use it; and enterprise resource planning systems, performance management systems, and related tools. These systems and processes ensure teams are equipped to maintain context, monitor what is working and not working, and make faster and more effective decisions. If you lack the hardware to track and update information, share data, and monitor progress, execution will struggle.

Many activities of execution, such as testing beliefs and assumptions, maintaining shared context, and allocating resources, are facilitated by efficient and effective hardware. When these work well, it makes the daily jobs and actions of the distributed leaders seamless. Inefficient systems and processes and daily work that is unnecessarily burdensome is one of the leading causes of employee turnover. Talented leaders want to create value by focusing on the right activities: appropriate hardware and processes can ensure that happens.

The issue that most companies face is not the number of processes, but the lack of fit between processes, the strategy, and execution challenges. Rather than changing and removing outdated processes, companies tend to add more over time, leading to confusion and redundancy. While processes do not need to be completely reset every strategy cycle; they do need ongoing refreshing, updating, and the ones that are no longer working need to be discarded regularly. Telles and his team at Brahma prioritized resetting the information and tracking systems early in the transition given the criticality of real-time data in winning their MWBs. More recently, organizations lacking data systems—or with infrastructure that traps and silos data across units—are struggling to get the gains from AI, and its learning potential, versus organizations that prioritized systems and architecture for leaders to share, utilize and learn from data.

Execution is not just about doing things right, but doing the right things, and then resourcing them appropriately. Systems to allocate resources are some of the most critical hardware to have in place. Companies in the execution survey consistently struggled to allocate resources to the activities that mattered most. Only 11 percent of managers surveyed believed that all their organization's strategic initiatives had the time, treasure, and talent necessary to succeed. Over half of managers, in contrast, believed that many or most strategic initiatives were at risk of failure, not because of market or technical uncertainty, but solely due to insufficient resources. Most survey respondents cited the number of priorities and the constant addition of new initiatives as the major obstacle rather than an overall lack of resources.

In a dynamic market, all allocation is re-allocation, but most companies surveyed struggled to transfer resources. Less than one-third of managers believed their organization re-allocated funds quickly and effectively, and more than half believed that re-allocation was too slow.

Hardware does not need to be hard. Systemic support can come from non-formalized processes and procedures, and companies should avoid adding processes along with new priorities. Using principles such as Simple Rules[2], assumption testing, and managing by commitments (covered in Chapter 10) can be more effective than adding processes, especially when operating in dynamic markets likely to change.

Software

Culture is your organizational software. **Culture represents the bundle of actions, behaviors, and values that guide how work gets done around the**

organization and what is required, recognized, and rewarded. When a company fails to translate strategy into results, many executives point to a weak execution culture as the root cause. Management guru Peter Drucker was famous for saying, "Culture eats strategy for breakfast." Of course, culture matters. But what's most important is the fit between strategy, execution, and culture. In the execution survey, we asked people to list their company values. The most cited values were admirable—integrity, honesty, trust, and excellence—but have little link to execution.

There is also often a disconnect between the official values and the deeply-held beliefs that shape daily behavior. In the same survey, answers to questions around hiring, promotions, or firings revealed that employees perceive a very different set of values in action from those listed. A company's true values only reveal themselves when managers make hard decisions, and few choices are tougher than people decisions.

Most values and behaviors embedded in culture support hitting numbers and delivering results. Building a performance culture is necessary for effective execution, but it is insufficient. To do well in uncertainty, companies need to support and reward adapting as circumstances change and supporting and coordinating with colleagues in other units. In our survey, only around a fifth of leaders said innovating or acting with agility would lead to promotions (versus nearly 60 percent who said past performance would). And only 25 percent said experimenting would be rewarded for success and not penalized should it fail, whereas over a third said failure would hit their career.

Part of the problem is the time disconnect between strategy and culture. Strategies shift every three years, if not sooner, whereas it usually takes three to five years to shift a company culture, with rare exceptions to be only two years and others taking over five. Your culture will need to support your current and future strategies, and so it must reinforce the bundle of values and behaviors that support execution over the long run. This means balancing not just alignment and delivery, but also changing, adapting, and coordination. At Brahma, Telles and his team worked to build the performance culture as a top priority, which included rewarding people for performance—not tenure—and recognizing and rewarding when leaders made appropriate shifts to the changing situation.

Examine your lived company values. Do they reinforce sticking to and hitting plans? What about coordination, trust, learning velocity, and adaptation? To Thrive, the execution culture must support the necessary adaptation needed for growth through uncertainty. In my work, I review company values to see if they support alignment, coordination, and adaptation, and when one of these three is missing, I know there could be problems. When the company shift strategies across cycles, their values may not be capable of supporting the next phase of execution.

Resetting the Black Box

After the MWB execution workshop, sit down with the Black Box. For each element ask how this lever will support the new strategy. Identify the gaps and where major changes are needed. This entails focusing relentlessly on building shared context of the new Reset strategy. You will need to pull on different aspects of your software, add and dismantle parts of hardware, equip distributed leaders with new skills and capabilities, and as a top team you may need to reassess your ability to steer and lead (covered more in Chapter 11). Be prepared to keep what will still work, but remove and change pieces that will not.

Summary and next steps

Transitioning between modes in the SRT journey is often harder than executing within the modes, and the move from Reset to Thrive is the hardest. You will need to start moving and executing, even as you are building the mid-term execution engine. I often watch teams stumble in this phase, slowly planning but never moving, looking left or right for another team member to start moving so they know it is OK for them to as well. Visualize your team, especially your MWB champions, as runners in the starting blocks at a race. As a leader you need to explicitly say "Go!"

Saying "Go!" will likely feel premature, but the alternative is losing a quarter of the strategy cycle in planning mode. Utilize the principles of movement, build internal predictability, set the execution rhythm, and be prepared to make bigger shifts in execution capacity across the Black Box.

At this point in the journey, you should:

✓ understand the principles of moving and testing out of Reset

✓ be building the components of internal predictability

✓ have detailed execution plans for each MWB including clear definitions, supporting battles, success statements, and metrics

✓ know what gaps in execution capacity you must close

Now it is time to explore Thrive, and what consistently high-performing companies look like.

Endnotes

1 Braham vs Antarctica: Reversal of Fortune in Brazil's Beer Market. Teach Case 2005. Donald Sull and Martin Escobari. Case number 305-150-1

2 D Sull and K M Eisenhardt (2015) *Simple Rules: How to thrive in a complex world*, Houghton Mifflin Harcourt

10

Thrive: Operating on Full Blast

"Ever tried. Ever failed. No matter. Try again. Fail again. Fail better."
—SAMUEL BECKETT

High growth is exciting, but challenging. It is even more difficult to sustain high growth through different market cycles—in other words, to Thrive in an uncertain future as circumstances change.

What does it take to Thrive?

I have spent more than 15 years working directly with high-growth companies setting, executing, and innovating their strategy journeys through changing conditions. In this chapter I cut through the truisms of what it takes to achieve consistent performance such as having a great team or strong culture. Not only are these too simplistic, I know leaders need more practical guidance on what it takes to build a company that can Thrive through uncertainty.

Recall that by this phase of the SRT loop, you should have the core pieces in place. Your organization has been through a Reset, is running in steady-state Survive, and is prepared to Thrive with a leadership team and culture committed to consistent high performance and willing to make the adaptations to get there. Let's start by recapping the ingredients of the recipe for Thriving:

- strong balance sheet
- strategic insights
- executing with agility and learning (*BLAST*)

The first two ingredients have been covered in previous chapters. You bring the balance sheet from Survive and the insights from Reset. This chapter explores the third ingredient, executing with agility and learning, and goes deeper into the bundle of elements that powers this differentiated execution approach. And you see I have now added a word: **BLAST**. This acronym is how I codify these elements that together describe what sets Thrive companies apart:

- Beliefs setting and testing
- Learning velocity
- Agility in decision-making
- Shared context
- Trust

Envision your Thrive organization as a rocket BLASTing into space and journeying to the next growth frontier.

You will recognize some of these BLAST elements from earlier chapters. Here I go deeper into each and show how they work together in a bundle to fuel performance through uncertainty. In this chapter, I explain each element, with particular emphasis on learning velocity, offer examples of what they look like in practice, and provide guidance on how to build these capabilities. I wrap with some overall recommendations of how to reinforce and build BLAST at your organization.

Beliefs

A major differentiator of high-growth Thrive companies is that they make decisions based on beliefs, not facts. This sounds like an odd claim to make: Don't we want more data-based decision-making? Yes, data matters, but data is only one input. Historical data and facts are the basis for forming insights about the current state, but relying on existing data alone for decision-making has traps in an uncertain world: we cannot assume past and current trends will continue. Strategic choices are about making sense of data, how it fits with other data, and then using this to inform your beliefs about what is going on now and what will shape the future.

Thrive is about getting ahead and staying ahead. By the time something has become a proven fact, it is no longer an advantageous insight—everyone has it. If you want to outgrow the industry, you need to act ahead and make moves on beliefs. Beliefs drive your choices.

Chapter 4 discussed assessing your strategic situation and setting your beliefs. Here I focus on the practice of using and testing beliefs. Swedish music streaming company Spotify is a great example.

CASE STUDY

Spotify developed its Data to Insight to Belief to Bet (DIBB) framework to prioritize, test, and execute its one or two year bets (in SRT terms, must-win battles), which are broken down from their mid-term "Northstar" goals (in SRT terms, their main intent) that stem from their beliefs (which are articulated from insights from the data they collect and analyze). Once Spotify executes on a bet, they track it on the Bets Board so teams across the company can understand how it is progressing, what its priority to the company is, and when and why it shifts. This formalized company-wide approach which combines top-down and bottom-up processes for translating beliefs to testable bets, as well as bringing insights from execution and learning to form updated beliefs, led to the launch and growth of Spotify's audiobook initiatives, among others. Spotify, which went public in 2018, grew from nearly €3 billion in 2016 to nearly €12 billion in 2022.

Once you set the beliefs, ensure they are communicated along with your strategic priorities or must-win battles, tracked and actively tested as you execute, used to inform decision-making including adaptations, and incremental investment in the strategy. Using and testing beliefs empowers you to Thrive by forming the basis for moving within and across the strategy stances.

Communication

As you are building shared context with the wider team, communicate your beliefs and not just the priorities. Emphasize that the team will be parallel pathing—actively testing beliefs while executing the MWBs.

Communicating in this way is powerful. First, you have given yourself permission to change. Restricting yourself to communicating priorities feels easier because you do not want to overwhelm the team. But when the situation changes, you are stuck. Imagine a few months after the strategy Reset, some major beliefs that led to a MWB are challenged. As a leadership team, you need to change something, now, but you do not want to go back to your company so soon with new priorities. When this happens leaders commonly either do not make the needed adjustments, or they change strategy but don't disseminate it within their organization. This means distributed leaders are watching their bosses not execute against the strategy they recently socialized, which gradually erodes their confidence in this strategy and those shared in the future.

Second, when you communicate beliefs, you are recruiting more people to help you test. When you are explicit that the organization has some big beliefs that could be wrong, and may need to be adjusted, it's a signal to your team to be heads up rather than heads down. You have multiplied by an order of magnitude the number of people who are going to monitor these beliefs, which will allow you to test and adapt faster.

Tracking and testing

After you Reset the strategy, your team has two trackers: one for your beliefs, as discussed here and in Chapter 4, and one for the MWB action plans (discussed in Chapter 8).

As part of your situation assessment in the Survive phase, build a Beliefs Tracker that includes the most critical trends and beliefs you are tracking. In the execution phase, actively monitor and use the Beliefs Tracker for strategy check-ins (see Figure 10.1). After a structured conversation and based on the team's understanding of the environment, you can update your beliefs on the tracker. For companies with Boards, getting Board members involved in updating beliefs is a great way to use their cross-industry perspective to provide guidance.

For each of the beliefs, include the summary of the trend, your current belief, whether it is tracking (such as through a color coded drop-down), and any notes or links. It is OK if some beliefs are not on track (i.e. green) all the time: if a Beliefs Tracker is constantly green, it likely means you were not clear enough about your beliefs in the first place.

Owners should be running tests, checking in, updating the tracker and others, and including links to sources and updates regularly. The wider team should revisit beliefs at least once and preferably twice a year. Passive testing—simple tracking or asking the team what's changed—is helpful, but likely not enough. For your major beliefs, set alerts to notify you if something moves. Recruit customers and clients to help you test beliefs. Translate the top two or three beliefs into specific questions and ask the sales team to incorporate them into their weekly conversations with customers. Run quick, five-minute surveys to get a sense of what is happening in the market. Food distributor GFS did this with their pulse surveys, as discussed in Chapter 4.

FIGURE 10.1 Beliefs testing tracker

Tracking these, updating these, as information comes in from the market

Trend	Key beliefs	Status	Comments
INDUSTRY: Telecom operators become more like banks	More and more telecom operators will get their banking license and offer banking services. More telecoms will launch more value added services for their consumers base	Tracking ✓	Singtel acquires banking license, but moving slowly
MACRO: Demographic shifts	As US population shifts to coasts and south, these movements will create new opportunities in food service.	Tracking ✓	Population from northern states is moving to Sunbelt states, but likely bringing northern values with them. ID, AZ, TN, SC, FL, TX, CO, and NC are the top 8 states with inbound moves. Inbound migration to TX coming mostly from CA.
INDUSTRY: Midterm oil price	Oil price will take up to three years to return from weak supply	Caution	Brent above $100/bbl and forecast for continued increases. Good for business performance, but likely to result in asset acquisitions and M&A being more fully valued
MACRO: Market perception of EP	For public investors, returns are first and second; but short-term cash vs long-term NAV is the focus of those returns today	Off track !	Oil and gas companies continue to show discounts to oil price recovery suggesting a continued focus on short-term cash generation and use
OPERATIONS: New models: pivoting to try new formats	Restaurant operators will be continuing to explore and push the boundaries of what a restaurant is—delivery only, micro-store/bodega, carry-out, meal kits, prepared meals	Tracking ✓	New formats include: experimentation towards what will be the future of brick and mortar (hybrids of delivery, mealkits, bars all in one). In addition to pivoting, new players are entering the scene who only know this model and will push the industry forward. Sense from our surveys is most operators plan to keep the changes to their business model that they implemented in 2020
INDUSTRY: Increase in smaller competitive brands	Digital shelves will create a polarization of the category between the brand leader (including us) and smaller brands/new category entrants, making it easier than ever for them to take share. Our products will have to rely on point of differentiation (claims, sizes, efficacy, etc.) and cultivating a better overall brand experience to compete	Off track !	No new entry of any sizable scale or traction in the last 18 months; little movement in acquisition space of smallest brands that were on our radar
POLITICAL: CO_2 regulations/carbon reduction	Countries and parliaments will push CO_2 emission regulation and taxes – especially in certain European countries and then only later the USA/UK. This provides us an opportunity to partner to help save CO_2	Tracking but watch ?	There is no movement on regulations, but we believe this is due to slowness of regulators and not that this will not happen. We still believe we need to be ahead of this to gain advantage when it happens while others struggle to catch up

Testing beliefs is done in a parallel path to strategy execution: you execute your MWBs while simultaneously stress-testing your beliefs. As beliefs are affirmed, their related initiatives are given more resources and attention, and as beliefs are challenged or disproved, the team makes decisions about how to move forward, which may include pausing or changing an activity.

For any critical, game-changing belief, design explicit experiments to test the assumptions behind it (see the "Learning velocity" section for more on experimentation). Get outside with your customers like Brooks Running Company did during 2020. The team had a hypothesis that running would do well even during lockdowns. To test this belief, they placed 45 field marketers in local parks at 4pm every day and counted runners. Every day their counts increased. This very non-technical field test, combined with daily digital sales that affirmed early beliefs, led to Brooks turning its supply chain back on six to 12 weeks before competitors. As a result, Brooks grew 27 percent in 2020, stealing market share from the bigger players.[1] They continued active testing, which led to the company surpassing the billion-dollar sales mark for the first time in 2021.

Decision-making

In non-Thrive companies, decisions are based on recency bias (e.g. a leader's most recent conversation with a customer), past experience (e.g. what worked at a previous company), or gut. Of the three, gut probably works best, but I still wouldn't bet a growth journey on it.

In Thrive companies, beliefs are the starting point for making new choices or adjusting existing ones. When decisions are made or changed, ask: *"What belief was challenged that is making us change this decision? What new information or data do we have about that belief? What would we have to believe for us to agree to this?"*

When Spotify increases investments in a bet, it links the investment back to its company-wide beliefs, and when these beliefs are challenged, related bets are stopped or de-prioritized. When Airbnb announced a major revamp of its website and offerings in 2022, they linked these changes to their updated beliefs around the future of business and consumer travel.

When MWB champions need to change their action plans or introduce new ideas, make sure they communicate the change at meetings while referring to the changing beliefs: We selected this supporting battle as a priority because we believed X, Y, and Z about our top customers. But we have learned that that belief was not correct, and now we believe A, so we want to reprioritize.

Using your strategy stances

A common mistake in strategy is using only a limited set of options available. Use your beliefs to help you explore the full set of strategic options your environment provides. I call these strategic stances. These stances help take beliefs to implication by opening more of the exploratory and outcome space. See Figure 10.2.

When it comes to strategy, we can prepare or we can act. Prepare stances involve waiting; they are decisions *not* to act, but rather to analyze, observe, or get ready to move. Act stances include shaping the emerging future, learning, or making a commitment to get results.

FIGURE 10.2 Strategy stances

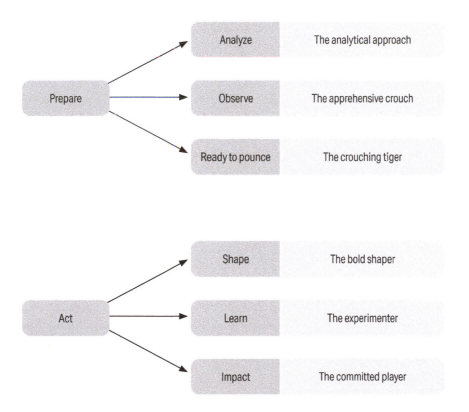

Using your stances to execute your full option set

Analyze	The analytical approach
Observe	The apprehensive crouch
Ready to pounce	The crouching tiger

Prepare →

Shape	The bold shaper
Learn	The experimenter
Impact	The committed player

Act →

PREPARE STANCES

A waiting stance can make sense when further research, analysis, or time is needed before acting. The most common is the analyze stance, where you use data and analysis to confirm a belief and then act. It requires building scenarios, researching trends, and trying to understand every facet of the environment. This can be useful, but represents time that could be channeled to other areas.

Some beliefs may be too critical and untested to act on yet, so you instead prepare by observing and watching the environment. In evolving environments, research reports and data sets may not exist, so we can learn from watching others in the market move and react. Waiting and watching is sometimes the right move, but can also lull a team into paralysis waiting for perfect knowledge that does not exist.

Waiting can also be a smart move when technology is changing quickly. Sometimes committing too soon is riskier than holding off. A well-known hotel chain was one of the first to install a CRM system and was seen as very forward-looking at the time. But within a few years, digital marketing and social media had transformed how hotels interact with their guests. The hotel's CRM system became a costly legacy.

The third reason to wait is to build capability in preparation for a move. I call this "ready to pounce." Here, you define the triggers that will signal to the team it is time to move into acting. In the meantime, you get ready. WHSmith, a UK high-street retailer, spent years watching and analyzing the small but growing e-card business before finally acquiring a player that, while not the market leader, had the best technology. By not immediately jumping into a business it didn't understand, WHSmith avoided making costly errors. At times it makes sense to be the second mover in an environment. You are poised in waiting mode until the belief is affirmed by another actor. Apple uses this stance to prepare and purposely not move first, as they did in smart phones and more recently their movement into the consumer AI space.

Strategic use of waiting stances is critical, but Thrive companies are always moving by employing the acting stances as well. This is another instance of parallel pathing—using varied strategy stances at the same time while actively testing all beliefs.

ACT STANCES

When we act in strategy, we also have three broad pathways. We can act for results; this is the most common and tempting act stance. But we can also act in two other ways: to shape and to learn.

Beliefs are critical to watch and test when you are committing resources to actions. Whether they are affirmed or negated may trigger movement back into waiting, or from waiting to acting.

When assessing your top beliefs, consider actions that will shape or form the environment in your favor—even if there are no immediate value creation opportunities. Purposeful shaping actions can include influencing regulation or legislation, employing land grabs, or implementing other high growth strategies. Of the acting stances, shaping the environment is the boldest and can lead to enormous market power. PayPal's movements into the financial space in the early 2000s created the opportunity for peer-to-peer transfers. They believed that this shaping action would open the playing field for them. They knew it could open it up for competitors as well, but that was OK. If they didn't open up this space, no one would be able to compete. Once the financial environment allowed for the necessary volume of peer-to-peer transfers, PayPal then shifted to ongoing acting to learn and acting for results.

More recently, Airbnb acted to shape. After they decided to shift to a fully virtual and global workforce, they realized other companies rarely did this because it was hard. It required navigating thousands of local employment laws and contract issues. Building the system was difficult and expensive, and the pay-off in terms of value creation would take a lot of time. Yet they decided to share how they did it and what they learned with their wider community. Why? The company had a critical belief that if they made it easier for companies to have a global workforce, more companies would do it, which means more people would stay in Airbnbs, and they would benefit.

The most underused and underappreciated stance by non-Thrive companies is the one most employed by Thrive companies: acting to learn. It involves experimentation, limited participation, or observing the mistakes of others to improve on their early offerings. **Acting to learn is explicit action not to get immediate results, but to learn about the environment so you can drive results in the future.** In times of high uncertainty, companies that learn the fastest relative to their peers gain a competitive advantage. During this stance, beliefs are tested in micro, frequent ways, as explored in the "Learning Velocity" section.

For most companies, most of the time, moving in the chosen direction beats waiting. This is because there is more to learn while moving than staying still as the path unfolds in front of you. Unfortunately, most strategy processes are limited to two stances: Wait/Analyze and Act/Results. But a lot of power comes from acting, even if not for immediate results. The evolving environment will keep providing opportunities, but you need to open up all of your stances, and test your beliefs as you move across them, to seize these.

Learning velocity

Learn faster, grow faster. This is the simplest, most powerful finding I can share from over 15 years working with high growth companies. Companies with the methodology, hardware, and software to learn faster than others will outgrow others.

Learning velocity measures the rate at which learning and knowledge acquisition in an organization occurs, is shared, transferred, embedded, and used to further performance at an individual or organizational level. Learning velocity is more than launching development programs, teaching classes, and tracking performance on a Learning Management System. Being a Thrive company involves moving from being a *teaching* organization to being a *learning* organization that is continually utilizing the "acting to learn" stance.

While often used to focus on individual learning journeys, the power for Thrive is in system-wide structures and support for learning. Thrive organizations are better at quickly scaling learning curves, internalizing findings, embedding and acting on learnings; they also have cultures that reward fast and efficient learning.

Most processes are built around collecting and analyzing data, making decisions based on estimates, and then committing resources. This is the analytical approach above, and the sequence is learn–think–act. What is less common but more powerful is an act–learn–think (also known as a test–learn–commit) approach where you take action to learn before committing significant resources.[2]

Instead of deciding on a prototype and testing it before launch, conduct experiments and then invest based on the learnings. With this approach, the research is linked to probing, rather than to a commitment of resources, as data about the past cannot tell you what the actual reaction to a new product will be—too much is unknown and unknowable.

Acting to learn is a form of experimentation. Under high uncertainty, the only way to find out if something works is to conduct experiments to probe reality and decide which has the highest likelihood of success. Such experimentation must be done cheaply, as most experiments fail. And that should be expected! A 2009 paper studying experimentation at Microsoft and other high-performing tech companies found that at most 30 percent of tests positively impacted the variable they were trying to affect.[3]

To dissect this concept of a learning organization that routinely employs "acting to learn," let's break it into four distinct pieces: learning loops, constant experimentation, implementing specific practices to reinforce learning, and supporting learning with execution capacity.

Learning loops

The critical connection between strategy, execution, and learning velocity is learning loops. **Learning loops are specific, iterative cycles of forming hypotheses, testing, learning, understanding, analyzing, and applying various forms of knowledge.** Accelerating learning velocity comes from identifying your most critical loops, shortening them, and increasing the velocity that team members traverse them.

Loops are a fundamental part of the growth journey. The best known is John Boyd's OODA loop: observe, orient, decide, act. The cycle begins with observation which leads to orientation on possibilities, then a decision on a course of action and then acting on that decision. The results are then observed, and the cycle starts again, with the critical link back from "act" to "observe," which makes it a loop.

In the organizational Learning loop, the stages are: Articulate (hypotheses or beliefs)—Act—Learn—Document—Share—Apply—Embed. Embedded learnings further the journey by leading to more assumptions and hypotheses, starting another journey through the loop. Accelerating learning velocity means shortening the time for each step and increasing the velocity at which teams make their way around them.

Consider the ideal learning cycle: a team member takes action in the market; learns something; shares that learning with others; that learning gets embedded in the organization for wider dissemination; and is then used to further the next action for future growth. This sounds great, but rarely happens. More often team members act, but the action was not taken based on a formulated hypothesis, so they are not actively looking for the learning. When they do have a learning, there is no easy way to share or record it, so it stays with them. It may be discussed in an ad-hoc way in a meeting or email, but the chances of it being applied by another team member are low.

Thrive companies identify critical learning needs related to specific MWBs and that offer potential strategic advantages, such as opening new markets or launching new products. Team members are trained to form testable beliefs or hypotheses that they can act on and learn from. Learnings are matched against the set of beliefs, and then tracked. This information is shared with others to further performance. It becomes embedded in the organization and a new set of hypotheses is formulated for the team to test. As teams keep going through this cycle, learnings compound leading to an order of magnitude more gains in the market. This formalization of learning loops and committing to shortening them is a secret weapon in breakthrough growth.

Celebrating experimentation, not failure

A popular idea—almost mythology—regarding entrepreneurial companies is that they celebrate failure. The assumption is that these companies get ahead due to their constant celebration of making mistakes and failing. But praising mistakes is missing the point: companies get ahead by creating an environment of constant experimentation and learning. Failure is not celebrated; the celebration is for resourcefully eliminating options that do not work.

The word "experiment" seems to bring much emotional baggage with it, so let's start by defining it. **An experiment is the testing of an assumption that if correct could affect the growth or profitability of the company.** Learning velocity is running as many good experiments as quickly and cheaply as possible. It is not about getting better at running *better* experiments, it is about getting better at running *more* experiments that are well-articulated, fast, and cheap.

RUNNING EXPERIMENTS

Imagine a grid where the X axis is a possible new customer segment, and the Y axis is a possible new value proposition (Figure 10.3). We want to learn which of these new intersections will be a possible new growth idea. In traditional companies, we need to justify the resources to run an experiment so much time is spent trying to increase the chance that this is the right experiment to run. Weeks are dedicated to making presentations and getting approvals. In doing this, we increase the odds that we are running the right experiment, but at most we have increased the odds of success to around 15 percent (as above, the highest performing teams only hit 30 percent).

A learning approach does not try to improve the likelihood that any of the boxes on the grid are the right experiment to run; it tries to run them all as quickly and cheaply as possible. In the first option, failure is getting the experiment wrong because we wasted so much time and money getting to an experiment that did not work out.

FIGURE 10.3 Redefine how you approach experimentation

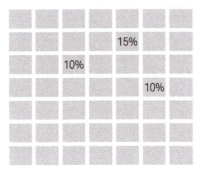

Solution grid for experimentation
All possible outcomes

Tradititional company approach
Trying three pilots

FAILURE: Getting it wrong

Experimenters's approach
Trying all your chances

FAILURE: Spending too much money
getting to the solution

Taking one hit and thinking
you're done

Not getting to all of the chances

But we actually made a bigger mistake: we have now framed the organization that "this [*whatever test we ran*] doesn't work here," which will be embedded in the institutional memory for years. Leaders may now look past or ignore growth opportunities in this area and prevent future tests. One or two poorly defined digital experiments led many large corporations to stay away for years due to this framing. I am already seeing this framing hold back companies from moving more quickly with AI applications. They jumped in early with a few heavily-resourced but poorly defined pilots, only to find their data systems could not support the tests, so paused everything leading to an unhelpful framing they were not "ready" for AI. In the Thrive approach, failure isn't getting it wrong, it is spending too much money getting to the solution, taking one chance and thinking you are done, or not taking all of the chances.

In retailing there are many new ideas for new ranges, pricing, and space allocation as part of "business as usual." At WHSmith, any potential change goes through a multi-step process where the idea is modeled with critical variables and expected metrics documented. Then a small trial of at most 10 stores is chosen to give the best read. Results are measured against a set of control stores, looking at average performance and performance distribution. If performance is widely distributed, a second wave trial is conducted. If the performance is clearly poor, the idea is dropped. If it is clearly superior, the company conducts a pilot of 50—100 stores to check implementation issues and consistency at scale, compared once more against a set of control stores. If the pilot confirms superior performance, the change is rolled out to all 500-plus stores.

Before this process was introduced, WHSmith relied on the experience and intuition of its senior people, which was hit and miss. Once the act-to-learn approach was established many obvious things became less obvious, so everything became fertile ground for testing and new learnings. While WHSmith's average failure rate of an innovation was about 30 percent (consistent with the Microsoft findings above), it became one of the highest performing stocks among UK retailers. In the eleven years 2003—14 it earned shareholders total annual returns of 29 percent.

DEFINING A GOOD EXPERIMENT

Experimenting cannot be just top-down or centrally controlled; you need team members testing everywhere. To empower the team to experiment within boundaries, define what an experiment is for your organization and where your boundaries lie. For example, UPS had an experimentation approach that encouraged wider testing as long as a test could not fail in a way that touches the customer moving with, paying for or interacting with a package. A few factors can help in defining a "good" experiment for your organization.

A good experiment tests only one variable at a time. Disentangle all possible assumptions into explicit variables and test each one, starting with the most critical. One-and-Only, the company from Chapter 4 that became Match.com, empowered its employees to run experiments within a few rules. They had to test one variable at a time, learn in less than two weeks, and if correct that variable had to contribute to the current 30 percent growth rate/month of the company. At the scale the site was operating, they could learn within a few days of identifying and running a test. Often team members could see the real-time revenue curve bend up or down within 30 minutes of a test.

A "pilot" is not a test: pilots should not be run until all the embedded variables have been tested. Whether or not a customer will buy a new solution for a certain price is not a testable experiment: you need to break this hypothesis down into all the assumptions around why customers would do this, and test the critical ones quickly and cheaply.

The best way to break down assumptions is to apply a lesson from the Survive phase, where we shift conversations away from "I think" or "Is this a good idea?" to the more powerful: **"What would have to be true for this to be a great idea?"** For the idea or test in play, ask this question to the team. Then take a flip chart (or virtual equivalent) and draw a line to create two columns: internal and external. Write down every assumption that must be true for the idea in question to be a great, not just good, idea. Once you have the totality of assumptions, agree as a team that if all those variables are true, this is a great idea. Rank these variables in terms of criticality then for each one ask: "Is this true or can we make it true?" When you do not know if something is true, design a test to find out as quickly and cheaply as possible.

For Uber, the most critical assumption that needed to be tested was "Would people get in strangers' cars?" for Airbnb it was "Would travelers stay in strangers' houses?" and for US-based online grocer Instacart, it was "Would consumers let strangers touch and pick out their groceries for a higher price?"

In experiments, **which customers you are testing with is one of the biggest considerations**. At its simplest, you have three options. If you have many customers, stores, or locations, you can run tests on a small number (e.g. <5 percent) then with a series of controlled experiments you can scale these numbers.

Most companies do not have business models with millions, thousands, or even hundreds of customers or locations, so your second option is to find your "New Zealand." This comes from Facebook's testing process. In its earlier days, Facebook mapped its connections and found this small country was ideal for testing new products and features: it was English-speaking, had mostly internal connections (most Kiwis' Facebook friends were inside the country), and had a low risk of big leaks outside, especially to the critical USA market, if something did not work.[4] When it comes to testing, I ask companies "where is your New Zealand?" Most of you have a group of customers or geographic area that is a safe zone for testing, that is, that represents a limited and contained risk. If the test doesn't work out with this group, the business will still be OK.

If you do not have a New Zealand, you will need to actively recruit "learning partners." Go to a small number of customers and explicitly ask them to learn with you. Tell them you know they want to grow, that you want to grow as well, and see if they will give permission to be part of your test and learn process. You will be surprised at how many customers want to learn with you!

TIME TO LEARN MATTERS

Organizations have three types of resources: time, treasure, and talent. But after a certain point, time is no longer prioritized as a critical resource even though it is THE most critical one a company has. The better an organization is at quickly testing assumptions and scaling learning curves, the less time you spend on things that do not matter—and the more time you have to resource the critical activities that are. My general principle is "two weeks is too long"—that is, if it cannot be learned in two weeks or less, the test is too complicated. You must break it down into a more focused test to get to faster learning.

Figure 10.4 provides a template for defining experiments at your company.

Learning velocity in practice

Learning velocity is more than running constant experiments, there are many ways to put act-to-learn into practice. It can start with ongoing **belief and assumption testing**. It can mean **redeploying** people across the organization so leaders have a more holistic understanding of how the company works and how things work together. Brahma, the brewer from Chapter 9, started a highly competitive trainee program where new employees spent

FIGURE 10.4 Defining experiments at your organization: A template

Increase velocity of testing assumptions by setting parameters of what an experiment is

Template definition per experiment for your company	Example of experimentation template
Clarity of assumptions and test: Must define what assumptions are testing, what variables are being considered, and what success and failure would look like.	**Clarity:** Have you clarified your assumptions, what variables are being tested, and what success and failure will look like?
Time investment: How much personal/team/unit time should be spent on each experiment? How much time can each experiment take before results are known?	**Time:** Will it take less than X weeks to conduct? Will you get feedback in less than X days?
Customer exposure: What is the exposure allowable per experiment? (%, certain population, etc.)?	**Customers:** Will it affect only our learning partners, or will it affect less than .5% of our customers?
Monetary investment: How much can each experiment cost?	**Investment:** Will it cost less than $10,000?
Risk exposure and tolerance (alignment with brand): Is it misaligned with our corporate values? Are there any obvious risks to blowing up the brand? If this were a story on the front of the *Wall Street Journal*, is that OK (e.g. Facebook emotional manipulation, Uber's Greyball).	**Risk exposure:** If the results of the experiment are published in the *Wall Street Journal*, are we OK with that?

their first four months rotating across every business unit. Then, when they landed in a spot they had a clear view of how the departments and units worked together. Future CEO Carlos Brito was an early product of this program. Explicit placements across different parts of the company furthers ongoing learning velocity as team members can translate and embed their learnings widely.

Another specific act-to-learn practice is **conducting postmortems and premortems**. Postmortems are structured discussions with cross-functional teams at the conclusion of a project to assess what worked and what didn't, and capture key lessons learned. Most companies do these infrequently and, when they do, they are long, drawn-out affairs that everyone wants to be involved in, which only leads to doing less in the future. Capturing, communicating, and storing these lessons and key takeaways in an easily accessible and shared platform accelerates and furthers future performance. Using AI, these lessons can be more quickly searched and summarized than ever before, making capturing them even more critical.

Premortems are even less frequently used, but can be even more effective. Before starting a new project or initiative, ask yourself: if we are sitting here in two years and this has not been successful, why might that be? Make a list of key reasons and then discuss what you can do to proactively address these issues.

Learning should be incorporated into your **operational rhythm**. Review your weekly huddles or standups, and add some learning points of discussion: What did we learn last week, and what do we need to learn this week? How do you learn from your customers? Do you treat customers like transactional vehicles or sources of learning? Thrive companies work with customers and clients to continually learn from them; this necessitates having structured methods for documenting feedback from customers and partners. No salesperson wants to spend even more time tracking data, so make it easy for them. Be clear about what needs to be learned and have easy ways to document their findings on a weekly basis. Short videos that team members record at the end of the week can be just as effective to learn from, and easier to do.

Structure to support learning: The Black Box of Execution

Learning velocity will not arise from one-off initiatives or the CEO saying it is important; it must be supported by the entire execution system. Keynote speakers herald examples such as Google's 20 percent flex time policy, where employees were encouraged to spend 20 percent of their time on side projects to foster creativity and learning, but rarely also mention it was officially discontinued in 2013.[5] These specific call-outs disguise the critical point: learning velocity must be supported by every piece of the Black Box of Execution from Chapter 9 (see Figure 9.1 on page 184).

- **Shared context:** How consistently is the importance of learning expressed? How many of the strategy conversations include what you need to learn and what you have learned? Ensure learning is core to your consistent messaging and strategy dialogue.

- **Top leaders:** Top leaders must model what learning looks like and how it supports the organization. Many executives espouse the criticality of learning but never provide practical examples of why it matters, how the company is doing it, and how these learnings are being further used. Too many leadership courses train executives to have all the answers, whereas in Thrive companies leaders know their job is to have the right questions.

- **Distributed leaders:** Are these critical leaders and managers distributed across the organization trained and coached in how to learn? Are they given the space to learn? This is an explicit capability that must be built and reinforced, it will not come naturally to most.

- **Software (culture):** Culturally, what do you reward? In the execution survey from Chapter 9, learning-related values were not in the top 25 of the aggregated and averaged values listed, and even companies that had a learning component as part of their values system did not frequently celebrate it. When giving shout-outs or recognition, do you recognize learning and testing and experimentation rather than just hitting the numbers and getting results? Reward team members who discover insights, including when those insights provide learnings they should not be working on this bet but should allocate attention elsewhere.

- **Hardware:** Processes, systems, and resource allocation procedures (i.e. your hardware) need to support and facilitate continual learning. Your Beliefs Tracker will be a start, but you will also need a document/platform for team members to quickly document learnings. The hurdle or perceived friction of using the system to track learning should be so low that everyone wants to do it.

Agility in decision-making

Thrive companies operate with agility. The definition of agility is simple but critical to understand: **Agility is making good decisions quickly aligned with strategy, and then resourcing them appropriately.** Aligned speed is a distinguishing characteristic of Thrive, and this is what agile decision-making gives you.

Agility is sometimes pitched as the opposite of alignment. I often see this confusion in practice: CEOs will tell me they are "not going to do strategy that year, as they want to be more agile." But **agility without strategy is chaos.** Thrive companies know that more alignment allows for more agility. True agility presupposes a strategy so that leaders can align day-to-day decisions with other leaders without needing oversight, micromanagement, or detailed guidance.

We must distinguish between an "agile strategy" and operating with agility. An agile strategy is one that is developed with the assumption the future is unpredictable (Chapters 1, 2 and 3). Success and milestones are often communicated in directions—not destinations (Chapter 7)—and actions need to be taken to learn (see above) and adjusted during execution. The SRT process is designed to build an agile strategy.

Executing an agile strategy requires operational agility, which is what we are discussing now. It comes from **clarifying decision-making rights, codifying what makes a "good" decision**, and **setting up people and processes to make more robust decisions**.

Decision-making rights

When lacking speed in execution, people often blame process or bureaucracy, but it is usually more basic. We lack clarity on who has decision-making rights, or these rights are not appropriately distributed. Say an ideal customer requests unique customization from a team member. But the leader doesn't know if they can make that decision, so they freeze and say "hold on" to the customer and ask their boss. But their boss doesn't know either, so they put it on the next executive meeting agenda or escalate it to their boss. Eventually the decision will be made, but it's likely too late, as the customer has moved on. Worse, those distributed leaders never build their decision-making capability.

Decision-rights are a shared understanding of who owns critical, repeatable decisions. Think of your organization: What are the most critical and frequent decisions your organization makes? Who makes them? If the answer is that you don't know, or that it is only the CEO, your organization will struggle to be agile. Operational agility occurs when decision-making rights are clear AND are given to the right people.

My favorite example of decision-making rights comes from Formula One (F1). If you think the business world moves fast, in F1 a second makes a massive difference, making speed is a distinct competitive advantage. One team prioritized this speed advantage and developed a simple practice: decision-making rights were owned based on the physical location of the car. If the car was in the factory, rights were owned by the head of operations; if the car was in transit, rights were owned by the head of the race team. While in the garage during a race it was the head of race engineering, and on the track, it was the head of race strategy. When something went wrong, the team did not stall, call a meeting, or waste time trying to escalate the problem up the ladder. Instead, they looked directly to the decision-maker to say what they are going to do or what help they need. I love this example because the most senior or experienced people on the pitwall did not automatically own the decision-making rights. The role of the more senior people is to give advice or stipulate decision-making criteria, but the experts with the best information make the decisions.

After your execution workshop, consider the MWBs and map out the critical decisions that need to be made to execute them, and authorize the right people to be responsible for them. Identify three to four critical, repeatable decisions for each MWB, determine who is in possession of the best information to make them, and give them the authority to do so. Wherever possible, give the final call to an individual (a top or distributed leader) rather than a group.

Are rights in the right place?

Companies tend to centralize decision-making during downturns, as they are optimizing spend, and decentralize in upturns as they are optimizing speed. Doing so sends the signal that you don't trust your employees when things get bad, which is a terrible signal to send. Thrive companies keep decision-making as decentralized as possible (not everything can or should be) regardless of the state of the market. This only works if the people with the decision-rights have the most relevant information at the point in time that the decisions must be made. To do so, they must be trained in decision-making (speed and robustness), have clear context on the main intent and boundaries of the MWB, and have a holistic understanding of how different pieces of the strategy fit together. Last, they must feel empowered and be willing to make the decisions. This happens when they are recognized and rewarded for making decisions within the set boundaries.

Not every decision should be decentralized; some aspects of competitive advantage may be purposely centralized. Airbnb centralized product development under CEO Brian Chesky in 2021. It took a similar approach to Apple while under the helm of Steve Jobs. Chesky decided the company would not work on more efforts than the CEO could be involved with and that all units (which he later collapsed) had to align around one roadmap. While it initially slowed some progress, it improved focus and teams felt it eventually led to speedier development, improved accountability, and more successful launches.

What is a good decision?

If you asked five leaders in your company what makes a good decision at your organization, would they all answer in the same way? A shared understanding of what makes a good decision at your organization is one of the most powerful ways to boost agility. It would be easy to say that a good decision is one that gives a good result, but that is not very helpful when you are taking it—and it is not always true. Some people can make a bad decision and get lucky. Thrive companies codify the features of a good decision, which then empowers team members around the globe to make them more quickly and confidently.

One law firm prided itself on its democratization of key decisions involving wide groups of partners and a complicated voting structure. As its global growth continued, waiting for infrequent meetings for votes began to significantly slow progress and erode competitive advantage. To speed things up without losing shared consensus, the managing partners agreed on the six variables defining a good decision, and then empowered partners around the world to make them as long as they fit within the rubric.

Your codified good decisions should fit your context and culture, but some common variables to consider include:

- whether it is in line with the company's beliefs
- use of data (do you need to use it, how much, and from what sources)
- time taken to make it (hours, days, weeks)
- who needs to be involved
- whether it is clear about the most critical assumptions
- whether the most critical assumptions need to be tested first.

A good decision tends to open up rather than close down future options, meaning it continues to open the opportunity set going forward (possible kickers) rather than prematurely forcing an organization on one path. Different approaches should be taken for decisions that are "no-regret moves," which can be made quicker versus those around your identified game-changer assumptions. What makes a good decision will vary by company, and that is OK. What is not OK is to not be clear on what a good one is.

Shared context

The CEO of one London-based professional service firm my colleague and I worked with met with her extended management team the first week of every month. She began each meeting by repeating the firm's strategy and key priorities for the year. She was delighted when their employee engagement survey revealed that 84 percent of the staff were clear on their organization's top priorities. She felt her effort to communicate the strategy seemed to be working.

Then her management team took my execution survey (introduced in Chapter 9), which asked them to describe the strategy in their own words and list the top three to five priorities over the next few years. The CEO was disappointed to learn that their descriptions of the strategy were all over the place, with little overlap. Fewer than one-third of her direct reports could name even two of the company's five strategic priorities—the same objectives she discussed in every management meeting.

This CEO was not the exception, but the rule. Most leaders believe that relentless communication is critical to leading execution, and most think they're doing a great job. The data tends to say otherwise. Across over 500 companies, on average only 56 percent of distributed leaders could name even one of their company's top priorities. Put simply, the most trusted leaders in the organization charged with strategy execution were given five chances to list the company's must-win battles and half failed to list even one. The situation deteriorates as you move lower down into the organization. Only 44 percent of top team members could list the company's top three priorities, a number that slipped to just over one-third among their direct reports. Further, only half of distributed leaders say they could easily explain the company's strategy, and another 17 percent say they mostly understand the strategy but question whether it is the right way forward.

Most CEOs and senior leaders I work with tell me they communicate all the time and are surprised when data shows how poorly strategy is understood throughout the organization. But frequency of communication is not the problem: 90 percent of middle managers agree that top leaders communicate the strategy frequently enough. So how can so much communication yield so little?

Because communication does not equal understanding; shared context does. Thrive companies create shared context, which is the common understanding of what matters, why it matters, how the pieces fit together, and what is and is not working.

Shared context cannot be measured by the input—volume of material communicated. Only the outcome matters, which is how well key leaders understand it. It comes from constant effort to build a shared understanding and reinforce this with your most critical leaders.

Here are four ways to build shared context:

1 **Simple tune that everyone can hum**: Strategy communication should be clear and to be clear it must be simple. Remind everyone about the Reset questions—what success looks like and the MWBs, and ensure all senior team members understand what they are and why they matter. If your entire leadership and management team cannot express the strategy in a few short sentences that reference the same points, you have not built shared context. Your outgoing communication is the starting point. Every company-wide announcement should go through a filter—does this reinforce our strategy and MWBs? If it does, describe how, and if it does not, ask why you are communicating it.

2 **Show what it looks like to win**: Success at the finish line matters. Consistent tying back to the definition of success (covered in Chapter 7), for both the strategy cycle and the year reinforce context. Everyone wants to win. If they know the finish line they are aiming towards, they can better align effort and make the daily trade-offs to get there. The London-based CEO was able to boost shared context after the survey results by consistently linking the top priorities to where they wanted to be at the end of the three years.

3 **Discussions, not lectures**: Shared context is built in discussion, which can be virtual and via shared platforms, but not just email or Slack. Review the agenda of your last meeting and the time allocation between telling and talking; if it wasn't majority talking, you are not building shared context. Building shared context comes from frequent, formal and informal, conversations with distributed leaders about what's working, what's not, and what they are seeing. Resist the urge to tell and ensure you are listening and discussing.

4 **Talk about what's not working**: It is just as important to discuss what is not working as what is. Even companies that score well on initial communication often fail to go back to the organization with updates on progress. It is these follow-up conversations on MWB progress and why things are working, or not, that build shared context. Having clear regularly updated scoreboard metrics for each MWB is another effective way to reinforce this shared understanding.

Offices are a great way to facilitate shared context. Steve Jobs knew the power of discussions and conversations in creating shared context. While designing the Pixar building, he moved away from a multi-building design to a single large building. In the center was an atrium designed to encourage employee mingling and unplanned collaboration. John Lasseter, Pixar's former Chief Creative Officer remarked he has "never seen a building that promoted collaboration and creativity as well as this one."

Chris Kane, former head of Corporate Real Estate at BBC, similarly prioritized the strategic asset of real estate to further strategy, and context when they launched White City in London and re-developed Broadcasting House. You can create context for collaboration and creativity around a virtual water cooler as well, but it takes explicit focus rather than leaving it to chance.

Trust

Trust means something very specific in the high growth context: Can you rely on others to do what they say they will do?

In Thrive companies, **high reliability provides adaptability.** Thrive companies execute with a considerable speed advantage as they have trust in commitments. Mindshare is powerful in growth; when team members can trust others to do what they are supposed to, you can focus on value creation and move faster than others on identified market opportunities.

Most people when asked to describe strategy execution detail the importance of communication and alignment through KPIs and objectives, and actually most companies are doing OK on vertical alignment. In my execution survey, processes to ensure alignment up and down the organization are among the highest scoring items. The problem with executing strategies in a changing world is that the biggest needle-moving initiatives usually cut across units. Here managers say they were three times more likely to miss their performance commitments because of lack of support from other units than they were because their own team failed to deliver on its commitments. Where the organizational chart supports vertical alignment, things seem to be working, but when things need to move horizontally, things break down.

During hyper growth, your organizational chart will change at least every 18 months. Most companies need less frequent structural changes, as the value creation gains from the adjustment must dramatically offset the effort and change management of doing so. Rejigging reporting lines every few months or for every initiative is impractical and usually ineffective. A more effective way to achieve greater reliability and trust is to rely on commitments. Making and delivering performance commitments is how companies execute strategy.

To test trust within their organizations, my survey asked respondents: "How much can you rely on your bosses/ direct reports/ colleagues to do what they say they will do?" 86 percent of respondents said they could rely on their boss all or most of the time, and this was the same for direct reports. The percentage fell sharply when outside of the vertical structure: 62 percent could rely on colleagues in other functions all or most of the time, and 53 percent could rely on colleagues in other units. The last finding was perhaps the most sobering: only 5 percent could rely on a commitment to come in from a colleague in another unit all of the time (see Figure 10.5).

FIGURE 10.5 The delivery of commitments: Reliability across organizations

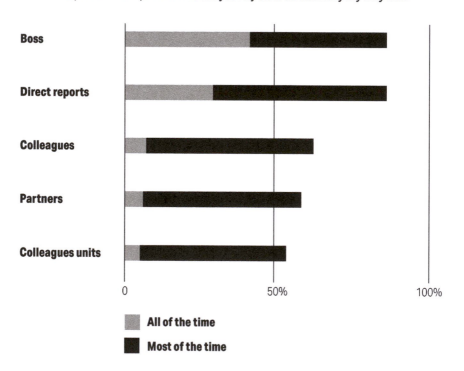

Who delivers on their promises?

Responses to the question *Who can you rely on to do what they say they will?*

Based on 442 companies and 11,890 respondents that took the execution survey 2011—2016

What happens when we cannot rely on commitments? We do a lot of dysfunctional things. We compensate by just doing it ourselves or double tasking it (asking two individuals or teams). We escalate the issue to bosses, call alignment meetings, and spend endless time sending follow-up notes and chasing calls and texts, and other means. But the scariest thing that happens when trust is low is what doesn't happen because we are too busy following up on stuff. Team members see attractive opportunities, tests they should run, and actions they could take to adapt around them, but they are too busy chasing or compensating to get to them.

Achieving reliability is deceptively simple: it's about training people to make better commitments and holding each other to account for doing them. It is the superior option over implementing process both in terms of time and money spent and in terms of results. A good commitment has five characteristics that make up the initialism: **AEIOU** (just like the English language vowels):

- **Active:** Actively negotiated in a conversation or discussion (not sent as a command in an email).
- **Explicit:** Absolute clarity on who is going to do what.
- **Intent-based:** Linked to the company's strategy and top priorities or MWBs.
- **Open:** Communicated with transparency, not made in a side conversation.
- **Understood:** Both parties agree to do it, sign up to the commitment, and understand what they are signing up to.

You might be thinking, "I don't have time to ensure each commitment follows AEIOU," and you will likely resort to sending quick emails and texts instead. But unless the commitment you are hoping to get meets all five criteria, you do not have the right to rely on it. Commitments demanded exclusively by email will erode the trust within an organization. Take the few days to help build commitment-making capability and then as a leader continue to execute AEIOU commitments. There may be fewer commitments in the system, which is OK: fewer commitments with higher reliability consistently leads to more results.

Summary and next steps

Thriving is the result of having the strong balance sheet from Survive and the strategic insights from Reset, and executing with BLAST. BLAST is difficult to achieve and harder to sustain over time. This is because its elements cannot be built as independent factors: there are strong linkages between them. Each element strengthens your ability to Thrive, but only when these elements reinforce each other does BLAST become a rocket ship to Thrive.

Thrive will only come through explicit choices, commitments, and actions. It takes system-wide support and relentless focus, but there is a playbook that works if you are committed to building the BLAST elements and reinforcing how they fit together.

You should now understand:

- ✓ the key characteristics of BLAST: Beliefs, Learning velocity, Agility in decision-making, Shared context, and Trust
- ✓ how to articulate, test, and act on beliefs
- ✓ how to shorten and accelerate learning loops
- ✓ how to increase agility by codifying decision-making rights and describing what makes a good decision at your company
- ✓ how to build shared context across your organization
- ✓ how trust and high reliability strengthens execution and improves speed

The next chapter will cover common traps leaders fall into and that stall the movement into Thrive.

Endnotes

1 Acquired Podcast (2022) Season 10, Episode 8: *Arena Show Part II: Brooks Running (with CEO Jim Weber)*, www.acquired.fm/episodes/arena-show-part-ii-brooks-running-with-ceo-jim-weber (archived at https://perma.cc/7JWN-7EXG)

2 See A Freeling (2011) *Agile Marketing: How to innovate faster, cheaper and with lower risk*, Goldingtons Press, especially pp. 68–77.

3 Online experimentation at Microsoft, Think Week paper 2009

4 A G Martinez (2016) *Chaos Monkeys: Obscene fortune and random failure in Silicon Valley*, Findaway World: Random House, p. 318

5 3M to current knowledge still has their 15 percent of time to experimentation rule in place.

11

SRT Leadership Traps
(And How to Avoid Them)

"If the leader is filled with high ambition and if he pursues his aims with audacity and strength of will, he will reach them in spite of all obstacles."
—CARL VON CLAUSEWITZ

Some things are simple, but that does not make them easy. Moving through the SRT loop is one of those simple things that is hard to do. In this chapter, I discuss the patterns of behavior that can make it even harder, specifically, the three main sets of traps leaders can find themselves facing. More importantly, I address ways to overcome them.

The first part of the chapter details the most common reasons that leaders don't get success from SRT, but then I discuss countering each one, with overall guidance on leading as an executive. Next, we explore how executives can use the trinity of direction, leadership, and management to move their organizations into Thrive. Lastly, I offer specific guidance for optimizing three key leadership roles: operations, finance, and people. What follows is a specific chapter, meant to better pave the way for your successful journey by learning lessons from others.

Trap set #1: Getting in your own way

The CEO, or top leadership role, is critical for leading the organization through the SRT loop. The SRT pathway often looks more straightforward than it is and just because you are eager and motivated doesn't mean that the ride will be smooth. As discussed in Chapter 2, our natural reaction to uncertainty as negative can get in our way, as can refusing to go into, or move out of Survive as discussed in Chapter 3. In addition to these Survive traps, below are other common reasons I see leaders getting in their own way, as well as practices to employ to overcome these.

1 "I've got this"

You have led companies through past shocks, so you are confident you can lead them through this one without a problem. You attempt to put in place the same steps for this Survive as the last time the company went into Survive. You don't bother to vet or test your old assumptions—things haven't changed that much. Or, after identifying must-win battles, you assume the team "gets it" as execution is execution, so you do not change anything in your operational rhythm. They'll figure it out.

What happens? From my experience: failure to reach Thrive. Different shocks present different kickers and killers. Your old assumptions may very well be worthless in a changed environment. Using them could steer the company directly onto the rocks or you could miss out on potential game-changing kickers just because you haven't looked for them. Executing a Reset strategy requires ongoing learning, testing, and micro-adaptations. If you don't build change into the strategy, you will struggle when it (inevitably) crops up.

How to overcome: Watch out for the framing or biases you may have about the next-order effects of situations. Move to active testing of your beliefs and assumptions, and invest incrementally as you learn more. Build strategic capability in the team to help you do this. Do not assume that as soon as you have set priorities the situation will stabilize.

2 Paralysis by analysis

You are facing uncertainty, and you are not sure what's going to happen next. You don't want to make any decisions yet; you want to wait until you know more. But the more you learn in the market, the more uncertain you become. You keep pausing any major decisions, effectively placing your company in an ongoing holding pattern.

What happens? Faster-moving competitors get ahead, the team becomes wary of the holding pattern, and you miss out on opportunities.

How to overcome: Build a system to actively test your top beliefs and assumptions, especially your "game-changers." Begin low-resource commitments and small bets as you test the market. Identify and execute on "no-regret moves," until you can fully reset your must-win-battles.

3 They "just don't get it"

You worked with the team to answer all the important questions for the Reset, but you feel they're too operationally minded, they're not strategic enough, and they just don't get it. You rip up the script and start over, this time on your own. You assume you have to do it yourself, as the team does not have the capacity or experience to understand this situation.

What happens? A strategy that only considers one perspective is going to miss something important, especially in a changing context. Plus, the team feels defeated, under-valued, and their trust in you starts wavering. They will not participate in strategy discussions going forward, as they believe they are a waste of time. They also start giving less energy and commitment to initiatives, assuming you will change your mind anyway.

How to overcome: Be selective in building your Reset team; if you purposely placed team members there to test their strategic aptitude, don't be surprised by the results. Use the guidance of the small team and move discussions from "What is a good idea?" to "What needs to be true?" Stress-test assumptions. Focus on building the capability of the team, as you need strategic distributed leaders to Thrive, and address gaps by working with your Head of People to bring in the needed skillsets.

4 Boredom

You successfully led through Survive and Reset. You have MWBs and champions. The champions are beginning to execute, and it's starting to work. The problem—even though you won't admit it—is that you miss the heightened energy of Survive or the strategic stimulation of the Reset. Executing a set of priorities doesn't excite you, so you look for things that do. Acquisitions, innovation projects, or other new, shiny things become your focus, and you start bringing your team into these discussions.

What happens? The team is confused about their priorities. They start to question the organization's commitment to the new strategy. Their attention is divided, which slows progress on those must-win battles.

How to overcome: Getting a set of MWBs to the execution phase is a great thing—embrace it. Find areas within the MWBs you are passionate about; otherwise get out of the way of the champions and their teams. Start the preparation for the next strategy cycle, but only in a way that does not distract or confuse the team.

5 False air cover

It's time for you and the team to go into the Reset discussions, but then you pause. The team is overburdened. You don't want to pull them away from operations. They're too busy to do strategy. There has never been a time when there was so much going on, and they can't be distracted, so you are going to protect their time. The issue is, they don't need it - the leaders are eager to reset the strategy!

What happens? The strategy never gets reset. You continue with a rolling, historic strategy, or downshift to a normal operating rhythm. Even if you achieve operational excellence—this is not strategy, and efficiency alone will not lead to growth. It feels like it's working for a time, but at best this gives you linear growth: it will not deliver breakthrough growth.

How to overcome: Do not make assumptions about other people's bandwidth: open the invitation to join the Reset team, but give them an easy out if they cannot. Carve out small but consistent windows of time to devote to the Reset. Daily grinding operations with no growth strategy in sight very quickly de-motivates a team in Survive. It reinforces the notion that neither the company nor their individual careers are being set up to Thrive.

6 Your Board becomes your customer

The Board wants more updates during the Survive phase. Quarterly meetings become monthly; monthly become weekly; weekly become daily. All the meetings need reports, PowerPoint presentations, and talking points. Then these meetings need notes summarized afterwards. More than half of your time—and that of the team—is spent managing your Board, instead of testing and learning from your market. You spend an order of magnitude more time talking to Board members than you do speaking to or about customers.

What happens? Spending more time on your Board than you do on the steering and guiding the business and interacting with customers will slow your progress through the SRT loop and likely cause you to miss out on opportunities emerging from the uncertainty in the environment.

How to overcome: Your Board is there for governance and direction, but it will likely not create value for you. Have an honest conversation with your Chairperson about the Board's role in the Survive phase and what you need from each other. Manage the preparation as much as possible, ideally from reports that can be pulled automatically from your systems. Have one Board member dedicated to Survive that can meet with your team member assigned to this mode in smaller, focused meetings that do not drag the rest of the team back.

7 Tinkering

You are anxious that not enough is being done, *and* you are afraid to make any big bets. So you tinker. Constantly. You keep changing the tracker and set of priorities or shifting the language to something new that you think might work better (for example, moving from KPIs to OKRs). You make micro cuts in all departments to cut costs, but you don't close the underperforming units that are really draining cash.

What happens? Your team becomes frustrated; all these changes are hampering their decision-making and they're spending way too much time implementing this month's new tracker. They burn out and down-shift to waiting to be told what to do. The business may Survive—but not in great shape.

How to overcome: Value creation comes from doing the few things that fundamentally move the needles apart: increase willingness to pay, decrease cost, or both. Lots of things cause the needles to bounce, but most of these are distractions. Prioritize what you are doing by their impact on value creation and effectiveness of helping to reach your main intent against the resources needed to execute it. Challenge yourself to stress-test assumptions on the big things.

8 **Overinvolvement**

You broadcast platitudes about having a great time and great people, but you don't show that in execution. You are quietly concerned that the team does not quite "get it," so you check in often with daily texts or calls. You assign activities to leaders and ask for reports on their actions. You jump in when a team member pauses and enjoy knowing you are the ultimate problem solver.

What happens? Team members do not build capability, they do not build trust, and they wait to be told what to do. You will not get to Thrive.

How to overcome: Great leaders build the context about where to go, they do not tell the team what to do. Your role is to set clear intent and boundaries, a system for tracking beliefs, and then get out of the way. The team will likely make different choices in execution than you would have. That's OK; they may be placed to make better decisions than you would have, and if they don't, they'll learn how to make better ones.

9 **Rushing the Reset**

A Reset sounds great, so you jump in, assuming one three-hour meeting will get the job done! Even though beliefs are new and untested, Right to Win is questionable, and you are lacking insights on "where to play," you plow ahead anyway. You set a list of must-win battles and now you're ready to execute. You think getting moving on execution is more impor-tant than getting the strategy right.

What happens? A strategy without insights is a prelude to underper-formance. Execution will start sooner, but at best will lead to linear growth. You will continue cycling through the same operational priorities, likely missing any potential kickers in the environment. Opportunities for breakthrough growth will pass you by.

How to overcome: Acknowledge that Reset takes time and commitment. Set a regular cadence of meetings. Remember a good strategy provides guidance to make choices *ex ante* (before the decision points occur), so when you're in execution, distributed leaders know what to do when they face them. The time you are spending now saves an order of magnitude more time in execution as countless meetings and follow-ups are unnecessary when distributed leaders have context. This allows your organization to move with aligned speed, a key competitive advantage.

10 You want things too simple or too complex

You love simple, you say, and you would love to have a simple strategy, but others can't comprehend the complexity of your industry! To the MWBs you add additional strategic priorities, principles, and goals. You add OKRs, rocks, or a new set of KPIs to the tracker, that may or may not be related to the MWBs. You don't want to miss anything, so you add more reports.

Or you err the other way. Six questions for the Reset are too many to remember, you think. You focus on just two of them. You do not spend time on the insights, just the final list of things to do. The list is indeed simple, but it is also generic with no differentiation or guidance.

How to overcome: What is complex is hard to understand. What is hard to understand is hard to remember. What is not remembered will not be done. If you want a fighting chance of this strategy being executed, it must be simple. But the paradox of a simple strategy is it does not start simple. It is easy to have a simple and stupid strategy. Just write that you'll be the leader in the market with innovative products and happy customers—done! But no one will know what they're executing. Visualize the possibilities of strategy as in the 2x2 matrix in Figure 11.1. The sweet spot between simple and complex is having all the insights of the complex strategy and then distilling it down to its essence for the team.

Not all leaders fall into these traps, but sometimes you can fall into more than one! Regardless of where you may be more inclined to occasionally falter across these, here are three pieces of guidance that I have found effective for leaders in staying out of their own way during their SRT journeys.

FIGURE 11.1 Simple vs complex strategy

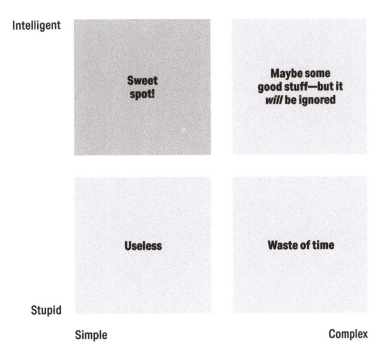

What I mean by simple

Intelligent

Sweet spot!

Maybe some good stuff—but it *will* be ignored

Useless

Waste of time

Stupid

Simple   Complex

Write an SRT memo

Write a memo to yourself on what the organization needs from you in all three modes: Survive, Reset, and Thrive. Where will your strengths be of most use, and where are your weaknesses a potential trap? How will you work with the team in Survive mode, and how will you manage the transition out? Where are you best in the strategic discussions of the Reset? How can you elicit the best strategic insights from the team? How can your network or contacts help in the fast testing of the assumptions? Where might your ego become a trap in the "Right to Win" conversations? Where may your biases prevent the right set of MWBs from coming through? In Thrive, where across the organization are you needed the most? Review the BLAST framework and write specific notes to yourself on how you can lead each one.

Share this memo with a trusted advisor or Board member to get feedback. Set aside some time to learn from others who have successfully gone through these modes already. Never hesitate to learn from another leader's journey.

Schedule an appointment with yourself to re-read your memo at least two times a year and at the entry into each mode. Hold yourself accountable for living up to it.

Scale yourself

If you want to scale your business, you will need to scale yourself. Eventually you must step back from some things to empower others and become ruthless of where you are most needed for value creation. In *Blitzscaling*, Reid Hoffman and Chris Yeh provide an excellent breakdown of ways to do this:[1]

- **Delegation:** Ask what in the organization you and only you can do, and then focus on delegating all other tasks to the team. Stop doing everything in which you do not have a unique value-add component and instead build a stronger team around you that can accomplish those tasks.

- **Amplification:** How can the time you spend and activities you do add more value to the organization? How can site visits be optimized? What about customer meetings or public events? Review your activities for the past week and determine how you can amplify at least half of them further. Some CEOs look to the Chief of Staff role to assist with this step.

- **Improvement:** Make yourself better. Ramping up your learning velocity is critical to helping the organization build its learning velocity. Seek and be very open to feedback. Prioritize specific areas of capability build each year. Remember, helping yourself is helping the company.

Do not tell your team what to do, tell them where to go

Draw from the wisdom of Prussian Field Marshal Helmuth von Moltke, who said:

> "...A leader who believes that he can make a positive difference through continual personal interventions is usually deluding himself. He thereby takes over things other people are supposed to be doing, more or less dispenses with their efforts, and multiplies his own tasks to such an extent that he can no longer carry them all out.
>
> The demands made on a senior commander are severe enough as it is. It is far more important that the person at the top retains a clear picture of the overall situation than whether some particular thing is done this way or that."[2]

When faced with uncertainty and complexity, you may feel like it's your responsibility to give more detailed guidance. This can become a potential pitfall. More and more details give your team less space to interpret and use their own knowledge and wisdom to execute when things don't go according to plan. Von Moltke also said: Detail is the enemy of clarity. The more detailed you try to be, the less clarity the team will have over what matters and what to do.

Your job is to set a clear intent and boundaries, and ensure your distributed leaders have the capabilities needed to execute towards the intent. Then get out of their way. A great team will push all the way to the boundaries without going over.

When things happen, avoid jumping in and doing it yourself. The easiest way to solve a problem is to do it yourself, but **the best way to grow a company is to empower others to do it and become problem solvers themselves.**

Trap set #2: Ignoring the leadership trinity

A long-ranging debate persists as to the difference between leadership and management. The debate began with Harvard Business School professor Abraham Zaleznik's 1977 article in which he proposed that managers are tough, analytical, persistent, and smart, while leaders are inspirational, passionate, and visionary.[3] He argued that managers seek control and order, whereas leaders not only tolerate lack of structure and chaos, they can thrive on it. The notion of control (managers) versus change (leaders) continues to divide the two.[4] But this distinction between leadership and management misses a critical element: direction-setting.

Stephen Bungay proposed that the tasks of the executive form a trinity of leading, managing, and direction-setting.[5] In the trinity, none of the three is more important than the other: All three are needed to move companies through the SRT loop (see Figure 11.2):

- **Direction-setting:** Directors set the definition of organizational success and provide guidance on how to get there. They guide development of the strategy with the team and plot its value creation potential in the strategic environment and according to the organization's capabilities. Directors then build context of this intent more widely across the team. Direction is critical in an organizational setting, and it should not be collapsed under leadership.

- **Leadership:** Inspiring people to execute toward the direction and achieve objectives is the role of leadership. An emotive element of the leadership role is maintaining the engagement of employees for successful execution. Leaders must balance their attention between the demands of the task (what needs to be done), the team (actions at the group level), and the individual (actions that address each member's unique needs). This is what John Adair calls Action Centered Leadership.[6]

- **Management:** Organizing and allocating resources to achieve directives is the critical task of management. Management involves understanding how to translate the direction into objectives and then track progress along the way. In SRT, managers are also responsible for continually monitoring and updating the Beliefs Tracker and testing grid. Management entails understanding what to do and how to do it, solving problems, and creating the right processes so others can organize their efforts efficiently and effectively.

FIGURE 11.2 The leadership trinity

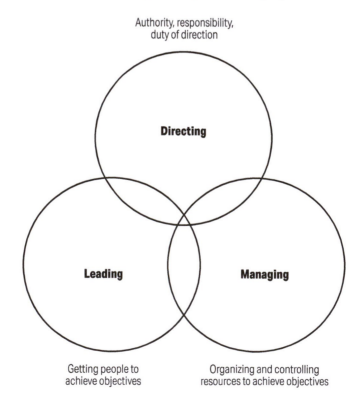

Leading an organization requires different mixes of directing, leading, and managing

Authority, responsibility, duty of direction

Directing

Leading

Managing

Getting people to achieve objectives

Organizing and controlling resources to achieve objectives

Leadership feels inherent to becoming Thrive and is certainly the most discussed. Management, while de-prioritized in the popular discourse, is of critical relevance for achieving the Survive and Reset modes and getting to Thrive. Do not undermine the role of managers: a successful journey demands them. Direction is unfortunately the least recognized and where the biggest deficits exist in most organizations. Direction is critical to leading the movement across the modes and guiding the insights from Reset to Thrive.

But it is not as simple as saying Survive requires management; Reset direction; and Thrive leadership. All three modes demand all aspects of the trinity.

The trinity describes types of work—and the skills this work involves—not individuals. Team members can gain skills and move into holding primary roles across the trinity over time. But as each aspect of the trinity demands different skills, it is highly unlikely a single individual is equally good at all three. Since your organization needs all three, the leader must be self-aware enough to provide the organization with what it needs at any point in time. Assess the strengths and weaknesses of your team and work to close any gaps. Very few people excel at all three, so the best solution is usually to build a team to ensure you can execute on all three.

Be careful in acknowledging if you have direction setting, which is the least understood of the three.

An optimistic leader will always believe something is possible, so often leaders assume because they are charismatic they are also good at directing. But if a leader does not have a complementary director, or the direction skill set, on the team they tend to ignore signs, not test beliefs, and have biased approaches, as they want to keep the team moving. This almost always leads the organization down the wrong path.

Average organizations over-index on management during triggered Survive and focus on KPIs and rhythm to keep the company running. Good organizations provide strong, clear leadership. **Thrive organizations prioritize not only leadership and management but also direction. They know direction is the key to growing through uncertainty.**

Trap set #3: Not optimizing for key executive roles

Building a Thrive company is a team sport, not an individual one. All leaders have a role to play in moving through the SRT loop. Three specific roles that are most commonly working with the CEO on the SRT loop are below

(CFO, CPO, COO), but in other organizations the Chief Commercial Officer or Head of Strategy could be more critical—it depends on the structure of your team, company, and industry. I have provided some brief guidance on the role and how to measure their performance on the SRT journey. These metrics are not meant to replace traditional metrics but provide additional insights into the movement to Thrive.

Chief Financial Officer (CFO)

CFOs should be growth partners, not just stabilization protectors.

CFOs are often considered the leaders in Survive, but to have a lesser role in the other parts of the journey. In Thrive organizations the CFO and CEO are true growth partners. In Survive, the organization needs the CFO to own the 4 Cs tracker (especially Cash) and work to strategically lead many of the power moves. Reset needs CFOs as a strategic thought partner helping to ideate and vet and test ideas. In the transition, CFOs work with MWB champions to quickly draft simplified budgets and P&Ls for the newly scoped initiatives.

A critical way CFOs support the journey to Thrive is through the budgeting process. Most CFOs I speak to lament that they are allocating less to certain areas because those teams still haven't spent what they asked for the prior year. This leads to persistent dysfunctional behavior where leaders scramble to spend their allocations at the end of every period to ensure they will get funds the next go around. Instead, CFOs should focus on rewarding the achievement of outcomes. Leaders who propose low-resource activities or shift to new ones and achieve greater outcomes should be recognized. Managers will not act to learn if they are allocated less budget next year for "not spending" their current year, even if in learning they saved the company overall and allowed an outcome to be reached faster.

Measures to master:

- **Cost to learn:** Organizations become risk-averse over time as failures often lead to financial or reputational losses. The CFO can help shift the mindset from risk aversion to learning by helping to track and measure learning. To build a culture of learning and experimentation, teams must be great at learning quickly and cheaply. It starts by being able to identify each assumption that needs to be tested. CFOs should help teams track the "cost" to learn: How can we significantly reduce the cost (including time) it takes to test individual assumptions? Can we move from $10,000 to test an assumption to $1,000 since we're getting better at identifying core variables and designing faster tests? Mastering this metric will dramatically increase learning velocity and moves the CFO to growth partner with the teams.

- **Reduction of uncertainty**: When presenting opportunities for investment, the first question CFOs ask is "What is the Return on Investment (ROI)?" This is a sensible question for investments with known variables and timelines, but not so useful when doing new things in uncertain environments. CFOs should focus instead on identifying the key uncertainties in the market funnel of assumptions. They should work with the team to tease out every assumption in the model (e.g. "We can price with a 20 percent premium over competitors," or, "25 percent of our existing customers will also buy our new solution line"). Once identified, rank them from most (pretty much a guess) to least (very confident in) uncertain. Then work with the leaders to test the most uncertain assumptions as quickly and cheaply as possible to reduce the overall uncertainty. The CFO sees the most assumptions of anyone in the business—they should leverage that knowledge by sharing learnings of how testing is being conducted across the organization. Being able to assess the uncertainty of assumptions and then reduce this uncertainty will further the organization much more than ranking initiatives by ROI.

- **Boundary defense**: This one is a way of tracking rather than a metric. Boundaries are the non-negotiable "rules of the game" that we must stay within while working to achieve our goals (Chapter 7). CFOs help guide the team to stay within these rules of the game versus optimizing for a specific value. Tracking in this case is about notifying teams when boundary breaches are likely, but not asking for more push. Picture the electric fence from Chapter 7: we want to track staying within the fence, but we don't want leaders staying in one place: we explicitly want them using all the yard space we gave them.

Chief People Officer (CPO)/ Head of Human Resources

A CPO should be a true business partner, not just the "people person."

Every part of the SRT loop is dependent on your people; they will determine the speed and effectiveness of the journey. The CPO's role as the pulse of the people is to be an effective partner and part of all the people-related conversations. In Survive the CPO is responsible for critical metrics and reviews of people so they can be allocated appropriately. They should own the "C" of Communication and work directly with the CEO on messaging. They can also own the employee engagement power move. In Reset, the CPO should be part of all the strategic dialogues, not just when people or talent are part of the discussion. They should not speak about "the business"—they are part of the business! To be an effective leader, they must understand how their organization creates value and what it takes from people to do this, lest they cannot be the right thought partner to their peers. In Thrive, the focus should be on accelerating learning velocity and driving a system that rewards results, not just completion of activities.

Three measures to master:

- **Days to value creation**: Organizations rarely measure the right metrics on talent attraction. Too many companies focus on cost to hire, which disincentivizes working with partners when needed, or time to hire, which fast-tracks searching or interviewing. Both lead to poor, rushed decisions and increased turnover, which has a significant cost. Instead, my favorite metric is "days to value creation," as this measures the lifecycle of recruitment. That is, how many days it takes to post a position, search and recruit, interview, decide, contract, onboard the new employee, and then have that employee create value in their new role. Every critical aspect is involved in measuring this—from writing a good job description to an effective onboarding procedure. Being able to measure days to value creation means you understand what it takes to create value in every critical role of the organization, which is key to moving to Thrive.

- **Length of learning loops**: Learning is the critical metric to measure, but too often organizations default to "activity" metrics such as number of training courses conducted or participant evaluations. Instead, start measuring your learning loops. Discussed in Chapter 10, learning loops are specific, iterative cycles of forming hypotheses, testing, learning, understanding, analyzing, and applying and embedding various forms of knowledge. Start with two of the organization's most critical MWBs and identify the critical learning loops within them (i.e., the areas where you most need to accelerate learning). This could be new key account signing or building partner relationships in new markets. Map them out and design ways to accelerate and shorten them. Then do the same for the other MWBs until you have a "loop dashboard."

- **Lived—not surveyed—engagement:** Engagement is a strategic element of triggered Survive, but more widely is proven to be directly linked to organizational performance.[7] While there is an established correlation between engaged employees and performance, this is an average. Additionally, your survey metric may or may not be linked to your growth if you are not clear on what you are measuring. As a team, decide what "lived engagement" will look like: How will you know whether your employees are engaged daily? Then measure that instead. Can you see engagement in how they approach work, how they build context in their area of the organization, or their decision-making effectiveness? The annual survey is a leading metric, which is great to track, but you should also measure and improve the lagging metric of how employees live engagement in their daily work. This forces clarity of what matters most and keeps the team focused on improving organization drivers not gamifying annual checkpoints (such as having the survey the same week as a big employee outing).

Chief Operating Officer (COO)

COOs should be strategic partners, not just execution partners.

An effective COO is the critical right-hand to the CEO during the entire SRT loop, leading significant steps in each piece, and sometimes needs to lead critical steps on their own. In Survive, the COO should own cost, drive most of the power moves, and guide the team in the defense to offense transition. At times, the COO may need to remain the owner of Survive while the organization starts to move to Reset. In Reset, the COO brings in views from the varied markets and functions and informs the team of how the possible MWBs will fit together in execution. The evolution to Thrive means moving from doing things right to doing the right things. A Thrive COO helps lead strategic direction setting, accelerating learning velocity, and steering teams to execute with aligned speed.

Three measures to master:

- **Outcome achievement:** A great COO measures outcome achievement, not activity completion, and builds a team that knows how to measure results instead of effort. To execute strategy we do things like make plans, build training programs, and negotiate new warehouse space. These are great, but they are not strategy. These activities deliver progress and outputs: plans are completed, timelines are built, and there is new warehouse space. To create value, we need outcomes. Outcomes are tangible results for the organization: revenue, profit, cost saved, customer churn reduced, and so on. Helping the team track this metric furthers the partnership with the CFO in allocating spend. I'll discuss outcomes more in Chapter 12.

- **Amplified—not just saved—time:** Many initiatives—especially fueled by the rampant growth of GenAI and its value-creating use cases—involve furthering automation, reducing costs, and achieving efficiency. Most companies struggle to show the results, however, and when they do these are tracked in terms of hours saved. The real power metric is "amplified" time. Consider a new digital platform, a touchless ordering portal, or an AI-empowered search of previous RFPs. For these, measure not just saved time, but how much the team member working with that system became more effective (for example, 30 percent more productive every hour). This is a multiplier. Saved time is helpful but not valuable unless time is reallocated to more value-creating activities, or productivity is increased dramatically. Being able to show, track, and continue to amplify time will further accelerate execution.

- **Decision-making robustness:** An under-looked measure is the quality and speed at which decisions are made. While some decisions will take longer than others, Thrive organizations have already codified critical aspects of decision-making, such as where decision rights lie and what makes a good decision (see Chapter 10). This means in execution distributed leaders should be making better decisions, at faster speeds. Being able to move with aligned speed provides distinct competitive advantage. Being able to track and improve how quickly you do this is another power move of execution. COOs should track whether critical decisions have decision-making rights codified (an output), the speed at which decisions are made (an output), and the quality of the decisions (an outcome).

Other critical metrics for COOs to master include economic value added (for businesses with capital investments) and profit per FTE (for businesses with intangible assets). Early-stage companies should focus on tracking "default dead vs default alive" from Chapter 3.

Summary and next steps

The Survive Reset Thrive playbook is purposely written to be simple, but it is not easy. Leading an organizational journey through Survive, Reset, and into Thrive is rewarding but hard. There are many traps that will stop even the most well-intentioned leader along the way. Luckily, these traps are avoidable, if you are willing to check your ego at the door, be honest about your biases, and scale your own learning curve.

Part of leading a successful journey is ensuring the organization has the right balance of direction, leadership, and management. Do not expect any single individual to excel at all three. Winning Thrive is a team sport, and all members of the leadership team have a role to play, including adding new metrics to their arsenal. Some final words on how to do so are covered in the next chapter.

Endnotes

1 R Hoffman and C Yeh (2018) *Blitzscaling: The lightning-fast path to building massively valuable companies*, Currency

2 In 1869 von Moltke issued a document called "Guidance for Large Unit Commanders", (Verordnungen für die Höheren Truppenführer). A translation is included in D Hughes (ed.) (1993) Moltke on the Art of War, Ballantine Books, pp. 171–224. I also pulled excerpts from S Bungay (2011) The Art of Action, op.cit.

3 A Zaleznik (1977) Managers and Leaders: Are They Different? *Harvard Business Review*, https://hbr.org/2004/01/managers-and-leaders-are-they-different (archived at https://perma.cc/R6F8-PB2F)

4 While some argue that these are very fundamentally different concepts (J Kumle and N J Kelly (1999) Leadership versus management, *Supervision*, **61** (4), pp. 8–10; J P Kotter (2006) Leadership versus management: What's the difference? *J. Qual. Participation*, **29** (2), pp. 13–17; R Perloff (2004) Managing and leading: The universal importance of, and differentiation between, two essential functions, talk presented at Oxford University, July 14–15), even to the extent that managers are not necessarily capable of being leaders, others argue these are complementary, if not overlapping roles. A breakdown of these debates is in my 2014 report for the UK Government: https://assets.publishing.service. gov.uk/government/uploads/system/uploads/attachment_data/file/302792/13-825-future-manufacturing-leadership.pdf (archived at https://perma.cc/5J7F-J5VV)

5 S Bungay (2011) The executive's' trinity: Management, leadership, and command, *The Ashridge Journal*

6 J Adair (1973) *Action-Centred Leadership*, McGraw-Hill

7 Numerous authors and reports have studied this link, more recently Gallup's 2020 report *The relationship between engagement at work and organizational outcomes*: www.gallup.com/workplace/321725/gallup-q12-meta-analysis-report.aspx (archived at https://perma.cc/5BNH-8CRW)

12

Making SRT Happen: Managing, Moving Through, and Measuring Change

"Some people want it to happen, some wish it would happen, others make it happen."

—MICHAEL JORDAN

Recently I was with a client in Dubai for their annual Top 100 conference to celebrate their high-performing leaders and build context for the year ahead. After a morning of discussing the Reset strategy, the CEO and I taught one of the masterclasses on Thrive execution. It was an exciting and engaging afternoon. Great questions were asked, role playing took place, and there was stimulating dialogue. At the end, the CEO asked how I thought it went.

"Half probably got it," I said.

His face fell a bit.

"And of those," I continued, "about one-third will do something with it."

Crestfallen, he asked "So, one-sixth?"

"If we are lucky."

These stats were not a reflection of the quality of the attendees—they were the top 100 high performers in the company—nor the quality of our teaching. Rather, they reflected an honest assessment of how much work and repetition it takes to build capability in an organization. Annual summits, town halls, and rollouts are great, but capability building to Thrive comes from ongoing effort. It is not something that can ever be checked off your list as "done."

This final chapter offers guidance on the how of that ongoing effort—how we manage the changes inherent to SRT, how we move through the loop, and how we measure progress.

Managing change

Don't just Survive... Thrive. It's a popular phrase, and one that inevitably starts circulating after market turbulence. The problem is that it misses a critical point: Just surviving will not get you to Thrive. If you are not prepared to go through a Reset and manage the changes that come with it—you will likely not get to Thrive. **The power is in the Reset.**

But Resets are hard because Resets involve change. Creating a new robust strategy is fundamentally about change. In setting and executing strategy we are making a series of choices to create and capture value advantage. Doing so involves adapting to the changing environment. As the market shifts and as we learn, we make changes to what we are prioritizing and how to set our organization up to keep winning.

When leaders ask teams to be more "innovative" or more "entrepreneurial," what they often really mean is they want them to be able to sense adapt to, and lead change, adapt to change, and lead change. Unfortunately, leaders often rank this amongst the lowest of the capabilities of their organizations. This is often due to the lack of honest conversations that need to occur when managing change. In my execution survey (introduced in Chapter 9), only one-quarter of distributed leaders said difficult issues were discussed in an open and honest manner, with more than a third saying only some difficult issues were discussed, or these topics were avoided altogether.

Concerns of "too much change management" often lead to scaled back, paused, or scrapped initiatives that were agreed upon during the Reset. These are valid concerns, but we should embrace having open conversations, learning faster, and building the capability to change rather than avoiding it. The major forces confronting our organizations today—digital transformation, AI adoption, the pressures of the ESG movement, and the continued turbulence of many industries—require change now, and the ability to keep adapting to win within this new world!

Thrive will come from embracing change, which means building it into your strategy, execution, and operational systems. It needs to be part of how your organization works. As a leader, you are also responsible for managing how changes are perceived. It might necessitate creating a sense of urgency. After all, there is a reason you are on the SRT journey and it's likely not because everything is chugging along smoothly. Your wider team needs to internalize this: A Reset requires change.

Just because you know what's next does not mean the organization does. Never underestimate how quickly the wider team will lose confidence the Reset will work and "check out." Keep building context for your teams around where you are, why you are there, and what you are doing now to move through Reset to Thrive. Many leaders find having a visual of the actual SRT loop where they visually show where they are at that point in time helps.

Be realistic about the change that will be required, but in a way that excites the team to go on the journey. There will be many challenges: be honest about them and openly commit to your role in removing (to the extent possible) these hurdles. And don't forget to deliver the quick wins. Even when major foundation-laying is needed for the Reset, continue to execute shorter term wins to keep momentum and energy.

Moving through change

SRT is a loop, not a line, and Thriving comes from your ability to move into and out of modes at the right time, with the right pace while seizing strategic opportunities.

If you have embraced steady-state Survive, when there is a trigger, you'll have less to do. Once your basics are stable (the 4 Cs) and you've employed a few power moves, you have set the stage for the Reset. Start moving at least some of the team into Reset. As mentioned, having one team member "own" the Survive phase allows other team members to move their mind-share to Reset.

Sometimes you move into Reset without a stop in Survive

When there is a major situation change or a trend that is affecting you (such as the rampant growth of AI), you may need to Reset immediately even if you did not have to pause in Survive mode first to stabilize. Cycle through the Reset questions and make calls on where changes must be built into the strategy, new beliefs monitored and tested, new capabilities built, and perhaps new priorities added (while others are taken off the list).

Reset should be the most time-limited of the modes—unless you are undergoing a hard Reset. If you determine you will need more time or this will be hard Reset, commit to having your DDDs (Define-Do-Deliver) completed within the next 90 days. Then update the DDDs on a rolling, three-month timeframe until mid-term priorities. Continue testing beliefs along the way.

Getting to the new Reset strategy involves triangulating the insights from your beliefs, Right to Win, where to play, and top challenges to determine how to get to your finish line. These discussions take more than a few hours: don't rush them. But also don't stall. Reset requires patience with the process *and* not letting the process overwhelm your team. Proceed to the next strategy question when you have enough insight to move, not when you are fully comfortable you know all you need to know. You never will, and that's why we build in the parallel path of active belief testing.

Transitions matter

A successful journey requires mastering the moves between the modes, not just the modes themselves. This is how you break the tension of the trade-offs—such as growth and efficiency, discipline and agility, and opportunity and distractions—that feel inherent to each mode.

Growth vs. efficiency

Breakthrough growth does not have to be growth that breaks the company. While moving into Thrive, maintain the discipline of steady-state Survive. There are very few exceptions when this should not be the case, namely, if you are employing a "land grab" strategy in markets where only one player can win or distribution channels must be controlled. This is rare, and land grab strategies should not be used when the assumptions do not call for them. For all others, avoid the rat race mentality of the growth phase. Don't assume you must grow at all costs and can return to efficiency when needed. By the time you do, it is often too late. Growth and efficiency do not need to be trade-offs: organizations that can operate in a steady-state are the ones that can consistently win.

Discipline vs agility

Moving through the loop is about finding, optimizing, and exploiting strategic insights in a disciplined and agile way. Throwing stuff at the market and seeing what sticks may be the quickest solution, but it is usually a wasteful idea. The solution to balancing agility and discipline is cheap, efficient information discovery and meticulous execution. You need to do both to ensure that you are learning as you are acting and making choices based on tested beliefs. A lean approach to discipline affords you the insights and guidance to be agile and THEN to exploit these opportunities with the right resources.

Opportunity vs distraction

During uncertainty, opportunities are going to appear, and it will be tempting to grab all of them. A charismatic leader will be able to justify going after any opportunity, but there is a fine line between distractions and true opportunities to exploit. How to balance execution with being open to opportunities is a common question I get. But if the insights in the strategy are clear, there is no major trade-off to make.

When an opportunity appears, and it does not directly support an existing MWB, ask if it is aligned with your belief set. If not, is it a challenge to your beliefs that needs to be tested? Or is it a distraction? If it fits your beliefs, is it aligned with your Right to Win, or what you are building? Use the same powerful question introduced in earlier chapters. Instead of *"Is this opportunity a good idea for us?"* ask: *"What would have to be true for this to be a GREAT idea for us?"* Separate these variables, rank them by criticality, and for each one ask: "Is this true, or can we make it true?"

If you find an opportunity that fits your belief sets, checks off all the variables that would make it a great idea, and can impact value creation, exploit it! At times this may mean pausing an existing supporting battle to ensure you have the resources to win this new opportunity.

I call this organizational **"swarming,"** which is when cross-functional teams quickly move and re-align on an emerging opportunity that fits within the strategic insights and boundaries, even at the expense of pausing other ongoing priorities. Swarming can be highly effective, but must be well-communicated, limited, time-based, and linked to the overall strategy to keep the momentum and engagement of the team.

Deliberate vs. emergent strategy

Acting to learn, testing beliefs, and thriving when facing extreme uncertainty are not new challenges only for today's organizations. The celebrated case of Honda's entry into the US motorcycle market over 60 years ago began the great, and still unresolved, debate between the virtues of "deliberate" and "emergent" strategy.

In 1959, looking for a reset of growth, Japan-based Honda sent some executives to the US to find a way of entering the market. The initial target was 10 percent of US imports. They had a lot of freedom, a budget of $1m, and the full support of founder Soichiro Honda. Their original bet was on large bikes as the best fit for the American market. While they had no time constraints, they were limited in the amount of cash they could spend, so they could not afford much market research.

They came, they saw, and they learned. Dealers showed little interest in them, and most bikers were enthusiasts with intact loyalty. What's more, the large bikes they did sell broke down because they were driven further and faster in the US than in the downtown Tokyo environment they were made for. The bikes had to be sent back to Japan to be modified.

So they changed their approach. The ultimate intent—penetrating the US market with 10 percent of US imports—remained the same, but the situation had changed, so they did too.

Honda happened to have a small bike available, the Supercub. Although the prospects were inauspicious, they decided to test whether this unique resource was worth anything. To their surprise, retailers who did not sell conventional motorbikes were willing to sign up, including Sears. The Supercubs became a huge success. Leveraging this win, they nurtured this new market with an advertising campaign: "You meet the nicest people on a Honda." It became one of the most successful campaigns in US marketing history. After that, they conquered.[1]

Honda was fully aware of the impact of scale on their business. They were passionate about market share and continued looking for ways of selling more volume. That was why they went to the US in the first place. On the back of the Supercub success, they started selling larger bikes. By 1975, they had established US import market share of 43 percent and set themselves up for decades of growth to come. In 2022, despite multiple new entrants, they remained the number three overall player in the USA market (and number one globally with nearly one-third of global market share).

Honda's moves show the power of direction-setting (penetrating the US market), and turning a killer (few bike sales, bikes breaking down) into a kicker (creating a new market) by adopting a series of evolving stances (see Figure 12.1). From their deliberate plan to enter the US market via large bikes emerged a new, much more successful plan to enter the US by creating a new market for small bikes. They were neither fully deliberate nor fully

FIGURE 12.1 Strategy stances and Honda

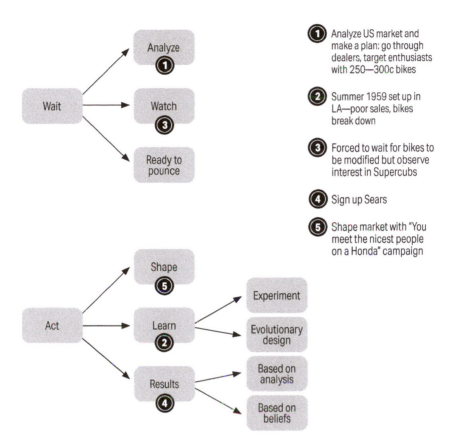

Honda motorcycles in the US, 1959—1964

① Analyze US market and make a plan: go through dealers, target enthusiasts with 250—300c bikes

② Summer 1959 set up in LA—poor sales, bikes break down

③ Forced to wait for bikes to be modified but observe interest in Supercubs

④ Sign up Sears

⑤ Shape market with "You meet the nicest people on a Honda" campaign

emergent; rather, their path to success was based on deliberately seeking emergence.

Honda shows how Thrive companies don't need to trade off between having a deliberate or an emergent strategy. They can benefit from both if they have internal predictability (from Chapter 9) in place. Honda had a clear intent around growth and tight boundaries they needed to stay within, mostly around cost. Decision rights were distributed to the leaders in the market, not with central headquarters in Japan, meaning faster action could be taken. Tight reliability meant the small team could execute quickly, knowing commitments would be maintained, and this reliability extended to their partnerships. And their organizational culture around learning allowed for the necessary adaptations which led to ultimate success.

Measuring SRT

What gets measured gets improved. It's a popular adage, often attributed to Peter Drucker, and it's a good reminder to reset your performance tracking and resource-rewarding systems along with all the other changes you are making during the SRT. If you don't make the change, your team will default to old ways of working and you won't get the gains your insights promised.

Effective measuring involves tracking and testing beliefs, not just priorities. It involves rewarding learning, not just delivery. And it involves managing by commitments, not just processes. At a higher level, though, it is important to adjust how you manage and track overall execution to ensure it is driving the change desired.

Consider the causal relationships involved in executing strategy. As a starting point, we have strategies because we want to deliver impact or change. Impact comes from delivering consistent and quantifiable results for the organization, or outcomes. Outcomes are what cause our value creation needles to move up (increasing willingness to pay) or down (reducing cost). Outcomes derive from outputs. Outputs are the effect of completing activities. Activities are things that we do. Figure 12.2 provides a visual breakdown.

Consider what happens in a typical organization. Impact is hard to articulate clearly or quantify, so we express it more generically. Impact statements displayed on posters all around the office center around safe, non-specific goals like industry leadership, growth, happy customers, and engaged and empowered employees. The typical organization also has a detailed list of resourced activities in their operating plan. Reviews track these activities and what has been accomplished. Rewards come with completion.

But what is the connection between the results of activity completion (i.e. outputs) and outcomes, and between outcomes and impact? These relationships are rarely delineated in a typical organization. And just tracking activities will leave you with a wide gap in delivering the expected change from your strategy, making the impact statement on the poster farther and farther from reality.

Clarity on activities does not guarantee clarity on the outputs to outcomes to impact chain.

This is why Thrive organizations build out the entire chain from Activities, to Outputs, to Outcomes, to Impact. They understand how to work back from impact to show how the company will deliver change, not just progress. They outperform against others as they consistently complete activities that deliver outcomes that lead to impact. One of their secret superpowers is they

FIGURE 12.2 AOOI

Activities, outputs, outcomes, impact: A breakdown
Deliver results from strategy

Activities	Outputs	Outcomes	Impact
Actions We see the team working on these What we do	**Effects** Completion of activities	**Delivering results** Effects leading to (ideally quantifiable) wins	**Change occurs** Lasting/higher-order results that make a difference
Make plans Build process Develop training	Trainings conducted Plans implemented Processes defined	Customer accounts won Cost of sales decreased	Significant market share won Major sales growth Establishment of brand as partner of choice
Build product roadmap Assess current innovation levels	Complete plan Train team on plan Develop innovation strategy Fill innovation funnel	Launch three new innovative products Increase revenue from innovation by 50 million	Establish brand as innovative leader CAGR of >10% from innovation
Defining metrics Establishing benchmarks Vetting suppliers Finding partners	Partnerships established Suppliers onboarded Benchmarks established	15% more employees retained Days from job posting to value creation from 100 days to 45 days Supplier risk reduced by 20%	Known as the place to work in the industry—magnet for talent Robust supply chain leading to sustainable growth and reduced risk

are always on the lookout for how to drive a tighter causal link from activities-outputs-outcomes-impact.

On the flip side, activity-obsessed companies micro-analyze planning documents, but do not spend time connecting the causal chain. They track and reward outputs—the completion of activities—not outcomes that move the value creation needles. Outputs may represent progress but if they are not leading to the desired outcomes, or not leading to them in a timely matter, they don't matter.

As a test, review one of your must-win battles' supporting battles in your Strategy Tracker (from Chapter 9) to determine the clarity of the outcomes and the percentage breakdown between outputs and outcomes. At first pass with companies, I often find over 90 percent are just outputs, or a re-statement of the activity. Why does this matter? Because your main intent must deliver impact to your organization. To reach this intent, each MWB needs to deliver promised results, or outcomes. Simply checking off multiple outputs will not lead to the finish line you set, as there will be no results, and you will dissipate resources and team member morale in the process.

A breakdown of possible activities, outputs, and outcomes in a digital-related MWB is in Figure 12.3.

Think of activities as the current best hypothesis of how to get to outcomes. Like all hypotheses, you are going to get some of them wrong. Empower team members to stop activities that no longer work and suggest changes during execution to get better outcomes. It is not only OK to stop some activities; it should be encouraged so you can resource the ones that will move the value creation needles. Build flexibility into the system and be prepared to change activities and outputs when they are not leading to the desired outcomes and impact, or change.

Making it happen

Leading a company through the SRT loop is demanding but incredibly rewarding. Every stage of the loop has potential pitfalls where progress can stall. When you see this happening, pause. Reframe where you are in the loop and why. Re-anchor on where you need to be at the end of each mode and what you need to get there.

As an executive team, use the trinity of direction-setting (orienting the company toward the goal), leadership (inspiring them to make the journey),

FIGURE 12.3 AOOI for a digital MWB

Activities, outputs, outcomes, impact: A breakdown
Deliver results from strategy

Activities →	Outputs →	Outcomes →	Impact
Actions We see the team working on these What we do	**Effects** Completion of activities	**Delivering results** Effects leading to (ideally quantifiable) wins	**Change occurs** Lasting/higher-order results that make a difference
Make plans Build process Develop training	Trainings conducted Plans implemented, Processes defined	Customer accounts won Cost of sales decreased	Significant market share won Major sales growth Establishment of brand as partner of choice
Build product roadmap Assess current innovation levels	Complete plan Train team on plan Development innovation strategy Fill innovation funnel	Launch three new innovative products Increase revenue from innovation by 50 million	Establish brand as innovative leader CAGR of >10% from innovation
Defining metrics Establishing benchmarks Vetting suppliers Finding partners	Partnerships established Suppliers onboarded Benchmarks established	15% more employees retained Days from job posting to value creation from 100 days to 45 days Supplier risk reduced by 20%	Known as the place to work in the industry—magnet for talent Robust supply chain leading to sustainable growth and reduced risk

and management (organizing and allocating resources appropriately) so that you can:

- leave Survive with a strong balance sheet
- leave Reset with strategic insights and a new finish line (success) and paths to get there (MWBs)
- stay in Thrive by executing with agility and learning—on full BLAST

Resets often lead to new awareness of the organization's gaps in capability; embrace what it will take to build them. Acknowledge that the Reset company may need new skills and leaders to form a more effective trinity going forward. Be aware that hard Resets may lead to a fundamentally different organization. Move forward and do not cling to the past. More often, though, Resets comprise micro adaptations that you develop and integrate without too much pain so that the company can quickly move on to Thrive. Embrace this as well!

Adopting the SRT approach contains a challenge and offers a prize. The challenge is for us to assume that we know less than we think we do. The prize is that if we do so, we can learn and grow more than we could ever imagine. Empirically, companies who have executed SRT are leading their industries, growing in new markets, and doing so with engaged employees helping to build the business for the next strategy cycles. And their leaders are engaged too. I have watched numerous CEOs reenergize around their organization's growth path after a successful SRT journey, as they have renewed energy and purpose.

Let's wrap up how we began—with an important reframing of uncertainty. Uncertainty is a series of future events which may or may not occur. Whether or not they are good or bad depends on what you are trying to do and how you are set up. My hope is that this Survive Reset Thrive playbook will support you in setting up and executing in ways that take advantage of uncertainty. Let's Thrive.

Endnote

1 C McKenna 'Mementos: Looking Backward at the Honda Motorcycle Case, 2003–1971', in S Usselman and S Clarke (eds.) *Festschrift in Honour of Louis Galambos, CUP*, reprinted in BCG e-panorama (2004) p. 11; R T Pascale (1984) Perspectives on Strategy: The Real Story Behind Honda's Success, *California Management Review* **26** (3), pp. 47–72.

APPENDIX

Downturns are a great time to grow

When a system shock occurs, our natural instinct is to view this—and the uncertainty it creates—as negative. And as organizational leaders, negative is often equated to a possible downturn. Earlier chapters asked you to reframe how you view shocks and uncertainty: rather than inherently bad, instead see this environment as one with possible upsides. Opportunities are always available to those who are prepared, stabilized, and willing to undergo resets.

But what happens when a shock does produce a market downturn, or recession? They are often accompanied by a self-reinforcing cycle of fear, which leads to panic and premature freezing of spending and investing, which translates into the slowing of capital flows and the beginning of layoffs, which leads to more panic. These effects can ripple through public and private markets into consumer sentiment, and the doom spiral begins. But macro downturns are not necessarily micro downturns. **If you have prepared—embrace these times, as downturns can be a great time to grow!**

This is not a catchy slogan—there is empirical evidence that supports this. While technological and societal advances (such as the iPhone launch in 2007) helped, some of the highest-performing companies of the 2010s (Uber, Airbnb) rose from the ashes of the 2009 Great Financial Crisis. And great companies emerged before them from other previous downturns: Microsoft (founded 1975) from the economic turmoil of the 1970s, Netflix or Google (founded 1997 and 1998) from the 2001 recession, and many more. And despite technology stocks falling more than 30 percent in the USA in 2022, by late 2023 several high-performing companies, such as Nvidia, were emerging with sustainable growth paths.

Many reasons make downturns a great time for growth; below are six of my favorites.

1 They are a great time to hire—and keep—talent

Financial capital becomes scarce in downturns, but human capital becomes more available. When there is a market shock, big public companies stop hiring and then start cutting management; technology companies freeze hiring and consider layoffs, growth companies get scared, and private entrepreneurial companies feel left behind if they are not in a cost cutting posture. While in the quarters before, attractive job seekers would have five or six offers, now they may have only one or two. **If you keep your mettle and have a clear growth story, this is a great time to hire talent.** More so, it's also easier to keep great talent as most of the siren songs of obscene wage offers have fallen silent. To take advantage of this opportunity you must have a clear and meaningful purpose, strong and compelling employee value proposition, and the credibility that you are or will soon be a Thrive company.

2 Focus matters; Scrappy forces innovative approaches

Focus provides clarity and enables you to channel your critical resources into the areas that matter the most. We often describe successful early-stage growth companies as "scrappy": devoid of the resources and brand recognition of larger companies, they are forced to be creative, resourceful, and agile. Scrappy is using limited resources to your advantage to force new, innovative approaches: it is not synonymous with severe cost cutting, which often leads to malaise and lack of motivation from talent. Companies that channel scrappiness over slowness focus on what matters the most for value creation and therefore enjoy more successful growth journeys. Airbnb CEO Brian Chesky consistently extols the powers of limited resources, focused work, and a "scrappy culture" in building novel solutions, and he credits this with the company's success—most recently in recovering from the 2020 pandemic. Over-funded and over-resourced companies often struggle, as excess resources can lead to over-hiring, failing to kill lagging projects, and sinking time and money into distractions. Execution requires focus. **Strategy is not about doing things right but doing the right things.** A downturn can bring scarcity, and scarcity when channeled as scrappiness forces you to focus on what matters most.

3 Customers make better decisions

While downturns feel scary as you fear losing customers and share of wallet, they can be the best time to retain and keep customers—if you have a differentiated offering. In downturns, customers make smarter decisions, and in upturns customers often make silly decisions. When inflation is low and cash seems limitless, both professional customers and consumers will try new things out of curiosity and overextend on options or subscriptions. **When things get tight, solid value propositions matter,** as customers will cull the excess and keep only the products and services that continue to solve critical problems or meet serious needs. For companies that deliver real value, downturns become a great time to solidify their customer base and accelerate growth.

4 Fundamentals matter

Fundamentals matter—unit economics, customer retention, cash flows, and the tradeoff between customer acquisition costs and lifetime value. Investors and leaders sometimes forget this—because overexuberant markets let them. When downturns hit, the sting of lacking fundamentals can be too much to overcome. For companies that have them in place, the base is built before the market tells you it needs to be. **Fundamentals provide a solid foundation for growth, enable confidence, and foster continued execution while acting as a launchpad** while others are floundering.

5 The Tourists have left town

In downturns the froth is blown off the ecosystem. Good companies often get punished in frothy markets because so-called "zombie companies" get over-funded, an obsession with growth at all costs takes over, and land grabs become the default business model rather than a conscious choice. More and more companies pursue dis-economic initiatives and get rewarded, and companies practicing prudent management of their balance sheet may feel outsized pressure to be more cavalier than what would otherwise be pragmatic. This leads to unrealistic expectations from investors and lenders, overwhelming consumer choice (usually exacerbated by companies pursuing customer acquisition with free or unsustainably low offers) and valuations (public and private) with unsustainable growth baked into them. True entrepreneurs love when froth leaves the system! **It's better to grow when competition is less intense, there are more acquisition candidates, and market opportunities are clearer for those that have prepared.**

6 Learning velocity increases

Longtime Berkshire Hathaway leader and Warren Buffet's partner Charlie Munger once remarked: "You have to keep learning… When the world changes, you must change." Downturns provide the most fruitful environment for learning, and as in chapter 10, those that learn faster grow faster. Limited resources focus lean test and learns and constant experimentation, sharpening the learning capability of the wider team. Customer feedback becomes more forthright: in macro slumps both businesses and consumers are increasingly candid about what they are really willing to pay more for, and what they are not. Learning loops become shortened as the pressure to move heightens, and these learnings—when captured and shared quickly— increase the velocity that they are embedded and used.

DOWNTURNS CAN BE GROWTH VEHICLES IF YOU ARE WILLING TO CHANGE.
There are growth opportunities available, and preparing your company to seize them can be a compelling call to action. But these opportunities come only to those willing to adapt and change. Part of why downturns are great is most companies are not willing or able to change: use your willingness to reset as fuel for your competitive advantage! Insanity is often defined as doing the same thing over and over again and expecting different results, and executing the same strategy as the situation shifts around you and your beliefs have been challenged will not set you up to grab growth possibilities.

GREAT DOES NOT MEAN EASY.
Being a great time to grow does not mean it's an easy time to grow. In a downturn, some things are much harder, notably raising capital. You can address this by employing steady-state Survive (Chapter 3), having solid fundamentals, and maintaining a strong strategic story. Having a strong cash runway allows you to weather the brief storm of capital flight while still executing towards Thrive. While valuations may take a temporary hit, leave your ego aside, and do not equate it with your company's performance potential. Try to avoid being in a position of a forced raise, sale, or other shareholder events. You may need to pause or slow a strategic priority that requires capital investment, which is OK. Keep testing your beliefs and assumptions and increasing learning to invest incrementally as the situation progresses.

As entrepreneurial leaders, we do not need it to be easy to be great. Uncertainty is inevitable, and it always contains growth opportunities, even in the event of a downturn. What separates high growth companies from others is learning velocity. If you foster a culture of empowered and agile learning while moving across the three modes of the SRT loop, you can grow faster, regardless of the market situation.

You can read more thinking on differentiated growth journeys at surviveresetthrive.com.

INDEX

Page numbers in *italic* denote information contained within a table or figure; those in roman numerals denote information within the prologue.

Looking for another book?

Explore our award-winning
books from global business
experts in Business Strategy

Scan the code to browse

www.koganpage.com/business-
strategy

Printed in the USA
CPSIA information can be obtained
at www.ICGtesting.com
JSHW070931080224
PP13318000003B/4

9 781398 607866